To be a Lady

TO BE A LADY

The Story of Catherine Cookson

Cliff Goodwin

CENTURY

Published by Century in 1994

1 3 5 7 9 10 8 6 4 2

© 1994 Cliff Goodwin

Cliff Goodwin has asserted his right under the Copyright, Designs and Patents
Act, 1988 to be identified as the author of this work.

Century
20 Vauxhall Bridge Road, London, SW1V 2SA

Random House Australia (Pty) Limited
20 Alfred Street, Milsons Point, Sydney, NSW 2061
Australia

Random House New Zealand Limited
18 Poland Road, Glenfield, Auckland 10,
New Zealand

Random House South Africa (Pty) Limited
PO Box 337, Bergvlei, South Africa

Random House UK Limited Reg. No. 954009

A CIP catalogue record for this book is available from the British Library

ISBN 0 7126 6159 X

Typeset by Deltatype Ltd, Ellesmere Port, Cheshire
Printed and bound in the United Kingdom by Clays Ltd, St Ives plc

Contents

To
Pauline

Preface and Acknowledgements

It is hard to think of any writer, living or dead, who has produced – and continued to produce – such overwhelmingly popular fiction as Catherine Cookson.

Between June, 1950, and the end of 1993, ninety million copies of her novels, children's books and personal recollections had been sold worldwide. An average of 5,800 every day – 241 books every single hour.

Cookson novels have been adapted into award winning television films. Musicals and plays based on her books have sold out within days and ran for weeks.

It is this popularity which has continually cursed her work with intellectual and critical scorn. Yet it is not great but popular art that has the strongest claim to be regarded as ahead of its time.

Arnold Bennett summed it all up when he said: 'Nearly all bookish people are snobs, and especially the more enlightened among them. They are apt to assume that if a writer has immense circulation, if he is enjoyed by plain persons, and if he can fill several theatres at once, he cannot possibly be worth reading and merits only indifference and disdain.'

Only recently has the academic world accepted and honoured the works of a writer whose basic message was truth and who devoted the greater part of her life to distilling that truth into popular art. Many of Catherine Cookson's earlier works are now being read and studied, not as fiction, but as records of social history. Students in Latin America, Australia and across the United States have, for more than a decade, regarded her work as educational as well as entertaining.

For more than forty years Catherine Cookson has been one of those genuine writers who remained bestsellers because she divined something at the root of the popular imagination. Her conviction and faith in a novel – frequently at odds with her publishers' advice – never deserted her.

When asked how editing on a television documentary was progressing the producer described it as 'nice'. 'Nice?' She snapped back, 'What kind of word is nice?'

But it is Catherine Cookson's inherent 'niceness' – her immediate likeability – which sets her apart from the majority of fellow authors. Writing, after all, is rooted in conflict and detachment and obsession. All of which were present in varying proportions during the first half of her life.

Add to this the constant pain and discomfort of her inherited blood disorder, and the legacy of a playground accident, and the time she devotes to her fellow human beings – in addition to her writing – make her unique.

Catherine Cookson is a woman of boundless compassion whose strength, common sense and bravery through years of suffering deserve respect. She is also an intensely private person whose international popularity has brought with it the double edge of fame and frustration. The boundary between publicity and privacy is well guarded. Details of her personal history – at least those for public consumption – are offered in carefully measured doses.

In the 1970s Catherine Cookson agreed to deposit thirty of her early manuscripts with Boston University. Since then she has forestalled any in-depth attempt to investigate her early life or explore her writing career. She has refused numerous requests to approve biographies and her will bans her literary executors from commissioning such a work. In 1991 her doctors informed her she had only a few weeks to live. Within days Tom Cookson had destroyed seventeen years of personal diaries. Only medical records remain.

In practical terms the fact that this book was 'unauthorised' was not such an obstacle to research as might be imagined. Numerous acquaintances of the Cooksons suggested sources and offered encouragement. Archives yielded a surprising wealth of background material. The list of those to whom I publicly and privately owe thanks continued to grow.

This book could not have been written without the help of a great many people. It is impossible to measure their contributions.

While some provided the greater part of a chapter others confirmed a date or provided a sentence.

For the chapters covering Catherine Cookson's childhood and teenage years my gratitude goes to Doris Johnson at South Shields Central Library; staff at Tyne and Wear Archive; Stephen Shannon at the Durham Light Infantry Museum, Durham; staff at South Shields and Gateshead Register Offices; the Commonwealth War Graves Commission; Dr Geoffrey Smith; Norma Kent; Rene Callendar, and Margaret Patterson.

I must also thank Chris and Violet Marjoram; Peter Adey; Reg Barton; Kathleen Simmons, and P. R. J. Coventry, of Essex County Archive, for material covering the Tendring years.

And, from 1930 to the present day, Jenny Johnson; John Ridd; Jim Clarke; Terry Jones; Joan Moules; Connie Langley; Peter Bolwell; R. E. Morris; Herbert Hoyle; Irene Marshall; John Barnett; J. A. Finch; Derick Rainton; George Coleman; Fred Swaffer; Heather Ging; Lizzie Hadden; Anthony Sheil; Michael Legat; Gill Coleridge; staff at East Sussex Record Office; Andrew Simpson at the RAF Museum; R. J. H. Hill at Hereford City Library; Beata Duncan; London Weekend Television; Tyne Tees Television; the BBC; staff at the Public Lending Rights office, Darlington, and The Sunday Sun and The Chronicle, Newcastle.

Permission to use copyrighted material was kindly granted by Bantam Press, William Heinemann and Headline. Every effort was made to trace and seek permission from those holding the copyright to material used in this book.

For additional information and permission to use photographs I am also indebted to Neil Fowler of The Journal, Newcastle; University of Newcastle Audio Visual Centre; Isabel Napier, and Jan Thompson.

But my deepest thanks must go to Dame Catherine and Tom Cookson who very kindly gave me permission to use family photographs and who never failed to answer my questions nor solve my problems.

My sincerest apologies to anyone I may have inadvertently omitted.

Cliff Goodwin, 1994

Part One

'Committed to memory'

One

I can smell memories of my childhood.

THERE WAS ALWAYS the noise. Day and night the sound of the steam engines and the railway wagons and the deep, whirring sound of the cranes in the dock and sometimes, if the wind was right, the high-pitched whine the timber made as it was cut into planks at the saw mill.

A thousand feet away – on the far side of the railway bridge and the four great, brick-lined arches – there was a different sound. South Shields Corporation had hired a local photographer to record the event. As he looked at the inverted scene on the ground glass of his camera's viewfinder, he could see men and boys in overalls and flat caps standing in groups beside two open-topped trams. Inside each of the trams, drawn up one behind the other, was the uniformed driver. On the upper deck of the first tram – its destination board showing Tyne Dock – he could see a cluster of civic dignitaries and guests. One face he recognised as that of William Black, a businessman and magistrate.

Black, who had first become a director of a tramway company as far back as 1884, was standing with his back to the goods shed at the dock entrance. He was watching the crowd at the junction of Hudson Street and Slake Terrace. When the photographer had completed his task, the group of men would sit on the wooden seats and ride the first tram between Tyne Dock and Frederick Street, South Shields.

The three-day-old baby girl lying in a make-shift cot beyond the staithe arches and the railway lines knew none of this. Her world was confined to the four walls of a room at No 5 Leam Lane. Her arrival – on Wednesday, 20 June 1906 – had been slow and painful.

The house was in the middle of a curved terrace on the right-hand side of Leam Lane where it opened out to join the Jarrow Road. The junction was known locally as Leam Lane End. From the front-room window you could look across the street to where another row of houses disappeared around the opposite corner. Looking left, to where Leam Lane started its steep climb up Simonside Bank, there was a second, shorter terrace built six or seven feet above the level of the road and protected by a brick wall. Between the two, leaning against the gable end of the second row, was a blacksmith's shop with a tall, narrow chimney and surrounded by a rough wooden fence.

Number 5 Leam Lane was a ground-floor house. The three-roomed property above, No 4, was occupied by a family called Angus. George Angus worked as a boilermaker. The two houses were the only up-and-down homes in the terrace.

In No 2, nearest the railway line and the dock, lived a family called Watson. The father worked for the North Eastern Railway as a shunter. Next door, No 3, was a public house owned by the Lilburns. At night you could hear the muffled sounds from the bar through the partition wall. The men called it 'Twenty-Seven' because they claimed there were twenty-six staithes or jetties within Tyne Dock and the pub was their final berth before they reached home. It was officially known by the grandiose title of the Alexander Hotel. Sometime after 1910 it was renamed the Alexandra, possibly to honour Queen Alexandra wife of the late King Edward VII.

In No 6 lived a joiner called Walton and his family. The house at the far end of the terrace was occupied by a family called Lawson who, to supplement the father's wages as a labourer, had converted the front room into a shop selling groceries. By 1911 the house had been taken over by a family called Lodge who, in addition to running the shop, earned extra money by taking in boarders.

Behind the row of houses, built almost into the railway embankment, was a gas works with a single gasometer. It was reached by a track which opened on to Leam Lane next to the Lawsons' shop. The smell of coal gas crept into every corner of every room. On washdays the women would take metal pails to the gaswork furnace to have them filled with hot cinders to start the wash-house boilers.

Kate Fawcett was twenty-two. Her face was flushed and red and she was running a temperature. Soon after the birth of her daughter, she had developed milk fever and her breasts were tight and painful. Already burdened by having to pay a doctor for attending the birth, the family could not afford more treatment. Kate's stepfather, a 'frustrated and licentious' man in his fifties, knew another way to relieve the pain. Kate could smell the beer on his breath and feel the disgusting bristles of his moustache as his lips tightened on her nipples and he sucked the milk from her swollen breasts.

KATE Fawcett arrived at South Shields registry office on 13 August with several misgivings. In her stepfather's eyes she had already committed the most heinous of offences against her family – she had given birth while unmarried. She was about to commit a second crime.

Kate had left the registration of her daughter to the last minute. The bout of milk fever had delayed her even more. Kate was proud but, like her mother, she was also a supreme realist. Her only concern now was to bequeath to her daughter at least the makings of respectability.

Convinced she would be prosecuted for the late registration – it was already fifty-five days after the child's birth – Kate claimed her daughter had been born a week later on 27 June.

To hide the child's illegitimacy Kate invented a new and respectable persona for herself. Believing the registrar, James Sedcote, would never see her again she gave her name as Mrs Catherine Davies, living at 5 Leam Lane. Her husband, the child's father, she claimed was Alexander Davies, a commission agent. Kate gave her maiden name as Fawcett which, at least, was true.

Even under the law as it stood, allowances would have been made for late registration because of illness. The legal time limit was forty-two days. The details of her fictional marriage were another matter. Kate had committed perjury and, had the registrar known, would almost certainly have been prosecuted. When the Perjury Act was passed five years later the maximum penalty was set at seven years' imprisonment or a £50 fine.

The birth certificate Kate carried out of the registry office bore the name of one other person: an identity three generations of women would do their best to conceal and which would surface, only once, thirty-four years later when Catherine Ann Davies was to marry.

JOHN and Rose McMullen had moved to the house at Leam Lane End with their fifteen-year-old son Jack in 1905. It was their ninth home since their marriage in 1890.

Rose Ann McConnell was born in Gateshead in 1858. She met and married her first husband, William Fawcett, before her twentieth birthday. A straight and decent man, Fawcett was employed as a roller in a Jarrow steelworks. He was also a devout Catholic and a Brother at St Bede's Church, Jarrow. In his early thirties Fawcett contracted and died of tuberculosis, leaving Rose and their five daughters destitute. The family were taken in by Rose's mother and father who cultivated a smallholding on the outskirts of Jarrow and were respected in the local community.

Rose, it would seem, was a woman acutely aware of her own future. Her decision to marry John McMullen may well have been influenced more by despair than desire. The marriage would allow her to leave the puddling mills at Jarrow, where scrap iron was reprocessed, and where the bosses attempted to stave off the exhaustion of the female workers by serving milk and beer at break times.

John McMullen had recently returned to England after serving with the Army in India when Rose first met him. He was living with his family in Jarrow. At that time his skin was burnt from the fierce sun and he still possessed at least some of his Army gratuity. John McMullen was already a sullen man. Perhaps Rose mistook his silence for strength.

McMullen had been born in a southern county of Ireland, one of triplets, with thirteen brothers. He never learned to read or write, a fact which possibly accounts for the variety of official documents recording the year of his birth from as early as 1850 to as late as 1856. He had never been back across the 'watter' since coming to England at the age of twelve, yet patriotism flowed through his veins as frequently as stout. Any man who slandered his memory of the old country was repaid with a beating.

On 4 May 1890 John McMullen married Rose Fawcett. It is quite possible Rose was already pregnant. Before the end of the year she had given birth to their only child. The boy was christened

John after his father, which was instantly shortened to Jack. Sometime between the death of William Fawcett and her marriage to John McMullen Rose's eldest daughter died, aged thirteen.

By the following year the family had moved to a house at 54 Albion Street, Jarrow. The 1891 census lists the occupants as John and Rose McMullen; John McMullen, aged nine months; Elizabeth Fawcett, thirteen years; Sarah Ann Fawcett, eleven, and Catherine Fawcett, seven. There is no record of Rose's youngest daughter, Mary Ellen, born in 1887. It is possible she was still living with the McConnells or one of Rose's two married sisters, Elizabeth Hogan or Margaret Hindes.

Within a year Elizabeth Fawcett, Rose's second daughter, had also died. She too was just thirteen.

The money did not last long. John McMullen joined his brothers in the docks, just as a new depression was hitting the shipping companies and heavy industry. Work was scarce. He would often walk the three miles from Jarrow to Tyne Dock for a single ten-hour shift. He would return, his skin and clothes stained with the red dust from unloading iron ore, with just 3s 6d (17.5 new pence) – less the money spent on drink on the way.

At one time in the early 1890s, when there was no work for dockers, John McMullen signed on at Harton Workhouse. The conditions were little better than imprisonment. He would spend each day shattering rocks with a sledge-hammer. The shift earned him one shilling, paid in the form of a voucher to be exchanged for food.

By 1894 the McMullens decided to move nearer Tyne Dock. They rented a house at 25 Napier Street, one of a triangle of streets wedged between Tyne Dock railway station and the dock itself.

The shortage of money and John McMullen's fiery temper led to the inevitable clashes with landlords. Within four years Rose had been forced to pack up and move her children to as many new homes.

Rose struggled to send her surviving daughters – Sarah, Kate and Mary – to school. She knew the benefits of learning. She also knew the price of life. The cost of sending her three children to school was 3d a week, and for that she could buy enough scrag ends of meat and vegetables to boil up a meal. While they were still too young to secure legal jobs, Rose set her daughters to work

7

begging, calling bare-foot at the bigger houses in Tyne Dock to plead for bread or scraps of food.

Like her sister Sarah, Kate was found a 'place' when she was twelve years old. The house was in Stanhope Road, not far from the McMullens' new home at 34 Napier Street, and was owned by a local butcher.

Kate was responsible for cleaning the entire house as well as doing the washing and ironing. In addition to the blood-stained aprons and overalls she would wash all the family clothes and linen, including those of the four young sons, by hand in a wooden poss-tub. It was so tall that she couldn't reach over the top to pummel the washing with a three-foot poss-stick and a special stool was made for her. Her day began at six o'clock in the morning and never ended before nine at night. For this Kate received 2s 6d (12.5 pence) a week, frequently paid several weeks in advance and handed over to Rose. She was allowed a half-day off each fortnight. After a year Kate was exhausted and left.

In the early winter of 1898 the McMullens moved from No 38 Frost Street to the relative luxury of No 6 William Black Street at East Jarrow.

Just over a decade earlier Charles Gidney, the owner of the St Bede Chemical Works, had conceived a plan to build clean modern homes for his employees. He chose a site half-way along the Jarrow Road, which connected Tyne Dock with his factory at East Jarrow. Surrounded by open fields, his men and their families would benefit from living away from the overcrowded and fetid streets of Tyne Dock and Jarrow. They would also be less than half a mile from their place of work.

The first three properties on the site were completed in 1888. Only one cobbled street had been laid. Gidney decided to name it William Black Street after a fellow industrialist and local magistrate. Number 2 William Black Street was a self-contained house with two rooms up and two down. Next door was No 4 – an upstairs four-roomed home – with No 6 below. Work on more homes continued sporadically until 1902. Two other streets and a terrace of bay-windowed, superior houses were added. The estate was known locally as the New Buildings.

By 1898 the chemical industry on the banks of the Tyne was struggling to survive. Homes for its workers were no longer a priority. Many of the properties were sold off or rented to dockers or railway hands.

When in work, John McMullen could vent his scabrous temper through sweat. When he was idle a few drinks turned him into a vicious fighter. He used his fists and steel-tipped boots on men half his age. His tongue John McMullen reserved for women. Any woman who crossed him, in the street or in his home, would be treated to a torrent of foul words and obscene suggestions.

A natural bully, his violence was never far below the surface. One morning, when the family were living in William Black Street his stepdaughter, Sarah, arrived home after spending a night at an aunt's in Newcastle. She was working in the city and had been expected the night before. John McMullen erupted in anger, grabbed a horse whip and lashed the twenty-year-old woman after cornering her in the back yard.

In 1900 the McMullens were forced to quit the New Buildings and move to lodgings in Straker Street, opposite the Lake Chemical Works at East Jarrow. The air in the narrow street stank from the concentrated chemicals. Men walked home, still wearing the crude cloth masks they used at work to stop the fumes burning their throats and clogging their lungs.

Within a year the family had set up home at No 1 Cleveland Place, a single street of two small terraces across the main Newcastle to South Shields railway line. The houses were old and isolated. A railwayman, who manned the near-by signal box at St Bede's junction, sold fruit and vegetables from his garden. At the age of fourteen, Jack joined John McMullen working in Tyne Dock. To get home after their shifts father and son faced the long climb up Simonside Bank before cutting across the fields of Cleveland Place.

In 1905, when John McMullen was offered a house at the bottom of Leam Lane and within touching distance of the dock wall, he lost no time in moving his family in.

MARY Fawcett had grown into a snobbish and volatile teenager. At the age of sixteen, while her mother and stepfather were still living at Cleveland Place, she took a job as a housemaid at the Ravensworth Arms, an inn at the village of Lamesley, south of Gateshead. Within a few weeks she was joined by her sister Kate as maid.

Although it had a population of little more than 5,000, Lamesley had its own railway station, due almost certainly to the proximity of Ravensworth Castle. The village and surrounding farmland, covering 7,167 acres, were owned by an exclusive triumvirate: the lord of the manor, Lord Ravensworth; Slingsby Duncombe Shafto, of Beamish Park, Tanfield, and the Earl of Strathmore.

The inn was an L-shaped building, constructed so that the upright of the 'L' – the front of the premises – overlooked a wide, paved forecourt. Its walls were faced with heavy stone blocks, engrained with the grime from the near-by pit and the smut from the passing trains.

By all accounts the landlord, John Hardy, was strict with his staff, although Mary had struck up a friendship with the daughter of the house, whom everyone called Miss Jenny. His customers spanned the extremes of the working class, from miners at near-by Kibblesworth pit to staff working at the 'hall'.

Accommodation for the staff at the Ravensworth Arms was sparse. All the female servants shared a cramped attic room, reached by a near vertical stairway. From the bedroom's single window Kate could look down on the blacksmith's cottages next door. In the rare moments when she was not needed at the inn she would call on Bella Thompson, the smithy's wife, to pass on a secret or share the village gossip.

Late in 1903 a stranger entered the saloon bar and ordered a drink. He was served by nineteen-year-old Kate.

> In the inn at Lamesley he had met an old gaffer and paid for the history of the district in two half-pints of ale.
>   His ignorance had spurred the old man on. But when later he left the inn it was not just the feeling of being weighed down with a great deal of local knowledge; but also with the fact that although nobody had asked his name, all those present in the taproom seemed to know who he was.
>
>   The Moth

Between conversations the young man studied the attractive teenager tending the bar and clearing the tables. 'She had two great azure blue eyes, with dark curving brows. Her hair was brown and abundant.' Kate had a good, if not full figure. Her smile was warm and full of good humour, but she looked prettiest when she was serious. Despite an accident as a child – which caused her left foot to pull inwards – she was light on her feet, as if she were about to break into a run.

Kate studied the man with equal curiosity. He thought of himself as a gentleman. There was no doubt he had class. He was dressed in a black top coat, trimmed with an astrakhan collar, and carried a silver-mounted walking stick and black kid gloves. By his second or third visit to the Ravensworth Arms, Kate knew she had fallen hopelessly in love with this gentleman who spoke 'different . . . lovely'. Very soon he had arranged to meet her on her day off.

The 'gentleman' never became a regular, but planned his visits to coincide with Kate's free time and treated her to outings and excursions. For a few brief hours each fortnight Kate became 'a lady'. She was never dazzled by the dream. She was well aware that the distance between them on the strict social ladder of the time was unscaleable.

For two years, month by month, Kate allowed herself to be seduced. Her companion's kisses became more urgent, his whispered suggestions more serious. Finally – in the last two weeks of September 1905 – Kate surrendered. She was a virgin. The result of this single sexual encounter, at the age of twenty-one soon became apparent. By the end of October Kate began to suspect the worst. During November she knew she was pregnant.

Kate returned to break the news to Rose and John McMullen at their new home at Leam Lane End. Her stepfather erupted into hypocritical indignation and Rose had to protect her daughter from a beating. For weeks Kate endured John McMullen's hostility and mock shame. His sarcasm, sharpened by drink, seemed never-ending.

Kate had left Lamesley without telling her lover of her condition. Weeks would sometimes pass before his next visit, although it is more likely she accepted the inevitable and said nothing. Soon after her return to Leam Lane she was told by her stepbrother, Jack McMullen, that a man was outside the house asking to see her. Rose spoke to him first. He seemed genuinely shocked by the news of Kate's pregnancy. He explained how he had asked at the inn for Kate's address and had come to sort things out.

Reluctantly Kate agreed to spend the day with him in Newcastle. They caught the train from Tyne Dock station, at the top of Hudson Street. As they walked arm in arm around Newcastle they began to make plans. They must, he insisted, be married at once. It became a happy and exciting day for Kate. Before they parted he gave her his address in Newcastle.

The atmosphere in the Leam Lane house was transformed. Rose was delighted, even John McMullen could find nothing to complain about. News of Kate's engagement to a 'gentleman' spread through the cluster of houses faster than the gossip of her return.

A week passed without news, not even a letter. Kate put the scribbled address in her handbag and caught the train to Newcastle. When she called at the address she was informed no one of that name or description lived there.

Kate was devastated. As the date of her confinement approached she withdrew into herself and the small, cramped house. The only person she truly trusted was the young Scots doctor who attended the McMullens and the other poor families of Tyne Dock. There was never any spare money at the end of the week to pay into a doctor's club. Yet whether Dr James McHaffie treated them at his Hudson Street surgery or visited the McMullen's home there was never any pressure to pay.

Dr McHaffie's manner was confident and self-assured and Kate liked him. She was more than a little pleased when she heard his car pull up outside the house on 20 June 1906.

CATHERINE was a progressive child, inquisitive and quick to learn. There were few restraints placed on her exploration. Almost as soon as she could walk she was allowed out unaccompanied.

Her world quickly expanded from the muddy track at the rear of the Leam Lane house to the waste land surrounding the gas works. Soon after her third birthday Catherine was venturing beneath the black, echoing arches to peer through the shop windows of Hudson Street or climbing the hill past the allotments and gazing through the wrought-iron gates at the big houses clustered around Simonside Lodge.

As Catherine discovered a bigger world, the ancestry Kate had conjured for her offspring was confined to the closed drawers and shallow minds in which families bury their secrets. The immediate problem had been to provide little 'Kitty' with a home. But the home to which she returned, grubby and scuff-kneed, was a noisy and confusing place.

Her 'mother' was older than most with children of Catherine's age. Rose was, by then, in her fifties. Tall and flat faced, with a nose that looked as if it had been broken at some time, she parted her dark brown hair down the centre of her head and tied it back in a tight bun. Around the house Rose wore an ankle-length apron and a blouse buttoned to the neck. When she went out she always wore a bonnet and cape.

The 'Father' – as everyone in the house called John McMullen – was thin and gaunt and looked much older than a man almost sixty. His receding hair left him with a large forehead dominated by thick, wide eyebrows above suspicious dark eyes. A bristly moustache helped to hide his empty, sunken cheeks.

Catherine's 'brother', although apparently kind to his step-niece, had inherited his father's aggression. Jack McMullen was earning his own reputation as a fighter. Arguments between father and son frequently escalated into fist fights. Anyone who attempted to intervene, as Catherine soon discovered, was ferociously flung aside.

Home was where Kate and Sarah and Mary returned. Home was the place Catherine ate and slept and played. It was hardly surprising that she accepted herself as a McMullen.

Kate had returned to service in the autumn of 1906, when her daughter was less than four months' old. She came home, like Sarah and Mary, only for brief visits. Even though her appearances were confined to her days or afternoons off, the Father exerted another kind of dominance over his stepdaughter – the blackmail of duty.

Kate was working in a baker's shop in Chester-le-Street, County Durham, two stops down the railway line which passed through Lamesley. From the train she could see the Ravensworth Arms. The brown paper parcel she carried on her return to Tyne Dock invariably contained part of her wages taken as bread and groceries. She was to blame for the child, the Father kept telling her, and the child had to be fed.

Rose exacted a more subtle sentence. Each time Kate returned she noticed her daughter was a little more distant, a little more reserved. When she was hurt or frightened, Catherine ran instinctively to Rose. She sought her grandmother's approval. And whenever Kate hugged her daughter the child was swiftly retrieved by Rose to be tidied and have her clothes set straight.

Once, not long after the Lodges' arrival at Leam Lane End in 1911, Catherine was invited to a birthday party by one of the Lodge children. The event proved a success for everyone except Catherine, who managed to snap a string of pearl beads her Aunt Mary had given her to wear. The result was a severe spanking.

Beyond the end of the terrace in which the McMullens lived and across the entrance to the gas works was the Dixons' cottage. Anne and George Dixon were a family of a different social class to the McMullens. To supplement George's wage as a trimmer, levelling the cargo of ships berthed at Tyne Dock, the couple kept poultry and pigs and grew vegetables and flowers.

Beyond the Dixons' cottage the road curved and rose until it reached Simonside and bridged the Newcastle–South Shields railway line. For official purposes the road was recorded as Simonside Lane; its postal address was Leam Lane; in Roman times it had been called Wreken Dike. At the far end of the village, overlooking the railway sidings and backing on to the graveyard, was Simonside Protestant School.

Catherine started attending classes when the school reopened after the long summer holiday on 2 September 1910. She was four years old.

On the same day a government inspector delivered his report, following an inspection of the classes the previous July. 'A pleasant tone prevails and the school presents some fairly satisfactory features,' he said, 'but much of the work shows a want of neatness and care, and the general supervision is rather lax.' Of the two youngest classes, the bottom of which Catherine had just joined, he added, 'The infants are under kindly and judicious control.'

Two teachers were responsible for the sixty-three infant pupils at Simonside School. Catherine's first teacher was a Miss Kere. The following year she moved up to Miss Oliver's class. Each autumn the headmistress, Miss Clark, personally tested each stream. Her verdict on Catherine's second-year class was that 'written arithmetic and spelling were creditable, the oral arithmetic was not so good . . . The writing and figures need care.'

Attendance wavered between satisfactory and poor. Outbreaks of mumps, chickenpox and measles rotated from class to class. In 1913 one seven-year-old girl had to be removed from the register after suffering a heart attack during a lesson.

The classrooms were cramped and chilly. In many cases conditions were far worse than in the children's own homes. A governors' inspection complained: 'The rooms were cold although the heating apparatus was in use . . . The boy's lobby is unventilated and is too small . . . The classes present a neglected appearance and some have no doors . . . Light and low portable screens would be useful when two classes are taught in one room.' Toilet facilities were no better. 'The boy's urinal is insufficiently screened from the playground and cemetery and there is no proper urinal for the infants.'

Each schoolday morning Miss Kere walked up Simonside Bank, collecting Catherine on the way. Rose always made sure she left the house in a tidy pinafore and with her reddish chestnut hair in tight, neat ringlets.

When Catherine returned from school her grandmother would be humming one of the few tunes she knew. Encouraged by the child she would lift Catherine on to her lap and sing the words:

> Love, it is teasing
> Love, it is pleasing,
> Love is a pleasure
> When it is new;
> But as it grows older
> And days grow colder
> It fades away like the
> Morning dew.

One day Catherine returned with a book. It was *The Chatter Box Annual*. She had borrowed it from the daughter of the school caretaker, a man called Taylor. Each day Catherine would read a new story from the brightly coloured annual. The days turned into weeks and the weeks into months. The book's increasingly threadbare appearance added to Catherine's reluctance to part with it. Years later Catherine could still not bring herself to look at the girl whose book she had stolen. It was to become her 'guilty' book.

Two

Everybody had to have a Da, they had to be borned. You couldn't be borned without a Da.

NOT LONG AFTER her sixth birthday – in June 1912 – Catherine joined the McMullens' other possessions on the back of a flat horse-drawn cart and was transported the half mile from Leam Lane to William Black Street.

The McMullens did not move immediately into No 10, their third and final home in William Black Street. For a few weeks John and Rose McMullen, young Jack and Catherine took an upstairs house further up the terrace.

Nobody told Kate or her sisters about the move. She arrived at Leam Lane on her day off from service to find the house empty. Fired with a mixture of anger and fear, she thought the worst. It wasn't until she saw Catherine swinging from a rope tied to a lamp post that she found out the family was still together. Rose was too poor even to write and tell her daughters where they had gone.

William Black Street was one of four partly completed roads which made up the New Buildings. None of the four streets was finished. Maps of the time included the outline of the complete estate, the wasteland already overgrown or used as allotments. It was an estate of sixty-nine homes begun to serve an already dying industry and left in no-man's-land between two Tyneside boroughs.

Although commonly known as East Jarrow, the New Buildings were actually within the borough of South Shields. The boundary between South Shields and Jarrow separated the estate from the true East Jarrow, an industrial outpost known locally as Bogey Hill, further along Swinburne Street and half a mile to the west.

From the open-topped trams – which had started running on a single track down the centre of the Jarrow Road late in 1906 – the buildings on Simonside Terrace, overlooking the road and Jarrow Slake, were an impressive sight. The two rows which made up the terrace had been built five or six feet above the level of the road, and most had small front gardens and steps up to the front door. Number 1 Simonside Terrace was in a class of its own. Constructed of heavy, grey-stone blocks it had two large bay windows each side of a flight of wide steps. The house had been built for the Larkin family, whose business empire had, at one time, included the Barium Chemical Works.

Three of the streets on the eight-acre site ran north to south. On the far left was Lancaster Street. Unlike the other homes the three houses in Lancaster Street had no back lane. Land between them and the front doors of Phillipson Street – intended for more houses – had been left vacant. The back yards of the nine houses in Phillipson Street, one to each household, were separated from the houses in William Black Street by a narrow cobbled lane.

Reflecting the working-class hierarchy of the time, each street included a larger house for a minor works' official. Number 2 William Black Street, with its gable end facing the enclosed rear of the Larkins' house in Simonside Terrace, was a self-contained seven-roomed house. The remaining houses in William Black Street were separated into upstairs and downstairs homes. The upper homes had four rooms while those who lived beneath were forced to live in three. Both shared a single back yard.

The downstairs house second from the far end of William Black Street was No 26. It was already occupied by Rose's sister, Margaret Hindes, and her son James when the McMullens returned to the New Buildings. Catherine called her Aunt Maggie.

Number 10 was also a ground-floor house. The front door opened on to a wide pavement and was used only for formal visits and special occasions. Across from William Black Street, and running the length of the road, was a black timber fence behind which grew cereals and occasionally potatoes. The field was owned by a farmer who lived opposite Catherine's Simonside school, and provided illicit pickings for the neighbourhood children. At election time some residents would paint the front step according to their allegiance; green for Labour or blue for Liberal. Catherine, dressed in a long-sleeved frock and with ribbons in her hair, stood on the doorstep to have her photograph taken during the summer of 1912.

From the tiny front hallway – with its heavy patterned wallpaper – you turned left into the front room. It was a room crammed with an excess of furniture. Stiff-backed armchairs, a long oval table and, wedged into an alcove, a double brass bed.

At the back of the house was the kitchen, warmed by the constant activity, yet never free from the dust and soot given out by the open range. The name of its maker – Grieve & Gillespie, Jarrow on Tyne – was embossed across the top. Each side of the black-leaded range with its heavy oven door was an alcove. In the left-hand space – beside an old chest of drawers – stood an outsize gas cooker Kate had acquired from a hotel; it was never connected to the supply. To the right of the range, tall wooden doors enclosed a cupboard. Beneath the opposite wall, and pressed behind a large leather-topped table, was a six-foot saddle or settee. And spread on the floor between the table and the range lay the family's clippy mat, twisted and sewn from oddments of brightly coloured material.

The narrow kitchen took up half the width of the front room. The remaining half contained the bedroom. To enter it you had to squeeze between a small kitchen table beneath the window and the end of the larger table and the saddle. There was little more space in the bedroom. Half the floor area was taken up by a brass bed, its head against the dividing wall with the front room and opposite a window. On either side of the door were a chest of drawers and a small marble-topped wash-stand; there was never a basin or jug. Also stored in the bedroom was an early box sewing machine.

The water tap, serving both the lower and upper houses, was at the far end of the yard.

Occupied or empty, the kitchen was dominated by the Father's high-backed wooden chair. It was placed at an angle to the range, with its front legs on the clippy mat and its back to the scullery and backyard doors.

John McMullen never forgot his Army life in India – and he never forgave Lord Roberts. Life on the subcontinent was hard, hot and squalid. When he was sober John McMullen spoke little of the defeat of the Afghans in the late 1870s or the march from Kabul to relieve Kandahar in 1880. But when the drink worked on him he would point an angry finger at a picture of Lord Roberts mounted on a horse and guarded by a native and curse the field-marshal.

The picture hung on the far wall opposite the range and young Catherine had not yet learned to distinguish between the noble lord and her step-grandfather. For years she thought the Father was chastising the black man for not holding his horse properly.

When he was drunk John McMullen would empty the kitchen of its inhabitants by swinging an iron poker he called 'Dennis' above his head before subsiding into songs of virtuous women and his innocent homeland.

> *I love a lassie,*
> *A bonny, bonny lassie;*
> *She's as pure as the lily in the dell.*

And at one or two in the morning, standing to attention to face 'old Ireland far away' beyond the blackness of the kitchen window:

> *Sing us an Irish Comaylia,*
> *sing us an Irish tune,*
> *for Patsy Burke has buggered his work,*
> *all by the light of the moon.*

IT was never doubted — least of all by Kate herself — that she should return to take over the running of the house and the nursing of her mother. Rose's health continued to deteriorate. She found it increasingly difficult to move around. Kate, unmarried and in service, was told she must come home.

Swollen ankles were an occupational hazard for thousands of working-class women prior to the First World War. Hidden by long skirts, it was an affliction to be ignored and endured. But in the months before the move from Leam Lane End Rose McMullen had put on so much weight that she found it painful and awkward to move around. Climbing the backyard stairs to the McMullens' first house in William Black Street presented more problems, and may even have prompted the second move.

Shortly after the family transferred to No 10 Dr McHaffie ordered Rose to bed. He diagnosed dropsy; today doctors would call it oedema, a condition caused by fluid leaking from the circulatory system and accumulating in the body's tissues, usually around the ankles and legs, where it arrives by gravity. Dr McHaffie had qualified at Glasgow before setting up his surgery at the Post Office Buildings in Hudson Street, Tyne Dock. He was well liked, possibly because he seldom passed judgment on the condition or causes of his patients' ailments. He was undoubtedly aware that Rose's dropsy was an indication of other, more serious, problems of the circulatory, respiratory or urinary systems.

Despite the hard, ceaseless work, Kate discovered relative contentment. The kitchen was the hub around which the entire household revolved. A composite world where everything happened: laughter; tears; gossip; struggles; drunkenness; fights. It was also a world which had to be fed and Kate enjoyed cooking.

Catherine would watch her mother making the bread from the corner of the room where she sat reading her 'guilty' book – 'I'll put that book in the fire! Get it out of your hand' – or be forced to shuffle along the fender – 'Move your backside out of that, get along there' – to where the cold metal caught her between the bottom of her knickers and top of her stockings. To test the bread Kate would tap on the bottom of the upturned loaf tins, acknowledging her debt by nodding at the oven.

In the mornings Catherine attempted to predict the day's outcome by reading the embossed letters on the range between the ticks of the clock. G – tick – R – tick – I – tick . . . If the letters fitted exactly she was sure the day would be a good one. Somehow they never did.

The young girls of the New Buildings often gathered around the gable end of William Black Street to play shops with boody – scraps of metal and glass which took the place of treacle and salt-filled boody jars used in shops. Catherine had the thick end of a broken beer bottle which, because of its deep brown colour, she pretended was a slab of toffee. One day in the autumn of 1913 the prized piece of boody disappeared. Catherine squared up to a girl she accused of pocketing it.

'I'll go down and tell me Da of you,' she threatened.

'You ain't got no Da. It's your Granda,' the girl retorted.

The revelation exploded in Catherine's mind. She turned and ran. 'Everybody had to have a Da, they had to be borned. You couldn't be borned without a Da.' And if her Granda wasn't her father that meant her Grandma was no longer her mother. One person would know the truth. Catherine would ask Kate. Looking up the yard, she could see Kate through the kitchen window. 'She had a cooking table under the window and I could see her busying and I knew when I looked at her that she was my Ma,' Catherine admitted many years later in *Our Kate*.

The task of fetching the beer was given to Catherine. From the age of seven she would take two or three empty bottles to be filled at the Alkali Hotel further along Swinburne Street towards Bogey Hill or to the 'Twenty-Seven' at Leam Lane. Catherine still bares the scars of one such expedition. She had been sent with two bottles to the 'Twenty-Seven'. As she opened the gate to the back yard a Dalmatian dog leapt at her and sank its teeth into her left arm. The dog was only dragged off when the barman heard her screams.

One friend who accompanied Catherine on her trips to the Alkali, although with strict orders never to go inside, was Flori Harding, who lived at No 20 William Black Street.

Flori's parents had moved to the New Buildings soon after their marriage in 1902. Jim Harding, although only a coal trimmer working at Tyne Dock, took the opportunity to buy two homes. He and his young bride, also called Flori, lived upstairs in No 20 while renting out No 22 below. Their eldest son Bill was born in 1902. By April 1913, when their fifth child, Irene, arrived, there were seven members of the Harding family living in four small rooms. Flori, born the same year as Catherine in 1906, became a close friend.

Irene Harding, now Irene Callender, remembers Kate as a 'kind-hearted woman' who would do anything for her neighbours. To solve the problem of knowing two Kates the Harding children dubbed mother and daughter 'Big Kate' and 'Little Kate'. To the other girls in the New Buildings Catherine was known as 'Kate-Kate'.

By the time she was eight years' old Catherine was carrying a stone jar the McMullens called the 'grey hen' to an outdoor beer shop in Hudson Street. Two shillings' worth of beer would fill the grey hen to the neck. It was so heavy when full that Catherine needed to walk with it resting on her hip.

Although Flori Harding would keep her friend company, Catherine was the only child from the New Buildings sent for beer.

The overheard comments of the neighbours filled her with shame. Other chores filled her with revulsion.

It was common practice in the New Buildings to supplement a family's food supply by keeping poultry. Hens or ducks ran free in most backyards. Soon after the McMullens moved to No 10 the Father decided he too would fill what little space there was between the house and the coal shed with low, wire chicken runs. He also kept rabbits.

Each evening before she was allowed to go to bed – rarely before nine o'clock – Catherine went into the yard with the Father to 'try the hens'. John McMullen would take the large run while Catherine worked her way through the hens in the smaller pens. The job involved inserting her finger into the bird's rear passage to determine how many of the hens would lay the next morning and how many in the afternoon.

If the prospect of fresh eggs looked bleak John McMullen was not beyond employing a little skulduggery to increase supply. One trick involved enticing his neighbours' hens into the McMullens' yard by laying a trail of corn down the back lane.

Trying the hens was not the only job which made Catherine retch. Another task she was expected to carry out without question was holding the ducks or hens while John McMullen slit their throats.

THE New Buildings had been built at the bottom of a U-shaped bay on the southern shore of the River Tyne. The Romans had landed and camped on its western shore. Centuries later it had been the site of St Mary's Monastery where the Venerable Bede had taught and preached, looking out over what was then known as the Bay of Ecgrid's Haven.

The twice-daily tide had deposited centuries of silt into the bay. The River Don, which once drained freely into the Tyne, now ran through to the open river in a steep-sided, treacherous 'gut'.

This wasteland – known as Jarrow Slake – was a natural magnet for the industrialists of the early nineteenth century. Tyneside was the centre of Britain's chemical industry and the area's largest factory, Jarrow Alkali Works, was built on the east bank of the slake. In 1857 a public house was built on Swinburne Street to serve the workers whose throats and eyes burned from the chemical fumes. It was called the Alkali Hotel. Fifty years later it was the closest source of beer for the McMullens. But its opening came too late. The chemical industry was already in decline and by the 1880s only two alkali works remained; Charles Gidney's St Bede Chemical Works, also on Swinburne Street, and immediately to the west, the Lake Chemical Works. In 1891 the Lake Works was bought by the Hedworth Barium Company and used to manufacture a disinfectant from a secret formula.

Originally the slake had extended further east toward South Shields. Countless schemes were devised for its use. In 1856 work started on Tyne Dock, reclaiming almost sixty acres from the mud flats. Three years later the dock – capable of loading up to forty ships at a time and berthing 400 others – was completed. By 1902 more than seven million tons of Durham coal passed through Tyne Dock.

Since the 1860s what remained of the slake was used as a seasoning pond for timber imported from Scandinavia; great chunks of roughly trimmed wood the size of railway sleepers were stapled together by iron clips. At high water all that could be seen were the tops of irregularly placed posts and the straight line of a make-shift fence marking the pond's boundary with the Tyne.

One other feature remained, although ignored completely by official maps of the time. A precarious cat walk, only inches above the rising tide, led across the slake to a floating isolation hospital. Moored at the edge of the main river, it consisted of a cluster of buildings on an extensive raft. The hospital was clearly visible from the New Buildings, yet the fear of cholera and other diseases brought in by the seamen exerted a strange taboo over any contact with it.

The timber ponds had a near-fatal attraction for Catherine and the other children from the New Buildings. One game was called 'playing the piano'. It involved jumping from one half-submerged plank to the next before the extra weight dunked it beneath the water.

One Sunday in May, before Catherine's thirteenth birthday, she took part in the procession of Our Lady at a Tyne Dock church. She walked behind the bier wearing a white dress, white shoes and socks and with a veil crowned with blue forget-me-nots. None of her family could attend the service, so Catherine walked home with two boys from her class at St Peter and Paul's school.

As the trio emerged from under the saw-mill bridge spanning the Jarrow Road, Catherine dared her companions to a game of 'playing the piano'. Forgetting her fear of water – which she finally overcame almost fifty years later – she led the way across the floating landscape. Timbers which sank, or had disappeared, were often replaced by a collection of rubbish. Skipping at speed across the timber pond, Catherine mistook some floating debris and plunged into the water.

Panic-stricken, her friends fled. Catherine, unable to swim, sank below the level of the solid raft. It was pure good luck that she floated to the surface and emerged in the narrow gap between the timbers. As she gasped for air, the water stifling her screams, two hands grabbed her tiny body and hauled her to safety.

Catherine returned, exhausted and shaken, to face Kate's ice-cold anger, her white outfit stinking from the filthy water.

A neighbour was not so lucky. In 1913 James Kilbride – a 'nice man' called Matty by his neighbours in Phillipson Street – decided to take a boat along the gut. He intended to row across the river to look at a ship moored on the Howden side. As he reached the open river the tide turned and he was caught in a fierce whirlpool. The boat capsized and he was drowned.

The tragedy swept through the streets, to be retold and embellished in every kitchen. Catherine used the incident almost forty years later in *The Fifteen Streets* when Katie and Christine die in the racing waters of the Tyne.

The accident did not stop Catherine accepting trips in a neighbour's motor boat – until a moment of panic almost caused a second tragedy. Jim Harding had renamed his boat the *Irene* after the birth of his youngest child in April 1913. Whenever the weather was fine he would take his older children and their friends for trips up and down the river. His oldest son, Bill, was allowed to steer the boat. On one occasion Catherine thought Bill was about to collide with something in the water and stood up before making a grab for the tiller. Jim Harding managed to regain control of the rocking boat but vowed never to allow Catherine aboard again.

A few months later Catherine was forced to watch from the shore as her friends witnessed the departure of the 27,000-ton battle-cruiser HMS *Queen Mary* from the tiny *Irene*. Both sides of the Tyne were crowded with onlookers as the massive warship, built at Palmer's Jarrow yard, left the river for the last time on 30 August 1913. The *Queen Mary* was sunk in 1916 at the Battle of Jutland. Only nineteen of her crew of 1,266 survived.

CONDITIONS at No 10 were cramped but never squalid, Kate saw to that. To bring in a few more coppers the family took in lodgers. Sometimes there were as many as six or seven people living and sleeping in the three-roomed downstairs house.

The lodgers slept in the bedroom with Jack McMullen. Rose McMullen slept where she spent most of her days, on the couch in the front room, with her husband sleeping in the brass bed. Catherine and Kate spent the nights on the saddle in the small kitchen. When even more lodgers were squeezed in, mother and daughter slept each night at Aunt Mary's, further up William Black Street, while Jack occupied the saddle in the kitchen. Mary had married Alexander Hamilton Charlton when she was twenty-five. They had moved to No 30, the downstairs house at the top of the street, within months of the McMullens moving to No 10.

The lodgers would come and go. One, who came almost as frequently as he was ordered to go, was Billy Potts. Like the Father and young Jack McMullen, Billy was a docker. He could have lodged with his relations who lived above a shop in Leam Lane, but for some reason Billy, a man who never failed to quench his own thirst, objected to their drinking.

Catherine had a soft spot for Billy, 'a rough, unintelligent lump of a man', mainly because when Billy was lodging she was let off the regular Saturday morning trek into Jarrow to fetch half a stone of grain and a stone of boxings to feed the backyard ducks and hens for the coming week. Billy had another way of keeping the birds supplied.

It was common for dockers working in ships' holds to hitch their trousers up beneath the knees with pieces of string or leather. The popular reason for tying 'yorks' was to stop the rats running up the men's legs. Whenever he was unloading a grain ship Billy would fill his trouser legs above the 'yorks' with grain. He would waddle, as naturally as possible, out of the dock gates and back to No 10. Kate would then make him stand on a canvas sack while she released the ties on his legs and retrieved his haul of grain.

But the stream of lodgers brought with it more than simply

money. The kitchen was filled with new stories of sadness and laughter and Catherine's head with a dizzy whirl of fresh hope. For Kate hope was a luxury. Life, she told her daughter some years later, appeared to be 'running out fast through a dark alleyway'. It was exhausting merely attempting to keep up.

In addition to cooking, cleaning and washing for the McMullen household – a routine which frequently began before six in the morning – Kate also took half- and full-day jobs wherever she could find them. The wash-house, with its boiler, poss-tub and mangle, was situated in the yard next to the upstairs staircase. Taking in washing allowed Kate to work from home, but it was a tough, exhausting day's work.

In 1912 Kate first met the man she was eventually to marry.

Jack McMullen was usually employed at Tyne Dock off-loading ships of iron ore for the steel furnaces at Consett. One day he was ordered to work on an ocean-going cargo ship, most of whose crew came from Maryport in Westmorland. Jack was quick to invite some of the men back to No 10 for free food and drink. The group of seamen included David McDermott and Jack Stoddard. McDermott, like his master mariner father, had spent all his working life at sea, mostly as an engine-room fireman. He was married to Stoddard's sister. At thirty-six he was quiet and jolly and enjoyed bouncing the six-year-old Catherine on his knee.

The visits became a regular occurrence. News of the ship's return filled Catherine with endless despair. Although they were clean mouthed and respectable enough the seamen also had money, and that meant drink. They needed little encouragement from Jack or John McMullen to hold a party at No 10. Unlike the family gatherings, the parties paid for by the seamen seldom ended in a fight. Bolstered by drink Kate, who had a natural and good voice, would sing 'I Dreamt I Dwelt in Marble Halls' while her daughter slunk into a corner of the kitchen or sat with her head bowed low and her hands buried deep between her knees.

Stoddard soon began to show an interest in Kate. Flattered by the attention, Kate knew that any attempt to set her free from William Black Street would be swiftly and ruthlessly dealt with by John McMullen. When the war started Jack Stoddard enlisted and was taken prisoner within months. Catherine wrote him letters in her spidery handwriting. Then one day Kate asked her daughter to stop sending the letters. David McDermott's wife had just died. Kate found herself caring more for the lonely seaman than his absent friend.

SOLITUDE was in short supply in the McMullen household. At night Catherine could lie with her eyes closed and watch the pictures in her head or lose herself among the maze of the pattern on the wallpaper. But when the house was awake there were few corners in which she could hide.

Driven out of the house – or afraid to go into it to be confronted by Kate – Catherine locked herself in the toilet at the end of the yard. The brick-built lavatory was divided in two and shared with the family upstairs. With the wooden lid down Catherine would pick thoughtfully at the white-washed plaster and peep at the world through the gap above the door. There was no pan or cistern, the dry toilet was emptied by a 'scavenger' who thrust his long-handled shovel into the toilet through an outside flap no matter who was using it at the time. The intrusion left her hot and blushing. Outside the neighbourhood children would chant as they followed the scavenger's cart up the back lane.

> *Cloggy Betty, on the netty*
> *On a Sunday morning . . .*

Catherine used the space between the rough beams and the roof as a place to hide her precious savings. A halfpenny saved from bringing back the beer. A penny from Uncle Jack. Coins for her future. For special days.

'It was my mother's birthday and I had saved tuppence-halfpenny,' Catherine recalled many years later. 'I had heard her say she loved a pear so I went to the fruit shop up Stanhope Road and I bought the biggest pear they had.

'I took it home and I can still see the pleasure that registered on Kate's face as I gave it to her. She cut it in half and gave one half to me. It was marvellous.'

The hoard of cash was not always spent on things which met with Kate's approval.

It was Guy Fawkes' Day. Catherine had been kept back from school to run an errand for her mother. She knew exactly how much was hidden in the lavatory without counting it. With the penny she had just been given she now had fourpence. She walked round to the small general dealers' shop in Phillipson Street and asked what was the biggest firework they had. It was called a One O'Clock Gun and cost fourpence.

Armed with her firework, Catherine decided the best course of action would be to hide. If Kate – who hated all fireworks – caught her with it she would be skinned alive. The safest place was the three-foot gap between the end of the backyard hen crees and the bedroom wall. Blocked by the rain barrel Catherine could crouch down or sit on the bedroom windowsill unseen and out of Kate's or John McMullen's reach.

Catherine peered in through the bedroom window. She knew exactly who was inside without looking. Whenever Billy Potts was lodging at No 10, Kate insisted on wedging the bottom of the sash window open about six inches because not only did Billy suffer from severe flatulence, but he was not too fussy about personal hygiene. This afternoon the docker was stretched out asleep on top of the bed in his long-johns. Billy always swapped his work cap for a different one when he went to bed.

Catherine was getting bored. Her plan had been to wait until her friends arrived back from school and then show off the firework before a ceremonious ignition at the top corner.

Catherine decided to light the long fuse hanging down the side of the One O'Clock Gun. She would let it smoke for a few seconds before snuffing it out. Instead the fuse spluttered into life, spitting out sparks. Catherine – who had never held a firework in her hand before – panicked. A wild notion came to her that if she flung the firework through the gap in the window it would roll under the bed and put itself out. Which is exactly what she did. The firework was not so obliging. The roar of the explosion rattled the window and drowned her screams.

As Catherine stood up to squeeze between the rain butt and the crees, the back door burst open. Billy Potts – still in his long-johns but minus his flat cap – shot through the yard. Catherine dived for cover as Kate and John McMullen emerged followed by whiffs of black smoke.

Billy left the next day and never attempted to persuade Kate to take him back.

THE dubious responsibility of juggling the family's meagre finances fell to Kate.

The McMullens were never truly poor. There were more hard pressed families among those who occupied the New Buildings. Money flowed into No 10 as frequently as it flowed out. Both John and his son were working in the dock, yet they considered a man's wages his own property. The only extra income came from the occasional lodgers. Kate – ever resourceful and ever proud – never failed to provide at least the basics of life. There was always debt. But it was new debt, weekly debt, money borrowed from Peter to pay Paul.

Kate readily took any paying job she could find. She would take in bundles of washing or clean and dust the homes of people she considered socially 'worse' than herself. She even took on jobs only offered to a woman because she would be paid less, such as painting and decorating or replacing whole window-frames. However back-breaking the work she never earned more than three shillings a day. From it odd sixpences and shillings would be kept back for 'some of the hard' when work was scarce.

Slowly Catherine became aware of a change in her mother. Traits she had only noticed during celebrations or parties began to surface whenever there was money in the house and the smell of whisky would be on Kate's breath. When she had been drinking Kate would sniff repeatedly, as if she had a slight cold. Walking up the street, the action of her left foot became more pronounced. The blue of her eyes appeared to change colour and her mouth would change shape.

Kate knew she was trapped by the inevitability of her fate. She had been shown a way out, offered a better life, and had the door slammed in her face. 'Don't stand there looking at me with his eyes,' she would shout at Catherine. 'Don't look at me like that. Haven't I got enough to put up with?'

Kate was also enduring a secret torment. Exhausted by the day's work she would spend most nights dozing in a state of fear. Jack, whose shyness and fear of women had become a family joke, saw nothing wrong in demanding attention from his half-sister. Kate fought to keep Jack from raping her and to stifle any screams which would have woken her daughter, asleep beside her in the bed. Once, dressed only in a nightgown, she fled through the kitchen and locked herself in the toilet until daybreak. The only nights she knew she would be safe were those when Jack staggered home drunk and collapsed in the kitchen.

In the spring of 1914 there had been a few, brief weeks of hope. Kate watched in despair as the money which could have cleared their debts literally slipped through her fingers.

John McMullen, then nearly sixty, had injured his leg in an accident while working at Tyne Dock. Prompt medical attention would probably have eased the pain and brought about a full recovery. His stubbornness and misplaced pride allowed the wound to worsen, until in the end he was reduced to sitting in front of the range with his leg raised or hobbling around with the aid of a stick.

He applied to the North Eastern Railway for compensation. After several weeks of haggling he was offered £100. There was one condition: that he would never be employed in the dock again. The cash, when it arrived, was locked in the little drawer of the box sewing machine.

The rent for No 10 was 4s 6d (22.5 pence) a week. Within a year of moving to the New Buildings the McMullens had sunk into arrears, never owing less than £3. Even allowing for the obligatory celebration, clearing the overdue rent and other debts, the compensation money would have kept the family housed and fed for the best part of a year.

John McMullen had other plans. He had waited long enough for a new suit; Rose would get a new outfit; Jack would get his share, and young Catherine was promised a new bicycle. Kate, still nursing her mother and increasingly at the beck and call of her stepfather, was promised nothing.

Each evening Rose would dip into the money and hand Kate enough for beer or whisky. A few pounds were spent on furniture and other oddments. The promises evaporated as quickly as the money.

Making her way back from Jarrow with the seed or carrying the grey hen full of beer, Catherine let her mind play with the new words she had learned at school or heard the lodgers use. The sound of a word would spark an idea and from the idea would flow a story which Catherine would, at the same time, both tell and listen to.

The stories diverted her from the taunts of her friends and the flickering of shame at Kate's drinking. At other times she retreated to the earth toilet at the bottom of the yard. Catherine would rely on her imagination to rescue her, to provide her with the one thing she wanted more than anything else – a 'Da'.

She examined, and rejected, several candidates. The problem was solved one day while she was on her way back to Simonside School. Dr McHaffie had called on John McMullen to examine his leg. Perhaps Catherine would like a lift in his car? She had never ridden in a car before. Watched open-mouthed by her fellow pupils as he delivered her to school at the top of Simonside Bank, his young passenger was not going to waste the chance to pay them back for their scoffing and doubts about the 'great big house' in which Catherine lived and the 'three servants and two cars and two horses . . . galloping ones'. Dr McHaffie was her 'Da' and she didn't care who knew it.

It wasn't the last time Catherine was to make use of the innocent doctor and her playground announcement. Thirty-six years later a young doctor becomes the hero of her first novel, *Kate Hannigan*. He too drives a motor car, delivers an illegitimate baby and finds himself named as her father. Happily for Dr McHaffie Catherine's desperate claim was never taken seriously.

EVEN before she was eight years old Catherine was forced to carry the guilt of adults.

In his naïve way Jack Stoddard still considered Kate as a possible wife. Although she refused to 'walk out' with the seaman, she did little to disillusion him. He was certainly unaware that Kate had attracted the attention of a man lodging next door. Unlike John McMullen, who had lost his brogue, this tall, handsome Irishman spoke as Catherine imagined everyone across the 'watter' spoke, with a 'thick, laughing voice'. One word he used quite frequently was 'marriage'.

Catherine got used to the Irishman spending more and more time at No 10. One Saturday evening Kate slipped out to buy some beer, leaving her suitor and Catherine alone in the kitchen. As the door closed the child felt the workman's hands lift her first on to his knee and then carry her to the old leather chair. He began to kiss her; not playfully, but in a sexual, frightening way. Catherine screamed and tried to push him off. 'Let me go. Don't do bad things. No. No.'

The fear of what John McMullen might do to the man if ever he discovered what the Irishman had inflicted on the child backed Catherine into a corner of silence. The thought that this man might one day become her father terrified her even more. Catherine kept her secret. But, after one particularly violent family row, the subject of marriage was forgotten.

Three

This environment was the womb in which my imagination was bred.

CATHERINE'S WAR BEGAN on Wednesday, 5 August 1914. Early on Tuesday morning the German troops had marched into Luxembourg. That night, at 11 pm, while Catherine slept beside her mother on the kitchen saddle the British government's ultimatum ran out. When she opened her eyes the next morning Great Britain was at war with Germany.

On Wednesday morning Catherine walked down the back lane and across the Jarrow Road to sit on the bank of Jarrow Slake. Ships were moving up and down the river.

Earlier that morning a troop of soldiers disembarked from a commandeered tram and marched through the Tyne Dock gates to seize the sole German ship berthed at the staithes. The steamer *Albert Clement* had arrived during the weekend from the White Sea loaded with timber. Its crew surrendered without a struggle.

War, Catherine knew, was a noisy business. All she could hear were the sounds of the river. The time for listening was over. She needed to talk to someone. Anyone.

In Phillipson Street she found Mary McArthur cleaning the front step of No 17.

'Mrs McArthur,' Catherine said, 'do you know there's a war on?'

The woman said she did.

'I've been sitting on the slake bank waiting for ages for it to start. They take their time, don't they?'

That afternoon an elderly Lord Roberts – whose picture had stood guard over the kitchen of No 10 for so long – sat with ministers and other senior officers at a Downing Street council of war to discuss a military response. On Tyneside life continued very much as usual. The front page of the *Shields Daily Gazette* carried a single reference to the crisis. Beneath a Fowler & Brooks advertisement – offering ladies' 'pirate' caps from sixpence three-farthings – was the announcement of an anti-war demonstration demanding 'England must be neutral'. The Grand Electric Theatre and the Picture House in Ocean Road, South Shields, were prophetically showing *The Port of Doom* and *Repentance*.

The men in the docks and yards were working longer hours. Blue and khaki uniforms were everywhere. Women queued outside the shops for food and, for the first time, Catherine was forced to wait in line for beer. Familiar faces also began to disappear.

One Friday evening in the late summer of 1914 Jack McMullen left the New Buildings for an evening's drinking with his friends. He returned late. The following morning he announced that the group of dockers had ended the drunken outing with a visit to a South Shields recruiting office. Jack McMullen had mistakenly given his place of birth as Tyne Dock, instead of Jarrow. It was a technicality. The Army needed every man it could get.

Instead of finding himself in France 24-year-old Jack was posted to 3 Durham Light Infantry (DLI), a reserve battalion made up almost exclusively of local officers and men. Its task, throughout the war, was to protect the Durham coastline with a series of trenches and machine-gun posts running from the mouth of the Tyne at South Shields to Whitburn. The most likely target for a German raid was the Royal Naval Air Service seaplane sheds just inside the river's South Pier.

The Army had taken over a number of South Shields schools and converted them to billets. Jack was stationed at Mortimer Road School. The building had been hastily closed and converted; spare classrooms were stacked with desks and chairs, and cupboards were crammed with textbooks and half-used exercise books.

Catherine spent most Saturday afternoons queuing for beer. One weekend, as she made her way back to the New Buildings, she met Jack in his khaki uniform. He was cheerful and 'solid and sober', and instead of the steel plates of his work shoes jangling on the cobbles his polished Army boots hit the ground with a purpose.

Before they reached No 10 Jack slipped Catherine a penny. It wasn't the only present he was to bring her on his days off duty. Sometimes he stole exercise books. Catherine opened one book to discover the picture of a little girl. She was sitting beside a blazing open fire, with a cup and saucer on a table and a kitten playing at her feet. The picture symbolised stability and comfort and stayed with Catherine long after she lost the book. Years later the image prompted her to write one of her children's books.

Aunt Mary's husband, Alec Charlton, lost no time in volunteering for military service, but he was rejected on medical grounds. The houseproud but still volatile Aunt Mary was to have two sons, Jack and Alex. When she considered Catherine old enough she asked her niece to baby-sit. As soon as the coast was clear, and the young boys settled, Catherine went from cupboard to cupboard examining the family's possessions.

Always a social climber, Mary had long coveted No 2 William Black Street, occupied by a family called Christopher. When it became vacant in the 1920s the Charltons moved in.

Mary's temper earned her few friends. Even Kate was not spared her sister's tongue. Each row was followed by a period of icy silence. Contact between the two sisters was broken. During one such period Mary gave birth to her third child, Theresa. Despite living only yards away Catherine did not see the baby for five months.

Mary's husband Alec shared none of his wife's petty grudges. He was a favourite of Catherine's, possibly because he was a clever man also intrigued by words. One of his hobbies was entering competitions. When crosswords began to appear in newspapers and magazines he became an avid fan.

As the Durham Light Infantry losses mounted on the Western Front, men from the 3rd Battalion were transferred to the 15th (Service) Battalion in France. John McMullen, the old soldier, was proud of his son.

In France it soon became apparent to Jack's officers that he was one of the best shots in his company. His battalion sniping officer ordered him to draw a rifle with a Ross telescopic sight. Snipers on both sides operated largely independently of their parent unit. Most wore camouflaged clothing. Few stayed in the trenches, but crept out at dawn into no-man's-land, moving from cover to cover until dark. In the relative calm between full-scale contact the snipers maintained a lethal guard over the enemy trenches. In one fortnight in December 1915, British troops lost 3,285 men killed or wounded. It was a deadly occupation, strangely suited to Jack's shy, rather isolated character. But Catherine noticed a change in her step-uncle when he returned on leave from France. He was no longer retiring or content to remain in the shadow of a conversation. Jack took Catherine's hand and toured the New Buildings, chatting to people he had never previously had the nerve to approach. When they met Catherine's Uncle Alec, an argument broke out. Jack had no time for anyone who wasn't 'doing their bit'.

Jack returned to France and Catherine continued to write him letters as she had done every week since he first went away. Her handwriting was so untrained and sprawling that Kate had to address the envelopes. In reply he sent her postcards with silk pictures woven on to them.

Each evening Kate would spread the *Shields Daily Gazette* on the kitchen table and read aloud the despatches from the war. She always began with Philip Gibbs's report from the Western Front. John McMullen, sitting in the high-backed wooden chair beside the range, never drank his beer while he listened. When Kate had finished, he would blow the froth from the top of his mug so that it sizzled and steamed on the hot coals. He would then offer Catherine a sip from the mug before drinking the rest of his beer in silence.

On Tuesday, 15 June 1915 – five days before Catherine's ninth birthday – the German Zeppelin L10 droned overhead on its way up the River Tyne. Kate, Catherine and John McMullen joined the other families on the waste land at the top of the New Buildings to watch the airship pass overhead. The younger children were snatched from their beds. In the dusk the Zeppelin followed a train of red-hot slag ladles from a near-by tip back to Palmer's Jarrow works. It dropped several bombs through the roof of the engine construction shops, killing seventeen men and injuring dozens more.

TO comply with John McMullen's devotion to the Catholic faith

Kate was pressured into removing Catherine from Simonside Protestant School.

Catherine moved first, early in 1913, to the Meases School at East Jarrow, where her friend Flori, and the three older Harding children, were already pupils. To get there the children would cut across the field next to Lancaster Street and behind Morgan's Hall. The hall, pretentiously called a lecture hall and topped with an impressive spire, was another example of the chemical industry's ailing fortunes. It was originally built as a social club for the workers at the Barium Chemical Works. Only the caretaker's quarters were ever put to use, taken over by a policeman by the name of Elias Morgan and his wife Nora.

Catherine's new school was half-way up Straker Street, beyond the tram depot and a Methodist chapel, and only yards from where John and Rose McMullen had once lived. Catherine considered the narrow main street with its factory entrances and cramped houses 'very slummy'. The move from the open country of Simonside to the heart of East Jarrow depressed her as much as it had her grandmother.

The Meases School was a half-way house for soon after her seventh birthday, Catherine was enrolled at St Bede's Infants School in Monkton Road, Jarrow. The school took its name from St Bede's Catholic Church next door, the same church her natural grandfather, William Fawcett, had attended as a Brother.

It was at this school that Catherine first experienced two factors which were to become such deciding forces on the rest of her life.

The distance, more than two miles from the New Buildings, made it necessary for her to take a packed lunch. Each morning Kate would give her daughter two halfpennies for the tram ride to and from school. Most days Catherine would walk one of the journeys. Sometimes the halfpenny would be spent on round, boiled sweets called bullets. More often than not it would be saved. Although the walk to or from school was not overly long, nor her lessons energetic, Catherine began to feel tired; very tired; 'funny tired'.

Secondly, for the first time, Catherine was forced to distinguish between right and wrong; good and evil; heaven and hell. Ordinary, everyday things – the Father's bad language, the smell of whisky on Kate's breath, keeping the 'guilty' book – were suddenly branded sins.

Catherine went to her first confession on a Friday afternoon immediately after school. 'As I knelt in the pew with the other penitents I went over in my mind what I had to do,' she recalled many years later for a television documentary. 'I had to tell the priest how wicked I was and when my turn came I did just that. The strong hand on my collar thrust me into a black box in which I could see nothing but a glimmer of light above my head, and in it an outline of a profile which had no resemblance to a priest or his master.' That night her 'black nightmares' began.

Enforced religion did little to ease the routine boredom of Sundays for the seven-year-old Catherine. 'I used to hate Sundays as a child,' she has admitted, a conviction which remained with her for the rest of her life. Early morning Mass was followed by a large Sunday lunch, 'mostly fat brisket and runny cabbage'. While the washing-up water was heating on the range, the men of the house would go to bed for the afternoon. 'I think it was probably because they didn't have any decent clothes to go out in.' Sometimes Kate and Rose would also retire, leaving Catherine to clear the dishes by herself.

As Catherine grew older, she attended Benediction on a Sunday evening. As well as offering a welcome diversion at the end of a frustrating day, the service unwittingly fuelled Catherine's interest in the ultimate power of words. 'I loved Benediction,' she remembers. Unaware of what the words – what the sounds – meant, she could sense the energy they contained. 'I could listen to the Latin for hours on end.'

One day, a week before Christmas 1915, as she walked along Swinburne Street Catherine noticed crowds of people at the entrance to a lane beside the tram sheds. The early train from Newcastle had jumped the points. Catherine watched transfixed as the dead and injured were carried from the wreckage, the stretchers laid in rows on the main road near the tram shed to be ferried away in ambulances.

The casualties included a teacher from the Meases School. Mrs Thompson had taught Catherine during her brief stay there. Although the teacher survived the crash, she suffered horrific burns and was badly scarred. When she eventually returned to teaching she always wore a fine white veil over her face.

Kate gave no indication that her daughter's daily pleas to be let off school were having any effect. If her tears showed no sign of progress, Catherine would make herself retch and vomit. Frequently to no avail.

Then, one day in 1916, Catherine was told she was changing schools again. This time to St Peter and Paul's Catholic school in Belle Vue Crescent beside Tyne Dock railway station.

The school had opened in the same year as Catherine's birth. The grounds included the presbytery, where Father Bradley lived. He was a long-nosed, righteous man whose toneless voice only added to Catherine's sense of doom. The parish priest had been joined in 1914 by the kinder and quieter Father O'Keefe.

Of the six hours' teaching each day at St Peter and Paul's a full third would be devoted to religion. The pupils' spiritual and educational welfare was guided by the headmistress, Miss Caulfield, one of three sisters teaching at the school. She was a teacher who appears to have relied on acid sarcasm and her cane to deal with most minor misdemeanours.

To counter Miss Caulfield's inflexible regime Catherine resorted to bribery. Passing Leam Lane End on her way to school, Catherine would stop at Anne Dixon's house in Leam Lane to buy a pennyworth of flowers from the garden. She would invariably stay too long. When she arrived at school Catherine would present the elder Miss Caulfield with the bouquet, only to be caned for her late arrival.

Catherine's first teacher at her new school was the youngest Miss Caulfield. She had also taught at St Bede's and had transferred at the same time as her pupil. When Catherine progressed to Standard Four she was taught by Miss Barrington; 'big Miss Barrington, kind Miss Barrington'.

Both teachers noticed their pupil's ready memory for poetry. Miss Barrington frequently posted a penny reward for the first member of her class able to recite a piece of poetry. Catherine would eagerly accept the challenge. She loved the waves of sound each line produced. She could not spell the words. Very often she did not even know what they meant. But their beauty fascinated her and from the base metal of sound came the currency of words.

Catherine soon realised she could buy the affection a young child in a house of adults craves. And, with the attention, came fleeting respect. Hadn't the kitchen fallen silent when Kate read aloud from *Handy Andy* or *Wee McGregor*? Or crumpled into laughter with *Tales from an Irish County Court*?

Standing with her bare feet on the clippy mat and with the warmth from the range toasting her back, Catherine recited the lines Miss Barrington had written on the blackboard.

> *And all went merry as a marriage bell;*
> *But hush! hark! a deep sound strikes like*
> *a rising knell!*

Sometimes the stories were of her own making.

'Granda, you know that little man you tell me about, the one that sits on the wall in Ireland, no bigger than your hand. You know, him with the green jacket and the red trousers and the buckles on his shoes, and the high hat and the shillalagh as big as himself; you remember Granda?'

'Aye, what about him?'

'Well, I've seen him Granda.'

'You have, have you?'

'Aye Granda. He was round the top corner.'

'He was, was he? And I suppose he spoke to you?'

'Aye Granda, he did.'

'And what did he say?'

'Well,' he said: "Hello Kate." '

'And what did you say to him?'

'I said: "Hello mister, my Granda knows you." '

John McMullen wiped his moustache with the back of his hand and raised his white eyebrows. 'You know what you are Katie McMullen, don't you, you know what you are? You're a stinking liar. Go on, go on. Either into the clink or into the money.'

FOR some reason Jessie Eckford never got round to having the name above her Phillipson Street shop painted out. Even to children who had never seen the previous owner, the low-fronted shop in Phillipson Street was always known as Cissie Affleck's.

When the McMullens returned to the New Buildings in 1912 Catherine soon made friends with Belle, the daughter of Jessie Eckford. Although she confesses to never having a 'best friend', Flori Harding and Belle Eckford were among Catherine's closest friends. The two William Black Street girls were also regular visitors to the Eckford's busy but well furnished flat. Downstairs Jessie habitually wore a floral apron while serving in the shop.

Cissie Affleck had had the shop converted in the late 1890s from the downstairs rooms. The twin front doors of the 'Tyneside' flats were replaced by a low stone frontage and tall display window. The recessed entrance to the shop was on the left.

The shop, third in from the end of the terrace, acted as a larder for the local community. Food was purchased in small quantities and consumed before it had a chance to spoil or turn sour. Children were sent to 'Cissie Affleck's' two or three times a day.

Inside, the bespectacled Jessie would stand behind the polished wood counter measuring a pennyworth of jam or beetroot from stone boody jars. A barrel on the floor contained thick, sweet molasses and corned beef was cut from a slab the size of an orange box. During the war, when milk and sugar became scarce, there were condensed milk and syrup on tap like beer.

Jessie did not close the shop on Saturday until ten o'clock. While the men were drinking at the Alkali or 'Twenty-seven', the women from the streets would stay behind to gossip. The conversation would fall away whenever a child came in to buy a lucky bag of sweets or a pennyworth of tiger nuts. Sometimes the youngsters would catch snatches of talk about 'that awful house in William Black Street'.

At Christmas Jessie would decorate the window and fill it with toys and stockings and special treats. One year both Kate and her sister Mary asked for several items to be put away. It was several months into the New Year before Jessie was paid. Each week she would send Belle to call on the two houses to collect something off the debt.

Jessie closed her shop each weekday evening at nine. Sweets or cigarettes and tobacco could still be had until midnight from a makeshift shop in the front room of a house in Lancaster Street. The shop was run by the father of the couple who owned the house. Catherine hated the prospect of being sent for late-night Woodbines. The old man refused to hand over her change until Catherine had kissed him.

Other attempts to start house shops were less successful. Most lasted little more than a few months.

Eva Romaines, who lived above the McMullens in No 8, was never put off by failure. One scheme involved opening her upstairs kitchen as a fish and chip shop; it soon closed. Other ideas included yet another sweet shop. A third the reselling of factory-made cakes.

Kate, never far behind, supplemented her days and half-days in service with various schemes. One was the bottling and sale of ginger and herb beers which she bought in bulk. It was Catherine's Friday evening job to scrub out the bottles in an old poss-tub and restring the necks to take the corks.

One favourite, particularly among the children, was Granny Dixon's pies and peas. The old woman lived next door to Kate at No 14. Each Friday afternoon her scrubbed back yard would be lined with youngsters sent to collect a family tea of home-made pies and mushy peas.

The McMullens' yard, littered with beer bottles and food scraps, was earning its own reputation. As was John McMullen. The foul-mouthed aggression he had always shown toward women was extended to children. 'He was a drunkard, a real drunkard,' recalls Irene Callender. 'There is no other way of putting it. He always seemed to be arguing and shouting at us. We were all rather afraid of him and kept our distance.'

AT the far end of Hudson Street – past the Post Office with its roofed letter box like a little house and the chemist where Jack had bought flea powder on his way back to France – was the Crown cinema.

Each Saturday Catherine escaped. Her arms would still be aching from lugging a stone of wheat for the chickens back from Jarrow or her fingers tight from polishing the steel fender in front of the range. But the afternoon darkness of the matinée was far more than simple entertainment. It was as if the flickering beams of light were somehow washing away the adult squalor and refilling her mind with childish dreams. Returning down Hudson Street and under the dock arches, Catherine walked backwards. She often walked backwards when she was happy.

But finger-tip adventures on the top of skyscrapers or inches from whirring buzz-saws were momentary distractions for Catherine. When Charlie Chaplin swaggered his way through *The*

Cure Catherine's attention was never focused on the little man's antics. She was examining – memorising – the splendour of the large house in which the film was set or the elegant women who populated the longshots.

The Saturday ritual was interrupted only once. It was to prove a painful experience.

For days the children who lived in the New Buildings had been talking about Belle Eckford's birthday party. There would be cakes and fruit and all kinds of special food from her mother's shop and her father's allotment. And afterwards games with prizes.

Catherine announced she was not going to the Crown. She wanted a clean pinny and a clean hair ribbon. Kate gently attempted to dissuade her daughter. 'It's no use, you know, hinny,' she said. 'It's no use.'

When she was washed and dressed and satisfied she was ready Catherine stood at the yard gate. Her friends passed in silence. In ones and twos they entered the backyard of No 5 Phillipson Street and climbed the stairway to the flat above the shop. As soon as the lane was empty Catherine walked down to stand opposite the Eckfords' gate. She waved at the figures moving behind the netted windows. She jumped up and down. She made noises. No one noticed her.

Catherine crossed the lane, entered the yard and knocked at the stairway door. Above her the flat door opened. One by one the faces of her friends looked down, some giggling, some feigning adult annoyance. Finally Belle Eckford appeared, her face 'flat-looking, full of self-importance'.

'You can't come up,' she whispered, as if trying to keep Catherine's arrival a secret. 'Me Ma says you can't.'

Catherine asked why.

'Well, me Ma says you haven't got no Da.'

When Catherine walked silently and slowly back into the kitchen of No 10, Kate was near to tears. 'Never you mind, lass,' she said, 'you'll see your day with them.'

The snub – which caused Catherine real pain – was apparently soon forgotten by her peers. Catherine, however, resolved never to forgive Belle Eckford. It was a childhood betrayal which festered in her memory of the north for more than forty years. She would come to see it – and use it – not as a single act of childish cruelty, but as symbolic of all the overheard remarks and catty comments.

Catherine felt the incident more deeply because, unknowingly, the Eckfords had come to represent something special. Jim and Jessie Eckford never saw themselves as anything but working-class people. Belle and young Jim played in the same streets as Catherine. Yet they had a pony and trap and a servant to look after the house. And everyone knew how kind Jessie could be. When Ena, their first 'woman', left Jessie Eckford agreed to give a place to a destitute woman called Lizzie. To secure her release from Harton Workhouse Jessie provided her with proof of employment and a new set of clothes.

There was certainly no adult hand involved in keeping Catherine out of the party. Belle Napier, as she was to become, simply recalls telling her mother Catherine would not be coming to her party. She cannot remember why she did not want her friend there. In any event from Belle's point of view it was soon forgotten and both girls were talking and playing together within days.

But Catherine's realisation that her illegitimacy was an open secret, and was quite obviously discussed within earshot of her friends, erupted in violence.

Always a bossy child, Catherine now took to confronting opposition to her game plots with a challenge: 'Aa feel like a fight.' The willingness with which she used her fists soon labelled her a troublemaker – until the day she clashed with Olive Swinburne, who lived across the back lane at 15 Phillipson Street. Olive landed the first punch and Catherine landed unceremoniously on her backside.

Her reign of terror was over. In one ego-bruising encounter Catherine lost the guarded respect her bullying had earned. For a few brief months the name calling had stopped. It had been a diversion, no more. Catherine, once again, overheard the word 'bax . . . tard'.

FOR weeks Catherine had been watching a drama played out inside her head.

A wild-eyed Irish girl with red hair and ringlets is running through a wood; stumbling; crying; pushing her way past the bushes and trees. Chasing her is a villain. A handsome, well-dressed villain; a gentleman. He wants the girl. He catches her and tries to drag her into a lonely lodge. Screaming, pleading, the girl breaks free and the chase begins once more.

Using one of the notebooks her Uncle Jack had stolen from Mortimer Road School Catherine began to write the story down. Her handwriting was untrained. The spelling phonetic. Even Kate could not decipher the words. Catherine gave the story – her first story – a name: *The Wild Irish Girl*. For the next four years, until she was fifteen, she would spend hours rewriting the plot. The villain never quite managed to drag the girl into the lodge because Catherine, already aware handsome gentlemen craved pretty females, still did not know precisely why.

ROSE's health continued to deteriorate. She began to suffer from shortness of breath, and even moving around the house became a struggle. Her face and arms looked puffed and swollen. Any exertion or excitement would trigger pains in her chest.

But during the spring of 1917 Kate noticed a more dramatic change in her mother. For the first time in her life Rose was apparently losing her spirit. Although she tried her hardest to hide it from her granddaughter, Rose was being smothered by a creeping lethargy.

Despite his injured leg, John McMullen had found wartime work in a Jarrow shipyard. Kate was taking any job she could find. During their absence Rose spent more and more of her time propped up on the kitchen saddle. By the summer she never left her bed.

Kate's moods became deeper as her future darkened. Without her mother to shield her from John McMullen's sullen cruelty and endless demands, she knew her life would soon become intolerable. She turned increasingly to alcohol; seeking courage from the very thing which brought her misery.

The night Rose McMullen died Catherine was lying, half asleep in the dess-bed in the front room. Her grandmother was in the brass bed in the far corner. The room seemed full of people: John McMullen; Rose's sister Aunt Maggie; Kate and her sister Mary; Uncle Alec. Jack McMullen was in France.

Catherine heard her grandmother vomit. A few minutes later Rose McMullen was dead. She was fifty-nine. When the child awoke the next morning she discovered the old woman had been laid out during the night. Catherine had not even been moved to another room.

Rose died on 13 December 1917. Later that morning Dr McHaffie arrived to sign the death certificate. He gave the primary cause of death as 'cardiac disease'. Chronic nephritis or kidney failure had also contributed to Rose's death.

The following day, a Friday, Kate took the tram into South Shields to register her mother's death. She must have suffered a chill of fear when confronted by the registrar, but James Sedcote failed to make the connection between the woman who now gave her name as Catherine Fawcett and the woman, eleven years earlier, who claimed to be Mrs Catherine Davies.

For three days Rose's dead body lay in a rough coffin in the front room. It rested on trestles with a bucket beneath it to catch the dripping blood and body fluids. Kate refused to allow a wake.

The weekend was bitterly cold. By Monday Jarrow Cemetery was covered in snow. Only Kate cried at the graveside, howling 'like a dog', the stale smell of whisky warming the icy air. Her mother's public display of grief disgusted Catherine. She wished it was her mother who had died.

Not long into the New Year Kate started working at a public house in Walter Street, Jarrow, less than a quarter of a mile from Palmer's shipyard. She never earned more than 3s 6d (17.5 pence) for a day's work cooking and cleaning. She seldom returned home sober.

IN 1917 the Army finally realised the effectiveness of its snipers and brought them under brigade or division command. Each company was ordered to supply its two best shots. Jack McMullen was an obvious choice. His reward was promotion to lance-corporal.

When Jack's letter arrived home announcing his promotion, his father was dismayed. John McMullen told Kate to write back advising Jack to turn down the stripe. 'It's the beginning of the end,' he warned.

At noon on 21 August 1918, the 15th Battalion of the DLI was moved through a storm of poison gas and high explosive to a position east of Beaumont Hamel. Two days later, at 11 pm its men crossed the River Ancre, north of the town of Albert, by footbridges. The men carried little equipment except weapons and ammunition. Their objective was the high ground south of Miraumont. The battalion achieved its objective despite heavy machine-gun, mortar and sniper fire and several counter-attacks. When it was relieved on 27 August it had lost fourteen officers and 268 men.

The War Office letter informing his family Jack McMullen had been wounded in action was followed a few days later by one from the battalion padre. It sounded hopeful. Jack was being shipped back to England.

The house needed to be got ready. Although she had no idea how badly Jack had been wounded, Kate decided she did not have enough bed linen. The next Saturday morning she took the tram into Jarrow. Before her mother returned with the new sheets Catherine answered a knock at the door. It was a telegram. John McMullen made her open it.

IT IS MY PAINFUL DUTY TO INFORM YOU THAT A REPORT HAS BEEN RECEIVED FROM THE WAR OFFICE NOTIFYING THE DEATH OF 3–11836 LANCE-CORPORAL JACK MCMULLEN, DURHAM LIGHT INFANTRY, WHICH OCCURRED AT 50 CASUALTY CLEARING STATION, FRANCE. THE REPORT IS TO THE EFFECT THAT HE 'DIED FROM WOUNDS RECEIVED IN ACTION' SEPTEMBER 5, 1918.

> *He felt terribly sick, he was actually going to be sick. He gulped in his throat, swallowed a mouthful of spittle, then even as his mind yelled, 'No! No! Not this,' he knew it was this.*
>
> *The Mallen Litter*

Jack McMullen was twenty-eight when he died. Exactly a month later the *Shields Gazette* formally acknowledged his death. Two lines in a list of 'Local Casualties'. He is buried in Abbeville Communal Cemetery Extension in France, near the mouth of the Somme. The Commonwealth War Graves Commission plot is on high ground overlooking Abbeville from the north. Beside Jack McMullen's grave is a rose tree bearing red flowers.

As his son's closest surviving relative, John McMullen found himself entitled to a War Office pension. He made sure of his entitlement by claiming Jack had been his sole means of financial support.

Every Tuesday morning John McMullen would meticulously wash and dress before walking to Bogey Hill Post Office in Straker Street. There the postmistress, a Miss McFarlane, would spell out his name beneath his mark. Not once on his return did John McMullen offer Kate any of the money.

ONE day in 1918 – as the war was drawing to a close – a solemn-faced Scotsman knocked on the back door of No 10 William Black Street. He was the first man to ask for lodgings in almost four years.

The stranger was carrying two suitcases. One was full of books. These he arranged on the top of the chest of drawers just inside the bedroom door. There were two rows. The first was a complete set of Shakespeare. The second included a biography of Donne, two books by Burns, one by Stevenson and a volume of poems by someone called Browning.

Despite an immediate warning from Kate to leave the man's library alone, Catherine found odd moments to read snatches from the books, usually when she should have been scrubbing the lino or blacking the hearth.

Another attempt to satisfy her appetite for reading proved just as risky.

No matter how short the money, Kate or the Father always managed to find the halfpenny for a copy of the *Shields Gazette*. At a penny, *Tiger Tim's Weekly* or *The Rainbow* were considered a luxury.

Catherine had been sent to the newsagents on the corner of Hudson Street and Lord Nelson Street, Tyne Dock, to collect the evening paper. She had spent the last of her coppers hidden in the toilet roof and was desperate for something new to read. On the counter beside the pile of newspapers was a copy of a comic called *The Rainbow*. Clutching the *Gazette* Catherine threw the coin at the shopkeeper and ran. As she picked up the paper she managed to hide the comic beneath it.

As soon as she was a safe distance from Hudson Street Catherine began to flick through the comic. But the shame of being discovered a thief was soon overtaken by the fear of eternal damnation. She could not read the words without hearing Father Bradley's soulless, faltering voice. Stealing was a sin. And all sins, the humourless priest never failed to warn her, had their price.

Four

Such little memories as these obliterate the pain of a lifetime.

CATHERINE WAS SAFE. There was no one on the Shields tram she recognised. On Mondays, when the rent was due, Catherine would be kept off school. Monday parcels destined for the pawnbroker included her dead Uncle Jack's suit or Kate's one good blouse, or perhaps a second suit borrowed from a neighbour in Phillipson Street.

The tram would swing right into Bolden Lane, past Mrs Brown's fruit and vegetable shop, then Catherine would get off at Tyne Dock Station. Two stops from the dock gates – a halfpenny –but it was worth it.

If there were not too many people about she would sometimes stop and read the posters on the wall of the Crown cinema, matching monochrome faces with the names of the stars. A train arriving or a familiar face would send her scurrying across the road and into Whitehead Street. Further along the street, almost opposite a school, Catherine would turn down the back lane which separated Bede Street and Dock Street. At the far end of Bede Street, three doors from where the tram had passed, was Bob's the pawnbroker.

Catherine resented her visits to Gompertz's pawn shop even more than she loathed her nightly errands to fetch beer or carry the illicit notes to pub landlords for whisky.

Catherine had become a slave to her mother's selective and snobbish fear of the law. Connecting Gompertz's back yard with Bede Street was a narrow alley. From there you could enter a number of individual pledge booths, the counters opening on to the main shop. It was illegal for anyone under the age of fourteen to pledge items in a pawn shop. The indignity of being summoned before a County Court to account for her debts held the same

51

horror for Kate as the workhouse had done for John McMullen. Answering to the school board inspector who regularly enquired about her daughter's weekly absences was a domestic matter – admitting the universal sin of poverty was not.

For Catherine, still only thirteen, the ritual was always the same. She would walk down the passageway and into Bede Street. There, with the parcel held out of sight in front of her, she would pretend to study the unredeemed clothes in Bob's window or look at the groceries piled high in the shop next door. Sometimes she could feel the idle groups of men watching her as they stood outside the Royal Oak on the far corner of Bede Street, where it opened out into Hudson Street. Stepping down into the shop was her only escape.

Catherine delivered Kate's plea for a certain price on the clothes. Bob examined them and offered no more than two-thirds. The deed was done. Catherine could now bow her head and occupy herself examining the displays of jewellery and musical instruments. Eventually an adult – always a woman, never a man – would enter one of the cubicles and Bob would ask if she would sign Catherine's pledge slip. If the pledge was more than 5s, Catherine made sure Bob passed the woman 2d. She could never bring herself to look the woman in the face.

Bob Gompertz was a kind, intelligent man. He knew more about each family's situation than many of their neighbours or relatives. Twice, sometimes three times a week, he watched Catherine leave his shop with just enough money to see Kate over the next crisis. He never asked where Kate was getting the 12s 6d (62.5 pence) a quarter to pay for Catherine's piano lessons.

Somehow Kate had managed to obtain £5 as deposit on a new rosewood upright piano. She also secured a good enough reference to allow her credit on the £95 balance, a sum large enough to pay nearly six months' rent. The piano was eased into the front room, with just enough room for Catherine to squeeze her spindly legs between the piano stool and the keyboard.

Each week Catherine was forced to ignore her fear of Mrs Dalton, her large, big-boned music teacher, to practise apparently endless scales and chords.

Kate's hopes for her daughter lasted less than a year. Struggling to meet the payments on the piano, the first 12s 6d was paid in two parts; the second quarter Catherine delivered whenever a spare sixpence or shilling was available. After six months Kate had fallen behind with the repayments on the piano. Mrs Dalton persuaded her to allow Catherine to continue studying for her first examination. Demands for payment – sent via her pupil – were finally eased when Mrs Dalton agreed to Kate paying off the outstanding fees in pies and peas, her current sideline.

Alone in the front room Catherine enjoyed practising, but the lessons became a nightmare. The polite, but firm, requests for payment compounded her mother's broken promises. Catherine performed her weekly lesson miserable with shame. Sometimes, when she would be carrying the grey hen along the Jarrow Road, she would see Mrs Dalton's three sons on their way to William Black Street to collect her next lesson in meat pies and mushy peas. Catherine turned her face away and pretended they did not exist.

Catherine passed her examination with honours. A few days later the Sunderland music store repossessed the piano. As the driver and his mate struggled to get the instrument out of the front room, Kate hid in the backyard toilet.

THE first Mrs Romaines was a secret drinker. The second Mrs Romaines was a woman intoxicated by ambition and of a 'better class' than the McMullens who lived below her in William Black Street.

James Romaines, a trimmer at Tyne Dock, remarried soon after the death of his first wife. Eva Romaines was as different and distant to her predecessor as John McMullen was to Rose's first husband William Fawcett. Secret drinking held no attraction for Eva Romaines, she preferred to shock her neighbours with bright clothes and make-up. She hated hard work and the chapped hands and swollen feet that came with it. Life was too short to be surrendered to drudgery and poverty. It was a philosophy Catherine found magnetic.

Early in June 1919, Eva Romaines asked Catherine what she would like as a thirteenth birthday present. To fulfil her wish, her neighbour took Catherine into South Shields and set her free among the shelves of a book shop. The volume Catherine chose was the complete *Grimms' Fairy Tales*. This was not a *Rainbow* or *Chatter Box* annual. This was a real book and it belonged to

Catherine. It became part of her life and part of her dreams. The characters rose up to live and breathe and act out their own fantasy in the drab reality of her surroundings. Each time Catherine sought refuge in the stories she re-entered their secret world through a different door.

Reading for pleasure was still an uncommon pastime among the majority of working-class households. Four doors up William Black Street near-sighted Aunt Maggie – known as Granny Hindes to the neighbourhood children – devoured books with a passion, reading by the pop-pop-pop of the gas mantle or straining to see the pages lit by the street lamp, which shone through her downstairs window.

Within a year Catherine had read Jean Stratton Porter's *Girl of the Limber Lost*; quickly followed by Charles Garvice, Ethel M. Dell, Arnold Bennett and Hugh Walpole.

CATHERINE opened her eyes. The pain in her leg was so intense it had woken her. She could hear muffled voices in the kitchen. Suddenly she felt safe, the fear and the pain draining out of her. Standing at the foot of the bed was her grandmother. Catherine was too confused to remember her grandmother had died two years earlier.

Weakened by pain and desperate for comfort it is not hard to dismiss the experience as a trick of delirium; the imagining of an already fanciful child. But it would not be the last time Catherine was to prove receptive to a spiritual power.

Confined to the little bedroom and ordered to sleep on boards, Catherine was recovering from a leg injury that was to plague her for the rest of her life. In later years the injury would develop into arthritis, and even getting in and out of a car would be painful. The damage to her leg and hip also left the hem on the left-hand side of her dresses an inch shorter than the right.

It was the winter of 1919–20, the end of the first full year of peace. Catherine had been playing with a friend in the yard of St Peter and Paul's School when she tripped and fell against the rough surface. The next day, a Saturday, she complained of a pain in her hip. Kate dismissed it as yet another tale. For days Catherine would suffer nothing worse than a dull ache, at other times attempting to carry the grey hen produced tears of agony.

There was snow on the ground when, one Monday morning, Catherine pleaded not to be sent to school. Kate was still unsympathetic. When Catherine finally arrived at school more than an hour late she collapsed. A doctor ordered her to rest her injured leg. By teatime she had collapsed again, this time to slip in and out of consciousness for days.

The playground accident had torn the sinews in her left leg away from the bone and muscle. It was a serious injury which required hospital treatment, but apart from the occasional visits of a doctor the damage was left to heal itself. It was the spring of 1920 before the pain and swelling had subsided enough to allow Catherine to hobble around the house. She was weak and thinner than ever.

Catherine would never return to school. Things had changed during the slow weeks of her recovery. Money was shorter than ever and girls Catherine had gone to school with had found themselves 'a place'. It was time, both mother and daughter decided, for Catherine to get a job.

LONG before her daughter's playground accident Kate had promised herself Catherine would never be forced into domestic service.

To Catherine the prospect appeared far less daunting. It was, in many ways, the short-term solution to her long-term plans. Catherine had lots of ideas for stories, all she needed was time. Time to improve her grammar and her spelling and to train her ill-disciplined hand. In the meantime she could clean house and complete other duties expected of a thirteen-year-old.

The Sowerbys lived at 27 Simonside Terrace. The six-roomed house had a staircase and two passages and was crammed with furniture, not oddments such as Kate and the Father had brought home over the years but stylish, well-made pieces which commanded respect.

The Sowerbys kept their distance from the other inhabitants of the New Buildings. Martha Sowerby was related to the Mayoress of Jarrow, a Mrs Alexander Johnstone. George Sowerby worked as a foreman-carpenter in Tyne Dock, where he was to be joined by his three sons.

Catherine was first invited into the Sowerbys' kitchen – reserved for cooking and never eating – one evening in the summer of 1920.

She had been waiting outside for a friend who was employed by the family as a domestic. Martha Sowerby, who had seen Catherine as she grew up around the New Buildings, took an instant liking to her teenage guest. When her friend was dismissed for some minor infringement Mrs Sowerby offered Catherine the vacancy.

The post did have its advantages. Kate knew the Sowerbys by sight as well as reputation. Despite the long hours – from eight in the morning until six at night – Catherine would still be living at home. And the 10s (50 pence), less stamp, her daughter earned weekly was badly needed.

Catherine – still recovering from her leg injury – found the work interesting enough to overcome the pain and fatigue. In addition to cleaning the six rooms, the backyard and a front room which overlooked the Slake, her duties included preparing the meals and helping with the washing. The atmosphere was warm and relaxed. So much so that Catherine often returned to the kitchen after hours to cook chips for the four men. There was another reason. She had developed a crush on the Sowerbys' eldest son.

During the day Mrs Sowerby was a strict but fair employer. When Catherine returned to the house in the evening she was treated almost as an impish younger sister by the Sowerby boys, a situation tolerated by George Sowerby but frowned upon by his wife. The line between employer and employee had been crossed. 'I dared fancy that I wasn't made for taking orders or working after other people,' Catherine later admitted in *Our Kate*. The job did not last long.

Each Sunday she attended eleven o'clock Mass at St Peter and Paul's Church beside her former school. She made friends with a girl whose father was a ship's master. The girl's mother, Gladys Cooper, was earning extra money and filling her husband's long absences by giving lessons in book-keeping and pen painting. One of her art pupils was Belle Eckford.

The charge was 1s (5 pence) for one hour's instruction. Catherine persuaded Mrs Cooper to give her a trial thirty-minute lesson for 6d.

From the moment Catherine picked up the pen she knew she had discovered an avenue of escape. Painting and writing were, after all, both forms of art. At the end of the lesson Catherine thanked Gladys Cooper. She did not arrange to go back. She would be too busy earning a living.

Household items – and the occasional luxury – out of reach of ready cash could be purchased 'on the club'. Sixpence or a shilling would be paid into a club at weekly intervals and withdrawn for special events like Christmas or birthdays. More commonly, clubs would be opened with corner shopkeepers or larger stores in Jarrow or South Shields against the price of specific items.

Catherine began canvassing relatives and neighbours for her own club. Each member who paid in 1s a week was offered two hand-painted black satin cushion covers or one large one. Within days she had twenty people on her books.

Filling the orders was harder work. Soon after Kate had cleared the breakfast things Catherine could set out the materials for the order she was completing, colouring in the transfers of daffodils and irises on the black satin cushion covers or the matching peacocks on a mantel border. As the day wore on the strain of the delicate brushwork only inches from her eyes began to tell. Her back, too, became stiff and sore. Catherine worked on into the evenings, the only illumination coming from the cold, yellow-green gas light and the glow of the coals in the grate.

Her days were longer than she had put in at the Sowerbys. It was a relentless, self-imposed regime for a fifteen-year-old, smiled over by Kate, but eased only by Catherine's conviction she was somehow fulfilling a destiny ordained by God.

Catherine had swapped the confines of the backyard closet for the quiet security of St Peter and Paul's Church. With Christmas or a birthday looming she would kneel among the pews to plead with God to keep Kate and John McMullen sober. 'I had never thought of going to heaven,' Catherine admitted many years later. 'My thoughts never ascended that far. I was either saying prayers to prevent me being thrust into hell or saying prayers to get somebody out of hell and purgatory. Heaven was a closed shop.' Each morning she prayed for God to give her strength. Each night she sought forgiveness for not working hard enough.

After purchasing the satin covers or mantel borders and the paints she needed Catherine never cleared more than 9s 6d (47.5 pence) profit a week. 'But you're your own boss,' Kate would tell her. 'And you're not dirtying your hands.'

Catherine spent what little remained of her money after contributing to the household expenses on herself. Most of her new possessions found their way under pressure from Kate to Gompertz's pawn shop. Each disappearance sparked a loud and spiteful row. But when Catherine confessed her anger to her 'first real friend', Lily Maguire, she felt ashamed at betraying her mother. 'I can't put up with it much longer,' she told Lily one night.

Catherine's hard work was being taken for granted. At home she responded by becoming sullen and withdrawn.

Her release from Kate's ever more noticeable drunkenness and swings of affection, was regular visits to the Maguire home. Mrs Maguire was a 'hard-working, patient' woman with a knack of producing an apparently endless line of babies. Mr Maguire was a pit man 'with a big voice', who greeted Catherine with an even louder welcome. Catherine had saved enough from her scant profits to buy herself the bicycle John McMullen had promised but never delivered and Catherine and Lily could now lose themselves in the narrow country lanes.

Through it all Catherine still found time to write. As a Catholic she believed in the imagination and the miraculous. She put aside the childish adventure of the little girl pursued through the forest by the lecherous gentleman and started work on a new story. This time she tempered her fantasy, at least partly, with first-hand knowledge. She called her new story *On the Second Floor*. It described how Christ returns to earth as a labourer living in a working-class environment. When it was completed Catherine counted every word: there were 16,520.

She enquired about having the untidy handwritten story typed. There was no way she could afford the 12s (60 pence). Catherine once again turned for solace to Lily Maguire.

Lily had a sister called Maisie. She was attending a local high school and, according to Lily, was a 'good printer'. It wasn't long before Catherine and Maisie had struck a deal. Each evening after school Maisie would laboriously copy the story into neat block letters, a task which took her several months and for which she earned 2s 6d (12.5 pence).

When it was completed, Catherine packaged the bulky manuscript and posted it to the *Shields Gazette* office in Barrington

Street. Thirty-two years later a retired Tyneside journalist wrote to Catherine describing the swift judgment meted out on her first submission. According to the reporter: 'The assistant editor came tearing out of his room with this bundle in his hand, saying "Some so-and-so, so-and-so, so-and-so fool has sent a sixteen thousand word story to a penny daily, can you beat it. Chuck it back." ' The story returned to No 10 less than seventy-two hours after it had departed.

CATHERINE rode her bicycle slowly away from the New Buildings. It had been a day heavy with shame and betrayal.

She was on her way to spend the rest of the weekend with her Aunt Sarah. Kate's sister Sarah – a big-boned woman who also liked her drink, but never let it blunt her straight talking – had married a miner called Mick Lavelle. They lived at Birtley, a pit village near Gateshead.

Catherine had eight Lavelle cousins. The four boys all went on to work in the mines. Sarah's eldest daughter, Mary, was a year younger than Catherine and often stayed at the New Buildings, where the air at least had the benefit of a river breeze instead of the smoke and grit of a pit village. In 1924, when Catherine was eighteen, Mary died of tuberculosis.

Catherine's seventeenth birthday, ten days earlier, had passed almost unnoticed. Moreover Kate had stubbornly refused to make any of the arrangements for her own wedding. Instead she sent Catherine to the registry office to pay for the licence and book the ceremony. After finally giving in to David McDermott, it was as if a solitary cowardly secret still remained between Kate and respectability.

David McDermott had become a regular visitor to No 10 William Black Street since the end of the war. The death of his first wife had left the quiet, loyal seaman free to pursue Kate.

Despite her drinking which, no doubt, prompted more male assumptions about her virtue, Kate had not had sex since the day in 1905 when she finally gave in to her gentleman lover. She remained celibate for eighteen years. Yet under David's quiet, unhurried attentions her mistrust of men faded. Kate seemed to speak more freely and give more ground to David than she allowed other men. It soon became apparent to Catherine – and no doubt to John McMullen – that Kate would eventually agree to marry David.

The Scotsman, whose books Catherine had secretly enjoyed, had been replaced in 1920 by a new lodger, James Tullock. The continued presence of other men in the house no doubt worried David McDermott. His return from an extended voyage in the spring of 1923 coincided with Tullock's departure. At forty-seven he decided he could wait no longer and proposed to Kate. To his surprise she accepted.

The engagement would, of necessity, be a short one. Work was already becoming scarce and David could not miss the chance of signing on for a new voyage. It was a prospect which suited John McMullen. His place as head of the household would be restored, while his son-in-law would be contributing £2 18s each month – half his seaman's pay – to the family income.

Love had little to do with Kate's decision to marry David McDermott. Kate was too old and tired to give in to the heady love of hope and longing she had experienced in her early twenties. Perhaps, like her mother, Kate saw an opportunity to secure a future for herself and her child and took it.

The couple married at South Shields registry office on 30 June 1923. David McDermott gave his address as No 10 William Black Street. Kate, eight years younger than her bridegroom, described herself on the marriage certificate as a spinster. The 'cold soulless' ceremony was officially witnessed by Catherine and a family friend, Allen McGill.

In her own way Kate had, at last, succeeded in giving her daughter a father. Yet, as Catherine watched her mother marry a man whose steady character and working-class background cast a drab colourless shadow over her future, she was even more determined to one day discover the identity of the man who had shocked her into life.

The kitchen gossip of Kate's seduction was far less romantic than reality.

Kate, it was claimed, had been working in a large house as a kitchen maid. Being bright and full of life, she had attracted the attention of one of the family's sons. Sexual harassment and even rape were treated by many young women in service as almost inevitable. Some openly encouraged flirtations. When Kate found herself pregnant she was either dismissed or left of her own accord. The story – certainly not unique – was common knowledge among the residents of East Jarrow and Tyne Dock.

There was never any doubt Catherine's father was a 'gentleman'. The suggestion that her mother's seduction was of a higher order than the gratification of a young man's lust came from Catherine's Aunt Mary.

Soon after her sister's engagement the scornful Mary redoubled her efforts to malign the likeable Kate. Why Mary should use the truth about her sister's love affair is hard to understand, especially when the story of her willing seduction at the hands of a lascivious employer was already in circulation and known to Catherine. It was the first time Mary spoke to Catherine about the well-dressed man who paid regular visits to the Lamesley public house. At last Catherine had a tangible link between her visions of grand houses and elegant ladies and her secret past.

In 1923 Catherine had little more than a sketchy description of her father. She did not know his name. Nor was she any closer to discovering his identity. It would be another ten years before her mother confessed to possessing a birth certificate recording Alexander Davies as Catherine's father.

Kate had always known she would some day need a birth certificate to give her daughter respectability. Inventing an imaginary husband and father for her child presented no real problems. Choosing a commission agent as a profession for her spouse left the edges so blurred it would have been almost impossible to prove Kate had been deliberately inaccurate. The description covered just about every entrepreneurial activity on both sides of the law. The choice of Davies, although not a north-east surname, could have been prompted by almost anything or anyone.

Which left the question of a Christian name. Once again any borrowed name would have served. Or, perhaps, the answer suggested itself the very morning Kate stepped out of No 5 Leam Lane on her way to the registry office. To everyone else the tiny, flat-fronted pub next door to the McMullens' home was known as the 'Twenty-Seven'. Kate would certainly have known its real name was the Alexander.

Several years later, when Kate finally admitted to the existence of her daughter's birth certificate, only one more lie was needed to end the affair. Kate informed her daughter that Alexander Davies – the father Catherine longed to reclaim her – was dead.

But Kate's lover – whatever his true identity – had already bequeathed his offspring something far more compelling than ambition and talent.

Within eighteen months of her mother's wedding Catherine was to suffer her first nose bleed. There was no obvious reason for it and it did not particularly worry her. In the years that followed the attacks became more frequent and more violent. Catherine was showing the first signs of a condition she had inherited from her anonymous father.

There is no evidence to suggest Kate's lover showed any of the classic symptoms of haemorrhagic telangiectasia. Neither Kate, nor her sister Mary, made any comment on the young gentleman's physical appearance. With hindsight it is safe to assume he would have been thin and pale; almost anaemic looking. He need not have suffered more than an occasional nose bleed. The severity and frequency of the symptoms have since been graded at 90, 50 and 10 per cent.

The chances of inheriting haemorrhagic telangiectasia from a parent have been rated at fifty-fifty. If the son or daughter of a confirmed sufferer is found to be free from the genetic disorder there is no chance of it being passed to a future generation. The first indication offspring have inherited the condition appears in late teens with sudden and unexplained nose bleeds. These are followed, a few years later, by blood-stained vomit.

There is little evidence to suggest Alexander Davies ever lived outside Kate – or Mary's – imagination. His name does not appear on any Parliamentary Roll for County Durham or Northumberland. His apparent profession, however, offers one tantalising clue.

Street directories covering Tyneside in the early years of the twentieth century include a firm of commission agents trading under the name of Davis. In 1905 E. F. Davis & Co operated from a yard in Lombard Street, not far from Newcastle Quayside. The firm, which appears not to have occupied any formal offices, was described as 'wherry owners'. A wherry was a small ferry or pleasure boat frequently hired for special occasions. Two years later the business had transferred to a similar yard around the corner and within the confines of the Exchange Buildings.

Any connection between a member of the firm and Kate Fawcett must remain circumspect. The fact that Kate's lover shared the same surname – the error in spelling is understandable – and occupation is intriguing, particularly as both were said to work and live in Newcastle.

The lifestyle of a younger member of a family firm would also appear to fit what little is known of Kate's 'gentleman' lover. By the very nature of a commission agent's profession – which could range from land deals to placing illegal wagers – dressing to impress was considered compulsory. A 'high hat, black coat with an astrakhan collar, kid gloves and silver-topped cane' would have suited a self-confident young businessman eager to please his elders. His time would almost certainly have been his own. Day-long absences every four to six weeks would have aroused little, if any, suspicion.

Confronted by the news of Kate's pregnancy Alexander Davies's action in following his lover to Tyne Dock may well have been honest. Their affair had never been a hurried, sordid one. It had lasted for two years. Returning home, after sharing a day in Newcastle with Kate, Davies announced to his parents his intention to marry, a decision even more shocking when he confessed his future wife was a pregnant barmaid whose family were dockers. Swift action would be needed to extinguish any possible scandal. When a worried Kate arrived at the Davies's residence two weeks later, a father's blackmail or a mother's snobbery had forced their son into disowning his lover.

Returning on the train to Tyne Dock Kate knew her situation was hopeless. She was determined she would not forget Alexander Davies's weak-willed treachery. Her child, whether a boy or girl, would one day know the name of its father.

DR McHaffie recognised the symptoms immediately. Catherine, never a teenager with colour in her cheeks, looked paler and more anaemic than ever. She complained of feeling so tired her hands and feet would often hang limp. Occasionally there would be a violent stabbing pain in her stomach. And, conclusively, there was a faint black line beginning to appear around the edge of her gums.

Catherine would have to give up the painting immediately. Two years of inhaling the fumes from the paints and allowing them to dry on her fingers had given her chronic lead poisoning.

The suggestion, even from Dr McHaffie, that her daughter was anaemic infuriated Kate. Like her mother Kate firmly believed that large quantities of food and basic remedies were the panacea for most ills. To cure Catherine of her constipation, a condition from which she had suffered since childhood, Kate relied on a crude and painful therapy. Catherine would have a piece of cheap washing soap inserted into her rectum and then be sat on a chamber pot of boiling water.

The prospect of Catherine's small but regular financial contributions – and the extra items Gompertz was so willing to pledge – coming to an end pleased Kate even less. Extra work for women was becoming almost impossible to find. John McMullen, now in his seventies, was still more tight-fisted and cantankerous. Kate would have to rely on the 14s 6d (72.5 pence) she drew each week from the Tyne Dock shipping office against David's pay. Mother and daughter clashed repeatedly before falling into moody silences.

Too ill to complete the remaining orders for cushion covers, Catherine dragged herself around the New Buildings to repay the money she had collected. The club, she informed her customers, was closed.

Catherine was approaching her eighteenth birthday penniless. Before she could find work she would have to find a shilling. Rather than ask Kate for the money she needed to sign on at the employment office in South Shields, Catherine turned to Mrs Maguire. It was the first time she had ever been in debt. She handed over her shilling to a dour-faced clerk and in exchange received the name and address of a woman seeking a child's companion.

Catherine arrived at Westoe village, convinced her luck had at last changed. Less than a mile from the centre of South Shields the tree-lined village street, with its white wooden railings and quiet respectability, looked as though it had somehow survived the last twenty years in peaceful isolation.

Behind the rows of elm trees stood solid, expensive houses. Country homes built for town families. These were different to the big houses Catherine had seen on the horse-drawn brake trips to

Shotley Bridge or Rowlands Gill in the Derwent Valley. The mistresses of these houses would never allow their husbands' work to contaminate their homes.

Catherine found the house she had been looking for and introduced herself to the wife of the owner. The woman approved of the shy but proud teenager standing before her. The family, which included a four-year-old child, was about to embark on a summer tour of Italy. The woman needed a companion for her son, 'someone still young enough not to have forgotten how to play, but old enough to have sense'.

Suddenly the woman asked her future employee if she was of any particular faith. Catherine readily admitted she was a Catholic. And yes, she did attend Mass. The woman, apparently stunned by Catherine's devotion in the face of a remarkable chance to travel, attempted to explain that any childminding duties would include Sundays and High Days. Catherine, however, heard nothing but Father Bradley's admonitions. Miss Mass, the priest was warning her, and you go to hell.

Catherine's next interview was at a large house surrounded by neat gardens in the centre of Harton Village. Less imposing than Westoe, it was still nearly two miles from the cramped streets of Tyne Dock. To get there Catherine had to walk past South Shields Union Workhouse, a sprawl of red-brick Gothic buildings dusted with coal from Harton Colliery next door.

The job was for a companion-maid to a small, quiet woman in her fifties. There would be no cooking. There was extra help to cope with the rough work, but perhaps Catherine wouldn't mind lending a hand with the washing?

Her wage would be 9s (45 pence) a week, with all meals and the use of a tiny bedroom. For that Catherine rose at six each morning and never got to bed before nine at night. Her duties, she soon discovered, included cleaning the high-ceilinged rooms and dusting and polishing the antique furniture, washing and ironing all the household linen and polishing the silver. She was also expected to receive guests arriving for the woman's frequent 'at homes' and serve most of the meals. It soon became apparent Catherine would never be called upon to act as a companion. Her employer had deceived her with a trick, she discovered, the woman had played on several other naïve teenagers.

For several months Catherine's plans focused on getting a new job in a chemist's shop. Ever since she had been taken to the pharmacist in Stanhope Road to be treated for the dog bite chemist's shops had become elevated in her imagination. They didn't smell of beer or dusty provisions. It was ladylike to work in a chemist's shop.

Catherine took every opportunity to visit one. Once she spent 6d on a tube of Pond's Vanishing Cream – it did. Straight to the lavatory among her secret hoard of pennies and threepences. Kate didn't consider it proper for women to put anything on their faces.

Catherine was allowed one afternoon and evening off each week, usually a Saturday. The afternoons she spent in the kitchen at William Black Street. In the evenings, she attended the whist drive and impromptu dance at the Catholic Boys' Club held in a classroom of her former school.

Saturday evenings at No 10 had become noisy, rumbustious affairs. The ageing John McMullen, although still gruff and outspoken, had mellowed enough to enjoy a weekly round of backchat and banter with Jackie Potts and his friends. Jackie was John McMullen's nephew's stepson. Like the Father he had noticed a change in Catherine.

Throughout her teenage years Catherine blossomed from a spindle-legged girl into a beautiful young woman. She considered her bust was growing too large and her legs were still too thin. But her cheekbones and thoughtful eyes proved irresistible. So, too, did her unwavering confidence.

It was at one of the Saturday-night socials that Catherine fell in love for the first time. She was fifteen. The object of her desire was a boy several years older. If he was aware of his young admirer he certainly did nothing to respond. Part of the attraction to Catherine was that the boy, employed in a bank, had announced his intention of only marrying a 'lady'. Although Catherine walked out with other boys, she kept a watchful eye on her bank clerk. Six more years would elapse before he considered her worthy of his attentions.

Unknowingly, someone else was also keeping an eye on Catherine.

Father Bradley had noticed the toll the fifteen-hour days were talking on Catherine. She looked tired and pale and her feet were so swollen they hung over the tops of her shoes.

Early in October 1924 Father Bradley approached William McAnany, a South Shields councillor and member of the Board of Guardians at Harton Workhouse. More important, McAnany was also on the board's House Committee. Part of its responsibility was the hiring and firing of staff. Something, Father Bradley said, should be done to see young Katie McMullen 'settled'.

A few days later McAnany spoke to Catherine at one of the weekly whist drives.

'How would you like a job in the workhouse as a laundry checker?' he asked. Catherine was too afraid to admit she didn't know what a laundry checker did. But anything sounded better than the demeaning slavery of domestic service.

Five

I can do anything I put my mind to.

MATRON HILL READ the reference a second time and then examined the teenager standing before her. There was a proudness in the way she carried herself and an arrogance in the way she spoke. The matron had seen it all before. She knew an upstart when she saw one.

Catherine listened as her new employer explained her duties.

She would work in the institute's laundry, checking the dirty linen in and accounting for its departure. As an officer she would be required to wear a uniform. She would start work at eight in the morning and finish at five in the afternoon. Her time off would include every Sunday, every other weekend and five hours every other evening between 5 pm and 10 pm. Once a month she would be allowed to stay out until midnight, but only if she applied for a pass. While not on duty in the laundry she would be required to stand in for staff on the infirm wards. In return Catherine would have her own room, four meals a day, and earn a little over £2 a month. When she retired, after forty years, she would be entitled to a pension of 6s (30 pence) a week.

Once again God had changed the course of Catherine's life for the better. Confronted by Matron Hill though, she was not entirely convinced.

Catherine was shown her room and the laundry where she was to work. Conditions had changed little since Victorian times.

She would spend most of her day in a glass-screened corner of the laundry, through which both the dirty and clean linen would pass. Sorting the soiled and foul-smelling sheets was left to two illiterate inmate helpers. Catherine would use her childish hand-writing to make entries in the ledger.

From her cubicle she could study the rest of the laundry. Only the officers wore black dresses with white aprons, caps and cuffs. They were helped by half-a-dozen paid hands, also distinguished by their white aprons. The more menial tasks were carried out by the inmates, who wore smocks and mop caps.

The equipment was crude but effective. Ironing was done on large benches, down the middle of which ran pipes to feed the wooden-handled steam irons. The two steel-bed presses were driven by exposed leather belts connected to a noisy drive shaft above the bare beams. Crumpled clean linen was dumped on the floor or tables. When it had been pressed it was returned to the main hospital and male and female mental blocks in heavy, square wicker baskets.

Catherine's arrival at Harton Workhouse was recorded in the House Committee minutes as 'Commenced: 22 October 1924 – Miss K. McMullen [sic]; laundry checker'. She soon discovered her standing among the other officers was just as lowly.

Staff meals were taken in the mess. Saturday afternoon teas were always a little grander and more relaxed than most, with cakes and tarts and a good deal of noisy teasing. As the newest and least experienced officer the job of serving fell to Catherine.

At first she tried to ignore the swearing and sexual innuendoes. Although Kate could do nothing about the Father's bad language, she had refused to allow any suggestive or smutty talk in the kitchen at No 10. Catherine considered any kind of profanity a sin. She could endure it no longer. She stopped slicing bread and rounded on the group of women with the knife still in her hand. 'Stop it this minute,' Catherine shouted. 'If I hear any more dirty talk like that I'll report you all to the matron.'

Out of the stunned silence came a single voice. 'Come off it, bloody St Catherine, and get a move on with that bread.'

SOUTH Shields was a borough to which poverty and disease returned with devastating regularity.

In 1866 cholera swept through the town. Four years later smallpox was ravaging the north of England. Four thousand cases were reported in the Tyneside borough alone. Destitution, despite various attempts to massage the official figures, proved just as resistant. In 1850 one in three residents of South Shields was registered as a pauper. The Poor Law Commissioners urged greater discrimination in giving relief. By the early 1870s the figure had fallen to one in twenty-three. But the three existing work-houses were still unable to cope with the demand for relief.

By 1903 the workhouse had been extended and could cater for 1,000 inmates. A hospital had also been added. Twenty years later the hospital consisted of three wings and a nursery. Infirm One treated the chronically sick and terminal patients. It was divided by a wide corridor, at the end of which were the workhouse staff bedrooms. The stench of urine from the wards hung in the corridor like an invisible blanket.

A second wing, often used as an isolation ward, frequently treated seamen suffering from infectious or venereal diseases. Linen from this ward arrived at the laundry stinking and stained with pus and discharges.

Norma Moore, now Norma Kent, joined the nursing staff in the summer of 1923. It was the first year in which the hospital had introduced a properly regulated training scheme for nurses. At twenty-three she was older than the majority of student nurses. Part of her early duties included delivering the dirty linen to the laundry. 'The junior nurse on each ward took the laundry list down each morning,' recalls Kent. 'There were large bags containing sheets and pillow-cases and other items. We counted how many there were of each and then the sister wrote out a list and ticked off whatever she had sent to the laundry.'

Late in 1924 Kent spotted a new and surprisingly alert face among the laundry staff. 'She was very pretty and very bonny. From the start I noticed how smart and tidy she was. Her hair and skin were beautiful,' said Kent. 'The other two women who worked in the room at the end of the main laundry were plain Janes compared to her. She always gave you a nice smile and said "Good morning, nurse." She always seemed to be happy and pleasant.'

Although Catherine was six years younger than the student nurse the pair soon found they had several things in common. Kent, whose mother was a teacher, appreciated any member of staff whose horizons extended beyond the workhouse walls. Catherine, meanwhile, welcomed any contact with the nursing staff. 'She was ever so anxious to become a nurse,' remembers Kent. 'She saw it as a kind of promotion. Something to aim for.'

Periodic outbreaks of smallpox were common. Two days before Christmas 1925 several cases of the disease were reported by Dr Shanley, the Medical Officer of Health at the institute. Catherine found herself lining up with other members of staff as Nurse Moore inoculated any new arrivals. In April 1927 a second more serious outbreak swept through the institution. It lasted for six months and seventy-eight members of staff, patients and inmates contracted the highly infectious viral disease. The laundry staff worked overtime to cope with the extra demand for clean linen. In one week they handled 19,000 articles.

Mental patients – known as defectives – lived in a separate block divided into male and female wards. The less seriously handicapped were allowed to walk freely around the buildings. Those who were capable were given light duties.

Throughout the 1920s, more and more families found themselves destitute and homeless. Accepted by the workhouse, they also found themselves physically and socially isolated. The men were confined to one block and the women to another. Any sexual encounter between husband and wife was a punishable offence. Their children were despatched to the Cottage Homes two miles away at Cleadon. Only 'well-conducted' old couples were allowed to live together in cottages.

Unmarried mothers effectually found themselves serving a fourteen-year sentence. Those who could not persuade a relative to offer them a home remained inmates until their child reached the age of fourteen and was old enough to earn a living.

One 1925 meeting of the House Committee was told there were 800 men, women and children on the workhouse books. During the previous four weeks there had been 168 admissions, 169 discharges, 8 births and 17 deaths.

In addition the Board of Governors was obliged to offer emergency accommodation to tramps and vagrants. The same four weeks had seen 258 casual men, 10 women and 4 children calling at the workhouse. Upon arrival each was given a bath and a clean nightgown and towel. Departing without completing an allotted task invited a sentence of seven days' hard labour.

Day-to-day management of the institution was left in the hands of the husband and wife employed as master and matron. Catherine did not see much of Master Hill. A favourite with the nurses, he was a 'great big, tall handsome man', recalls Norma Kent. 'Nobody ever saw him cross or angry.' To keep down the rats which lived beneath the institute buildings and occasionally scurried across the grounds in the half-light of the evening the Master, as he was universally known, kept a dog. The only time the terrier left his side was when it scented a rat.

Matron Hill was responsible for all the female staff, both nurses and workhouse officers. Men invariably found her charming. Her black dress uniform and starched matron's cap and cuffs complemented her 'womanly figure'. She distinguished herself from the other members of staff by never wearing an apron. From the start Catherine saw her as a 'little tartar of a woman'.

The Hills' combined salary of £33 a month – considerably more than Catherine was earning in a year – allowed them to live in their own house near the institute.

They were a couple who ruthlessly applied the will of the Guardians and dealt with transgressions by using punishments laid down when Dickens was still alive. The Master could also show unexpected kindness. A 22-year-old male inmate was reported for displaying 'refractory conduct' and sentenced to twenty-one days' hard labour, but on the same day in 1925 Master Hill sought permission from the board to purchase a 'wireless headphone' for an elderly male patient who had built a small wireless set but had no money to buy the headphones.

Those lucky enough to be employed at the workhouse often faced claims of favouritism from the growing number of jobless. It was true a large proportion of the board and staff, including the master and matron, were Catholics. To some it seemed to be the only qualification needed.

Fear of unemployment drove staff to extraordinary lengths to protect their income. In February 1925 the House Committee was informed by Master Hill: 'That owing to complaints of an unpleasant odour emanating from the person of the Assistant Cook (Main Building) he had caused this officer to be examined by the Medical Officer, with the result that he was found to be suffering from a very bad ulcerated leg.' The cook was treated in the hospital and then sacked.

Catherine's fear centred not so much on unemployment – she never doubted her ability to find another job – but more on the possible interruption to her saving plan. From her first month at Harton she had deposited 5s, a quarter of her monthly wage, with the South Shields Building Society. She was also paying 1d a week to insure Kate's life. The austerity of her grandmother's funeral had deeply shocked Catherine. She needed to know that when Kate died there would be enough money to pay for a proper funeral.

CATHERINE owed her new life and contentment to her religion. More specifically, she felt, to the Virgin and the Holy Family. 'I neither questioned nor probed but accepted it,' she said many years later in *Our Kate*. 'It sustained me and comforted me.'

She could not walk down Boldon Lane on her way home without kneeling before the altar at St Peter and Paul's to beg Our Lady to keep Kate sober and out of debt. On her way back to the workhouse after an evening or day at William Black Street she would stop to give thanks in the unlit church.

Ironically it was after one visit to the church that Catherine found herself drunk – for the only time in her life.

It was Christmas Eve. Overpowered by a dread of the day to come and the inevitable drinking in the kitchen at No 10, Catherine left the institute to attend Midnight Mass. When she returned, in the early hours of Christmas morning, she called in at the mess room.

Two of the officers were still up. The mess had been decorated for the festival and the tables were already laid with bowls of fruit, plates of mince pies and bottles of wine.

Catherine was invited to have a celebration drink. 'I told them I didn't drink,' she remembers. 'They said that what was in the jug was non-alcoholic and they poured me out a tumbler.

'When I smelled it – and remember, I could smell whisky and beer a mile off – it smelled very nice. So I drank it and it was lovely. Then I had some more, and a couple of mince pies.'

Two hours later Catherine found herself hammering on a bedroom door and shouting Christmas greetings through the key hole. The room was occupied by Miss Taylor, the laundry manageress. Egged on by her giggling colleagues she visited every door on the corridor, repeating the performance.

'On Christmas morning I woke up and my head filled the entire

73

room,' Catherine recalls. 'It was a very small room, more like a cell, but believe me, my head seemed to fill every inch of it. I felt ill and I couldn't even remember getting into bed.'

Christmas Day was inmates' day at Harton with all the staff waiting on the workhouse residents. Catherine staggered through her duties feeling sick and with her head throbbing. When she finally arrived in the mess for Christmas dinner she was greeted first by a deafening roar and then by waves of laughter.

Laughter was Catherine's escape route, the smoke-screen she could either create or hide behind. She used it to defuse the passions she most cared about. She was always striving to improve her looks, a vanity which bordered on obsession. But a fellow officer could reduce her to fits of giggles during sessions of physical appraisal – Catherine's bust was too high; her neck too short; her knees too bony. 'People could kill me with laughter,' she said.

Catherine's attempts at improving her social status provided amusement for her colleagues. There was a piano in the officer's recreation room, but Catherine knew the staff would never allow her to practise in peace. She needed something smaller and more portable. After a tour of the Tyne Dock second-hand shops she returned with a fiddle. It came in its own case with a bow and a lump of resin and Catherine had paid 10s (50 pence) for it.

Weekly lessons cost a shilling a time. Catherine took to carrying the black leather case everywhere and practising wherever she could find an empty room. Warning of her arrival was given by the assistant matron's dog. Whenever it spotted Catherine approaching with the case under her arm, it dived for cover and let out a pitiful series of howls. The eighteen members of Catherine's mess were less tactful. 'They were so sick of my fiddle they threatened to do me in in eighteen different ways,' she remembers. 'I think they thought I was a bit of a crank.'

After twelve weeks she concluded there must be something wrong with the fiddle and gave up. Her next accomplishment would be French. This time, her teacher informed her, there was something wrong with her accent. Catherine turned to swinging Indian clubs.

She had not written anything seriously since the rejection of her 16,000-word story by the *Shields Gazette*. The friction between the workhouse staff and those employed in the hospital blocks gave her the plot for her first play. It was written as a comedy and attempts to get the other officers to read the parts inevitably ended in uproar.

Her spelling had improved little and her grammar was atrocious, but Catherine was proud of the play. If she was to become a writer she knew she would need tuition. One national correspondence school was offering to appraise manuscripts before taking on new postal pupils. Catherine submitted her comedy. Several weeks later it was returned. There was no covering letter or criticism. Scrawled in red ink across the final page was the verdict: 'Strongly advise author not to take up writing as a career.'

THE talks between miners and coal owners had broken down. At one minute past midnight on Saturday, 1 May 1926 a million men walked out of Britain's pits – 190,000 of them in Northumberland and County Durham.

Faced with a deepening depression and a glut of imported coal, the pit owners were desperate to cut production costs. They informed the miners that each man would be expected to take a 13.5 per cent reduction in pay and work longer hours. Herbert Smith, the president of the Miners' Federation, replied with the slogan: 'Not a penny off the pay, not a second on the day.'

The dispute set in motion a frenetic game of tit-for-tat between Government and unions.

The miners described the action as a strike. The pit owners kept face by claiming to have locked the men out. Stanley Baldwin's Government condemned the dispute as a challenge to the constitutional rights and freedom of the nation, an attempt by the unions to set up a state within a state. The Trades Union Congress responded by issuing a national strike call to its 4,350,982 members for the following Tuesday. Ministers feared a bloody revolution. The TUC gave instructions that there should be no violence. 'We are not fighting the public nor are we attempting to overthrow constitutional Government,' said a Congress statement.

On Tuesday, 4 May, a silence charged with anger and hope descended on Tyne Dock and the New Buildings. Nine days later the General Strike was over, defeated by Government power and planning. The TUC surrender was unconditional. But the miners refused to return to work. Throughout the long, hot summer of 1926 they starved the nation of coal and reduced work at Tyne Dock staithes to a trickle.

For the first and only time Kate enjoyed relative prosperity compared to her neighbours. She was still receiving her weekly allowance of 14s 6d (72 pence) from David's wage. The majority of families depended on the North Eastern Railway and its dock complex for a living and were forced to seek social security assistance. The Guardians of the South Shields Union offered additional relief in the form of food vouchers. To the residents of the New Buildings it became known as 'living on the pineapple'.

Each family would be issued with a weekly voucher, similar to a store bill. On it would be printed a list of essential foodstuffs: flour, yeast, potatoes, bread. It would also state the maximum amount the supplies were to come to.

Jessie Eckford soon found a way of allowing her hard-pressed customers something extra. She would add a half-stone of flour or potatoes to the chit, giving the families a 4½d packet of cigarettes or a tin of pineapple in its place. To claim her money for the supplies Jessie would send eighteen-year-old Belle with the vouchers each month to the Master's office at the workhouse.

Coal was in short supply. With the police guarding the timber ponds, so too was wood. Jim Harding, laid off from his job as a coal trimmer at Tyne Dock until November, dragged his motor boat ashore at Bogey Hill. He broke up the *Irene* and distributed the wood for his neighbours, including Kate, to use as fuel.

John McMullen, by this time in his mid-seventies, still enjoyed a good brawl even if he wasn't young enough to take part.

In July the Durham Miners' Association began distributing a 5s grant to each union member on strike. The money had been collected by local lodges through public subscriptions. Its distribution presented the South Shields Union Guardians with a dilemma: how could they continue to provide the same relief for those laid off by the miners' actions when the strikers themselves were financially better off? The Board side-stepped the issue. The extra cash, it decided, was solely for the benefit of the miner while the weekly food vouchers were officially issued to his dependants.

The decision enraged the workers whose families were being

forced to endure deepening poverty with no union support and through no fault of their own. Hundreds marched to the Board of Guardians' office in Barrington Street, South Shields. When the staff refused to meet a delegation, the crowd threatened to burn down the building. The mob refused to disperse and was finally scattered by a police charge. It was the town's most violent demonstration of the entire summer.

One of the officers who took part was 33-year-old PC Billy Baines. Stationed at the police box built into the Tyne Dock entrance he regularly spent his shift directing traffic at the junction of Hudson Street and Slake Terrace. There were several local characters on his beat, which included the dock arches and Leam Lane End. One of them was John McMullen.

'He told me the next day he had watched the demonstration from the doorway of a tearoom,' remembers Baines. 'The men were going into a churchyard to get stones to throw at the police. John said a little policeman had caught one of these chaps coming over the wall and, he says, "I saw the best fight ye'll ever see."

'I told him, "You shouldn't have been there, you know. The police can't pick the corn from the chaff."

'You know what John McMullen said? "If you can find the policeman that scrapped with that man, I'll give him ten shillings."'

CATHERINE decided to make a second, more determined, attempt to train as a nurse.

She had first flirted with the idea five years earlier when she was fifteen and in service at the Sowerbys. She called at the Presbytery to see Father Bradley, a man who had the unnerving look of someone who could examine your very soul. The priest had connections with Harton Workhouse which, as Catherine knew, employed a number of nurses. His rejection was characteristically blunt. Not only was Catherine too young, she did not have a good-enough education.

At twenty Catherine was now old enough to realise her lack of education would continue to be a stumbling block. The shortfall would take years of hard study to make up. At least she could do something about her knowledge of the human body.

She bought a copy of *The Naval Book*. Compiled as an essential training manual for Royal Navy sick-bay attendants, it included the treatment for almost every medical eventuality except childbirth. Shut away each evening in her room at the institute, Catherine worked her way through its pages, struggling to pronounce words she never understood. On her Sundays off she would sit in the kitchen at No 10, painstakingly redrawing the pictures of bones and muscle groups.

Catherine knew it was pointless applying to train as a nurse at Harton, where she would be handicapped by professional snobbery. A trainee nurse who failed her exams could be downgraded to household duties. But a laundry worker was never considered a fit person to be upgraded to the nursing staff.

Catherine applied, in secret, to a Newcastle hospital. Nursing, she was told at an interview, was a popular profession for young women. Her name would be added to the list of hopefuls. What Catherine wasn't told was that her illegitimacy would have meant almost certain rejection.

As 20 June 1927 approached Kate had no choice but to concede the inevitable. Catherine had grown into a very beautiful young woman.

The two-and-a-half years living away from home had burnished her daughter's character. In it Kate could see many of the traits which had attracted her to Catherine's father. Her daughter had become a stranger whom she respected as well as loved. She was also a young woman drawing strength from Kate's own weaknesses. Catherine, who had once cowered under John McMullen's hand, was challenging the male control her mother had accepted without question.

St Peter and Paul's used a small patch of land it owned as a tennis court. The players were exclusively men, among them Jim Eckford, Belle's older brother. Catherine set her sights on breaking the monopoly. But first she needed a racket and a pair of tennis shoes. Kate took out a club with a Jarrow store to buy Catherine the equipment as a twenty-first birthday present. Although she developed a fearsome overhead swing, Catherine found the teamwork of doubles too restrictive, she found it irksome to rely on another person for her own success.

IN September 1927 the assistant laundress, a Miss Scott,

announced she was leaving to take up a post elsewhere. Catherine immediately applied to fill the vacancy.

After considering three other applicants, and with the grudging approval of Matron Hill, the House Committee agreed to Catherine's promotion. As assistant laundress she would now be paid £3 12s 6d a month. The Guardians valued her board and lodging at £60 a year. Her new wage was less than her predecessor's, who had been paid 4s 2d a month more, but it was a considerable advance on her £2 as checker. Catherine's place behind the glass partition would be taken by a girl raised from childhood at one of the Cottage Homes.

Catherine had already decided that if she wasn't good enough to be a writer she was certainly up to the task of managing a laundry. She would work her way up the ladder as quickly as possible. It was a resolve which almost evaporated in a moment of panic.

An inmate named Margaret Lalley had been feeding bed linen into the six-roller calender. Caught in the folds of the sheet, her hand had been dragged between the first set of steel rollers. Catherine heard the 37-year-old woman's screams. Realising what must have happened she turned and fled. Catherine had passed several other workers and pushed her way through the main laundry doors before she managed to pull herself together and return to help.

Throughout the winter of 1927 and 1928 staff at the institution had been raising money for an ultra-violet lamp. It would cost £146 15s 2d. In return they would be allowed to use the primitive 'sun-ray' equipment when it was not being used to treat patients.

The mercury vapour lamp was installed in March 1928. Catherine lost no time in benefiting from the machine, which left her skin tanned and healthy. Once a week she would join colleagues and sit in her underclothes around the cumbersome, crackling lamp. As the women took off their protective goggles at the end of one Friday morning session, a young officer noticed a large sore on Catherine's waist. There were others on her thighs and bottom.

Catherine dismissed the spots and blamed the fried food she was eating. In addition to her own breakfast at 7.30 am, she would frequently finish a leftover plate of cold bacon and eggs during her ten o'clock break. Catherine dressed and returned to her duties.

Her arrival at the laundry was swiftly followed by a message ordering her to report to the hospital. Her reception there was cold and stand-offish. Catherine was taken to the 'lock ward' and ordered to undress. The room had a bare floor, two wooden chairs and a scrubbed wooden table. Nurses were only allowed to enter if they were wearing rubber gloves and a rubber apron. No one would tell Catherine why she was there.

Dr Shanley arrived to examine her. Catherine recognised and trusted him. With him was Dr Stocks, the hospital's female physician, the ward sister and a nurse, and a sour-faced Matron Hill. From their expressions Catherine knew she was the subject of guilt rather than pity. The examination ended as abruptly as it had begun. The doctor took off his rubber gloves and spoke re-assuringly to Catherine. The matron, who appeared bemused by his change in manner, said nothing. Turning his back on Catherine, the doctor brushed past Mrs Hill. 'You're mistaken,' he said curtly. 'Never been touched.'

The following Tuesday Kate arrived to visit her daughter. Although still confined to the 'lock ward' the attitude of the nurses and other officers had lightened. They laughed and chatted freely with Catherine. The ward sister still refused to explain the reason for her sojourn.

On her way to the ward Kate had been to see Mrs Hill. The matron had been informed of her assistant laundress's background within days of Catherine's arrival in 1924. There was more than a hint of sarcasm in her voice when she told Kate: 'You've got a very good daughter, Mrs McDermott. She's a very good girl.'

Kate, who had dressed for the occasion and bunned her hair, contained her anger until she was alone with her daughter. The fact that Catherine was still a virgin came as a revelation to the priggish Mrs Hill. Two weeks earlier she had delighted in reprimanding Catherine for not returning from a party until two in the morning. Kate knew exactly what she had expected to find. But the idea her employer might even be pleased that Catherine had contracted syphilis was as enlightening as it was irritating to the 21-year-old.

Catherine considered the assumption she would make the same mistake as her mother an attack on her faith. 'I was a good

Catholic up to then,' she said. 'But these people in this institution, they were waiting for me to become pregnant. Waiting for me to follow our Kate. They tried to take my good name away, the only thing I valued in my life was to keep myself pure.'

The realisation the Catholic Church was not the encompassing shield she had been promised began to take hold. How could those who respected the same right and wrong – who claimed to fear the same good and evil – remain no better than back-yard gossips? How, Catherine asked herself, could she entrust her future to a divinity which allowed others such malicious freedom?

When Catherine was allowed to return to her room and the officers' mess the following week she was no longer naïve and gullible. She was still 'bloody St Catherine'. But this time she would earn the title.

CATHERINE had never read any book by Elinor Glyn. To do so would have been a sin. The Catholic Church said so.

Since the publication of her first novel – *The Visits of Elizabeth* – in 1900, Glyn had explored the shadows of romantic fiction, allowing chinks of light to fall across the Victorian morality which divided marriage and sex.

In 1906, the year Catherine was born, *Beyond the Rocks* told of transgressive sexuality and pain within a marriage. A year later, her most famous novel, *Three Weeks*, glorified a brief affair which leads to a wife's murder by her brutal husband. Glyn had not simply dared to unlock the cupboard door, she had flung it open. To the Catholic Church the light was blinding. Her books were damned from every Catholic pulpit.

In 1925, the year after Catherine began work at Harton Institute, Glyn published her most controversial novel, *This Passion Called Love*. Written in the form of a guide book, it contained chapters describing 'How to Attract the Man You Desire'.

But it was a well-worn copy of *Three Weeks* which was currently doing the rounds of the workhouse staff. Catherine could never understand why a quote from the book – 'He did but kiss her little feet' – should trigger such hysterical laughter. The novel, bloody St Catherine informed her fellow officers, must be a 'mucky book' written by a 'bad woman', a pronouncement which produced equal uproar.

A few days later Catherine returned to her bedroom to discover someone had crept in and left a copy of Glyn's 1916 novel, *The Career of Katherine Bush*. In the isolation and security of her room Catherine was defenceless. She was tempted and she fell.

'To say that my life changed at this point is absolutely true,' she admits in Antonia Fraser's *The Pleasure of Reading*. 'I've often said that I think Elinor Glyn was put on this earth for the sole purpose of enlightening an abysmally ignorant north-country girl.'

Already fascinated by the coincidence of the names, Catherine discovered the story was a reflection of her own dreams. It plots the social success of a secretary who eventually marries a duke and becomes a 'real' lady, his love becoming even stronger when she confesses a previous affair. Half-way through the book the duchess for whom she works tells the secretary: 'The first essential of a lady is to be well read and the book you must get to base your education on is *Lord Chesterfield's Letters to His Son.*'

The next day Catherine hurried to South Shields library. It was the first time she had entered a public library or attempted to borrow a book. The assistant, impressed by her choice, had to search the basement stockroom before Catherine could leave with the first volume of the earl's letters under her arm.

She felt as though she had at last discovered her personal tutor. Catherine listened to Lord Chesterfield's words inside her head as though he were sitting opposite her in the tiny room. Was this man not her natural instructor? Was she not his natural pupil? No one could have such a devoted, persistent and brilliant guide. He never failed her. And she never failed him, bolting her dinner to return to her room, reading and re-reading the letters until she fell asleep with the book still in her hands.

There was another affinity which Catherine cherished. The letters were written to Philip Stanhope, an illegitimate son born in 1732 when the earl was thirty-eight. From the first, written in 1732, to the final brief note penned late in 1771, Lord Chesterfield had one mission – to educate and elevate a single person so high that he would never be betrayed by the lowness of his birth.

Catherine found in the letters the true education she had searched for in the pages of *Cassell's Weekly* or the simply-titled *T.P.* Not only did the letters teach her history, they also showed her the geographic stage on which history was enacted. 'From then on a new world opened up for me,' she adds in *The Pleasure of Reading*. 'I was given my first taste of mythology, history and geography, and in going through further volumes I was introduced to names of authors such as Voltaire, Plato, Pope, Swift, on and on.' Attempting to complete the earl's reading list was not easy. 'Many of those I got from the library were beyond me. I was never one for skipping my reading, but I found more than a few of the books verbose and boring.'

Lord Chesterfield himself lacked hyperbole. He was a writer of plain English. He set the standards Catherine was to live by for the rest of her life: 'Dissimulate, but do not simulate'; 'Disguise your real sentiments, but do not falsify them'; 'Go through the world with your eyes and ears open and your mouth mostly shut'; 'He that is gentil doeth gentil deeds.'

But 'growing learned so that everyone will be fond of you' was one thing. Communicating that learning was another matter. Catherine took to reading the letters aloud, following Chesterfield's advice that all ladies and gentlemen should 'articulate correctly'.

The readings stopped when she discovered the mentally handicapped inmates regularly gathered at her keyhole to enjoy the strange sounds of a new language.

During private moments Catherine worked hard on her appearance. Kate's words echoed around her. 'Get Charlie off your back!' After the playground accident she had walked with one leg in the gutter to correct the problem with her hip and spine. Now Catherine trained herself to walk from the hip. Concentrating on each step. Holding her upper body rigid during the two-mile walk between the institute and the New Buildings.

Her attempts at improving her deportment were frequently mistaken for aloofness.

Billy Baines, the Tyne Dock policeman, first noticed Catherine when she was 'a pretty teenager weighed down with a bundle of clothes'. A few years later, Baines recalled, 'she carried herself as if she were walking past for the first time and never wanted to see the place again'. Baines also remembered watching as Catherine regularly broke out of her rigid isolation. 'When she smiled she was beautiful,' he said.

On her evenings off Catherine would catch a tram as far as the dock gates and then walk the rest of the way to the New Buildings. She would pass the sullen groups of dockers, careful not to give any sign of approval or disdain. They were hard men. Sometimes she would spot a face she recognised. Catherine would relax her pace and exchange greetings with Billy Potts, the lodger she had blown from his bed with the One O'Clock Gun. Once a month the ritual would change. Billy would step forward to chat and Catherine would dip into her purse for a sixpence or a shilling. 'Ta, lass,' Billy would say. 'Ta, lass. I'll not forget you.'

By the time she reached William Black Street she was once again a 'lady'.

'At that time she was very haughty,' remembers Irene Callender, by then a teenager herself. 'She might smile as she passed, but nothing more.' To her one-time friend Belle Napier, Catherine had turned into 'a loner, a bit of a snob'.

Standing for eight hours a day on her feet was no reason to neglect her clothes. Catherine bought herself a pair of shiny, black patent-leather shoes. This, after all, was the 'pseud business' of impressing others as she later described it.

'I knew these were the accomplishments of a lady and my unknown father was supposed to have been a gentleman, so here was me giving myself all the things I would have had if he had owned me.'

ONE afternoon in 1926 Catherine was getting off a tram in Talbot Street, South Shields, when she recognised a young man getting on – 'he was too beautiful for a man'. They did not speak. Catherine watched in silence as he boarded with a well-dressed young woman.

The beau was Hughie Aixill. At one time he had, literally, been the light in her life.

Catherine was eleven or twelve. She had walked past the dock gates on her way home and was just emerging from under the first of the Tyne Dock arches when she saw Hughie Aixill coming toward her. He, too, was in the well of sunlight between the dark of the arches.

'I kept my eyes on him while all the time feeling I couldn't bear it, I'd have to look away,' she told to a television audience many years later. 'And then a strange thing happened. Hughie became lost in a great white light. It spread out from him; it enveloped the great black arch and blotted out every material thing in the world. There was nothing but this great white light; and I walked into it.

'When I turned round, I was beyond the fifth arch. I walked back a few steps and looked through the arches, and there he was at the far end of the last one.'

Catherine was to use the experience, thinly disguised, in her novel *Pure as the Lily*. Mary Walton watches as Hughie Amesden vanishes in a 'lovely but frightening' white light, mysteriously passing her to re-appear a full street away.

Hughie Aixill had been the first boy to catch Catherine's attention. There was also Tot Lawson, a boy with 'dreamy eyes', whom Catherine attempted to lure with sweets passed via his sister Ruby.

In her early teens, while working for Mrs Sowerby on Simonside Terrace, Catherine had developed a powerful crush on her employer's eldest son. He ignored her childish flirtations, doubt-less guided by his mother. When, at eighteen, he considered Catherine old enough to pursue it was too late. Her heart had moved on. This time it was Catherine who was biding her time.

Catherine waited patiently for her bank clerk until 1927. In the meantime she enjoyed the attention young men were beginning to pay her. Tot Lawson finally noticed her and, briefly, she agreed to be his girlfriend. Then there was a pitman called Mickey Moran. Catherine also went to parties with Jackie Potts, the relative who had instigated the Saturday evening gatherings at William Black Street. Most of her boyfriends came from big families and similar backgrounds, although Catherine considered their homes inferior to her own. She took none of the young men seriously.

In 1927, after her promotion to assistant laundress at the age of twenty-one, Catherine finally began a relationship with the man she had convinced herself she was going to marry.

Whether her bank clerk considered her enough of a lady to propose is not clear. Marriage was certainly discussed. Catherine teased him by saying she would only marry him if he helped her discover the identity of her father, a promise she had no intention of keeping. Reunited with – and rescued by – her gentleman father Catherine would have considered even a bank clerk beneath her.

During his irregular and brief visits to William Black Street, her boyfriend made no attempt to disguise his contempt for Jack McMullen and his disapproval of Kate. Each visit was followed by an argument. And after each row Catherine was informed that their courtship was over.

For the first time in her life Catherine was in love. Each rejection sent her huddling to her room to cry herself silently to sleep, or back to No 10, where Kate recognised the signs. Her life had become a roller-coaster as breathtaking as it was painful. Catherine made only one attempt to get off.

She returned to the Presbytery and Father Bradley. The interview was characteristically brief. Unaware that the priest had had a hand in her appointment at the institute, Catherine stammered out an appeal for guidance. Six years before she had asked him to help her train as a nurse. This time she wanted to become a nun. Father Bradley rose from his desk. He walked to the door and opened it. 'Go,' he told her, 'and think some more.'

Early in January 1928 the woman who had managed the laundry since Catherine's arrival left to get married. Matron Hill refused even to consider Catherine's request to take her place. Two more attempts to have her name placed on a list of applicants were also dismissed. At twenty-one, and after less than four months as assistant laundress, the matron considered Catherine too young and inexperienced to take over the running of such a large laundry.

Despite several advertisements the Guardians failed to attract a suitable replacement. As a temporary measure they re-engaged a former laundress who had left the institute to manage a small hand laundry. She was paid two guineas a week. Catherine soon found she was doing most of her new superior's tasks as well as her own work.

The Guardians approached Mrs U. Stephenson, the assistant laundress whose place Catherine had taken. When she agreed to return as head laundress Catherine's ambition could take no more. Plunged into another round of rejection by her boyfriend, Catherine made up her mind to find another post. She began scouring the pages of the *Poor Law Journal*.

It took her almost a year to find what she was looking for. In March 1929 the Board of Guardians at Tendring Workhouse, advertised for a laundress. Catherine applied and was invited to Essex for an interview.

Catherine had to keep her plans secret. Mr and Mrs Hill had resigned the previous August to take over the running of a similar institution in Birmingham. They had been replaced by a new master and equally rancorous matron. Catherine knew Matron Hill's replacement was even less likely to allow her more than a day's leave. On Friday, 29 March Catherine feigned illness and retreated to William Black Street. Not a hard thing to do since her nose bleeds had now been noticed by most of the staff. A few days later she was on a train south.

The letter offering her the post managing the laundry at Tendring arrived in mid-April. Kate's words were ringing in her ears as Catherine stood before the Matron to announce her departure. 'You'll see your day with them, hinny. You'll see your day.'

THE tram which had rumbled through the first weeks of her life as a baby in the Leam Lane house was now taking Catherine away. She had used it for almost two decades to take her to the very edge of her world. Catherine knew Jarrow and South Shields, but only the main streets. From there the North Eastern Railway had taken her on to Newcastle no more than six or seven times; once to Durham; once to Gilsland; a few times to Birtley to visit her Aunt Sarah's family; and once, in 1928, on a day trip to Edinburgh.

At twenty-two Catherine was not leaving to explore the world beyond. She was escaping from the world within.

Catherine had watched the social conditions of Tyneside decline with the employment. For someone who saw work – hard work – as the only way out, the silent shipyards and the shuffling job queues were a threat. 'The only thing I knew about the North was work, that was my culture,' she recalled. 'And during my teens I saw the work gradually fading away. In my twenties it vanished. It wasn't the only thing that made me leave the North, it was a number of things, but quite prominent was this feeling of depression.'

It was as if her surroundings had become so concentrated, so insidious, that they had finally seeped into her very soul. The poverty and the squalor and the grime of everyday living –

compounded by the indignities suffered by the workhouse inmates – began to disgust her. She was sick of the drunkenness, the Friday-night beatings. Sick of turning her back on the open sores of rape and incest and abortion. Of turning her head away from men who did things in the street that a lady would try not to know.

Less obvious was her need to distance herself from the man who had broken her heart. Kate, who silently shared her daughter's longing, had wisely allowed the relationship to run its course. Catherine knew she was being used and humiliated. Sooner or later she would fight back. The end came when, yet again, her beau attempted to reject Catherine and her family. This time there were no tears. She described it in *Our Kate*: 'it was like performing an operation on myself without an anaesthetic, and although the wound healed the scar remained'.

One truth remained for Catherine to discover. In the days between her resignation from the workhouse and her departure from East Jarrow Catherine made the journey by train to Lamesley. When she called at the Ravensworth Arms where her mother once worked she was sent to the blacksmith's cottages next door. Catherine introduced herself to Bella Thompson. Over a cup of tea in the back kitchen Catherine learned the secret of Kate's 'gentleman' lover. Her father, Bella told Catherine, had been employed by Lord Ravensworth at the nearby castle as a footman. He was dismissed early in 1906 and returned south where he was born.

Kate stood at the back gate. She was crying. John McMullen walked Catherine down the cobbled back lane, past the gable end of Phillipson Street and between the two front terraces to the tram stop.

For days Catherine had been reciting the words of a poem she had discovered in *The Happy Mag*. The page on which the poem – 'Believe This' – was printed, together with passages and notes from Lord Chesterfield's letters, were in the suitcase at her feet.

> *I will succeed I simply cannot fail,*
> *The only obstacle is doubt.*
> *There's not a hill I cannot scale*
> *Once fear is put to rout.*
> *Don't think defeat,*

Don't talk defeat,
The word will rob you of your strength.
I will succeed, this phrase repeat
Through the journey's length.

As they waited on Swinburne Street looking out across Jarrow Slake, Catherine could see the Father was also holding back the tears.

The moment that I can't is said,
You slam a door right in your face.
Why not exclaim I will instead,
Half won then is the race.
You close the door to your success
By entertaining one small fear.
Think happiness, talk happiness,
Watch joy then coming near.

Part Two

'Out of the Darkness'

Six

I have never wasted time, no matter how I have felt.

CATHERINE ARRIVED IN Clacton-on-Sea for the second time. It was Saturday, 25 May 1929.

Her interview had been held in the Board of Guardians' office in the centre of the Essex town. The workhouse itself, she was told, was situated at the near-by village of Tendring. Naïvely she had assumed the institution would be within walking distance of the town centre. As she emerged from Clacton and Southcliffe railway station she asked directions to the workhouse. Tendring was ten miles away.

The village was served by one coach a day. Called the Silver Queen, it crawled through the flat countryside to make unhurried stops at the villages of Little Clacton, Thorpe-le-Soken and Weeley. The fare to Tendring was 5d (2 pence).

Catherine watched gloomily as the silhouette of the workhouse appeared beyond the hedgerows and trees. As the Silver Queen pulled up in the centre of Tendring village, she realised she had swapped her narrow world along the banks of the Tyne for an existence equally confining.

Tendring, which even at its peak had little more than 1,000 inhabitants, clung to a stretch of road that dog-legged its way into the distance. The workhouse was situated at the eastern end of the village. Its nearest neighbour was an isolated farm. The village boundary was marked by two public houses, the Live and Let Live opposite the workhouse gates and the Cherry Tree two miles away. Between these were three general shops, a butcher's shop, a blacksmith's and a third public house. Education for the village and workhouse children was provided by primary and elementary schools, spiritual guidance from the village church.

Catherine walked through the wind-swept porch to announce

her arrival. She was shocked by what she discovered. At least the Harton workhouse had allowed itself to be nudged into the twentieth century. Quarantined from the sensitivities and prejudices of town dwellers, Tendring operated in a late-Victorian vacuum, its outmoded traditions fiercely defended by the Master and Matron, Mr and Mrs Harry Burden.

The Union Workhouse at Tendring – centre of the old Tendring Hundreds of Saxon times – had been completed in 1838. It was designed to accommodate a maximum of 244 men, women and children from the thirty-five surrounding parishes.

Externally it had changed very little since the year after Queen Victoria came to the throne. Built mainly of yellow brick with small, prison-like windows, it provided much the same refuge as Harton Workhouse. The sick and 'mental defectives' were treated in the main hospital while the destitute were confined to the workhouse. The separation enforced on families was even crueller than at Harton. Children were taken from their mothers and brought up in a children's home situated on another part of the eight-acre site. Attempts by parents to make contact with their offspring were a punishable offence.

But where the doss houses and alleyways of South Shields also provided shelter for vagrants unwilling to submit to institutional rules, Tendring provided the only refuge in a bleak landscape. Each afternoon Catherine watched as the tattered figures began to gather outside the main gate. Every man, woman and child would be expected to complete a full twelve hours' work before being allowed to leave. Mealtimes were signalled by a blast from the hooter at the porter's lodge, which was also used to warn the outside workers from the village of starting and finishing times.

Visitors were openly discouraged. The entire site was surrounded by a twenty-foot hedge. All gates and doors were locked at dusk during the winter months and at no later than 6 pm in the summer. After dark the unlit grounds sank into a black world of frightening noises and strange shadows.

THE laundry was housed in a separate building away from the main hospital and workhouse. Behind it were neatly laid-out plots where the mentally handicapped patients were shown how to grow vegetables. They were forbidden to grow flowers.

Even the increase in wages did nothing to lift Catherine from the depression she felt at inspecting the 'biggest and best' laundry she had come to manage. Along one wall was a line of deep sinks. The machinery was belt-driven from a long shaft which ran the entire length of the opposite wall. As in all the buildings, the predominant colours were brown and green.

Catherine had been employed as laundress at an annual salary of £65 – the same rate as the assistant matron, the hospital staff nurse and the cook – and an increase from her wages as assistant laundress of £43 10s. Her total salary, with emoluments, was now valued at £130 a year. From her net monthly income of £5 2s 11d would be deducted 5s 5d (27 pence) for superannuation and 2s (10 pence) for National Insurance.

At the end of each month Catherine would sign the officers' account book before receiving her salary. She was still spelling her Christian name with a 'K', the way she had been taught at school.

In the final days before leaving Tyneside Catherine had opened a policy with the Prudential Assurance Company. She was saving regularly, but needed to know that Kate would be taken care of if anything untoward should happen. It was not a new fear. After the shame and penury of her grandmother's funeral, the eleven-year-old Catherine had insured her own life for £50. She was about to make her first train journey alone from Tyne Dock to Birtley and paid 2d at the ticket office for railway accident insurance. Catherine hoped at least part of the money would have gone towards giving her a 'proper' funeral.

The Prudential agent had asked to see Catherine's birth certificate. Too frightened to raise the matter with Kate, Catherine told the insurance company she did not have one.

Her predecessor at Tendring, a Margaret McFall, agreed to stay on for ten days until Catherine was confident about taking over the day-to-day running of the laundry. Although the laundry itself, and the institute it served, were smaller than Harton, the antiquated machinery and the restricted numbers of staff made the work tiresome.

Violet Marjoram, who was born and brought up in Tendring, worked in the laundry during the 1930s. The conditions had not changed since Catherine's time there.

'There were seven women workers and three inmates,' she

recalls. 'We had to do all the different jobs. I would be in the wash-house with one inmate for one week; then a week on the calender, where the bigger washing, such as sheets and draw-sheets, went through heated rollers. The next week it might be ironing. We all did this in turn.

'The wash-house had two big washing machines, one for the cleanest washing, one for the soiled drawsheets. The nappies and finer washing were done by hand by the inmates in the large sinks. There was a spin-drier which looked like a font with a lid.'

The nurses' uniforms, children's home dresses and shirts were dried in a heated cupboard, she recalls. 'You pulled out one section, filled it with clothes and closed it, and then pulled the next one out. They were all metal and heated from the boiler house. The nurses' and officers' aprons had to be starched. Four people were ironing all the time and from there the clean and pressed things were taken to the clean linen room by an inmate.'

The master and matron oversaw the accounts with miserly relish. Mrs Burden refused to allow Catherine to condemn bed linen until it had been patched at least five times, no matter how stained or discoloured. And patients or inmates who required glasses were found a pair from the 'dead stock box'.

BY October Catherine was again scouring the pages of the *Poor Law Journal*.

Any sensation of self-respect and control over her own destiny had been quickly smothered by loneliness and guilt. 'I was a foreigner there,' Catherine remembered. 'I think I only left the place once and that was to go to a fête in the village.'

The isolation came as a culture shock after the noisy familiarity of Harton and was heightened by the surrounding countryside. The sounds of metal on metal; of shipping and railways; of endless activity: all had been replaced by a peace Catherine had never experienced. She felt confined and threatened, a sensation which in later years was to spoil several country holidays.

Although Kate was missing her daughter, it was the ageing John McMullen who fretted most over his absent 'bairn'. New faces confused him. At night he could not settle. During the day he spent more and more time sitting in the high-backed wooden chair lost in his silent memories. He would shuffle to the door to meet the postman to collect Catherine's twice-weekly letters, demanding Kate stop her cooking or cleaning to read them aloud.

Catherine also began to suffer severe personal remorse at the loss of absolution. She had not been to Mass since her arrival in late May. The nearest Catholic church was ten miles away in Clacton.

In December 1929 Catherine answered an advertisement in the *Poor Law Journal* for a head laundress at the workhouse in Hastings. She wasn't even sure where Hastings was. On Thursday, 19 December Catherine arrived for an interview and was immediately impressed by the resort's apparent air of prosperity and well-being, everything 'seemed to be on a much higher level' than she had grown up with in the North. The laundry, however, did not impress her.

There were three other women shortlisted for the post. Catherine arrived wearing an imitation fur coat she had bought from a shop in South Shields, which had allowed her to put 'a little aside each week' and a brown velvet hat. All took their turn to be interviewed by the Board of Guardians in a room which resembled a lecture theatre. 'All the women were fat and the men were thin,' Catherine recalled.

During a tour of the laundry Catherine's frankness was never far below the surface. Bundles of soiled linen were sorted outside the laundry building on an ash-covered area of ground. The dust made washing the items harder and was picked up and brought into the building by the staff. It was obvious to Catherine that the area needed to be paved. When a woman member of the board asked Catherine what she thought of the laundry, she replied, 'Madam, I think it's dirty.'

Catherine was recalled to the interview room. It was only her honesty, she was informed, that had got her the job.

Her appointment was officially minuted later that day. 'The Guardians this day interviewed candidates for the above appointment at the Frederick Road Infirmary and Miss Catherine McCullen [sic] of the Poor Law Institution, Tendring, was appointed at a wage of sixty shillings weekly to live out, but to be given a dinner each week-day and otherwise on the terms of the advertisement and the application form signed by her.'

Little did Catherine realise as she returned to Tendring by train and bus that she was turning her back on one storm only to walk into another.

Catherine tendered a month's notice. Matron Burden, who had previously shown her laundress only kindness and respect, attempted to forestall her departure. She wrote to the Hastings Board of Guardians, urging them to change their minds. At twenty-three Catherine, Mrs Burden claimed, was 'too young and inexperienced' for such a post.

On Saturday, 1 February 1930, Catherine walked through the main gate of Tendring Workhouse to await the arrival of the Silver Queen. It was 253 days – 'eight lonely months' – since her arrival.

Seven

I get depressed sometimes but I believe in the therapy of work.

CATHERINE HAD COMPLETED a remarkable journey. She had travelled almost the entire length of England – and succeeded in traversing a complete social class.

Hastings, she sensed, was a place which reflected her own limitlessness. At last she was enjoying the freedom of spirit – of ultimate achievement – that had eluded both Rose McMullen and Kate.

Less than twelve months before Catherine had been earning £43 10s a year. As head laundress at Hastings Catherine would receive £156, little short of what Mrs Hill had been receiving as matron and two-and-a-half times more than the head laundress whose job she had been denied at Harton. It was an unheard-of amount for a single working woman of twenty-three on Tyneside. The average weekly wage for a miner was just £2. A time-served craftsman could expect no more than £3 7s 6d. Even the eleven staff in her charge at Hastings would receive little more than £1 for a week's labour.

The bulk of her £3 weekly wage would once again be put aside. When she had enough to support her, Catherine would enrol on a nursing course. 'My aim then was to become a midwife,' she said. 'I didn't intend to stay for more than a year.'

Early in January 1930 Catherine had written to the matron at Hastings informing her she would be taking up her duties on the first Monday in February. Her immediate concern was finding somewhere to live.

The problem was solved by George Morris, a local shopkeeper who played the organ in the workhouse and infirmary chapel. Recommended by the master and matron, he offered to rent Catherine a bedroom above his shop at 31 Clifton Road. She could also have the use of a downstairs living room.

Catherine had no problems finding her lodgings. The shop and the Morris's house occupied an entire corner on Clifton Road less than two hundred yards from the workhouse gate. To reach the shop door she had to climb four wide stone steps. Its walls and windows were covered by posters extolling the virtues of Nugget shoe polish, Robin starch and Lyons' tea.

George Morris, a bespectacled man who always wore a brown grocer's overall, ran the shop with his wife. They had three sons. The youngest – whom Catherine called 'young Tom' – remembers that his father and Catherine shared an interest in books. 'She would also sit for hours in what we called the front room writing,' he recalls.

When she reported for duty on 3 February Catherine was greeted by the fall-out from her 'dirty laundry' remark. Her comment about the cinder area beside the laundry had received considerable publicity. It was later discussed by the full Board of Guardians and duly reported by the local newspaper. While her new staff awaited her arrival with a mixture of admiration and apprehension, Catherine's ultimate departure was already being predicted. 'You won't be staying long,' the matron told her new laundress. 'Anyone who starts on a Monday doesn't stay long.'

FOR the first time in six years Catherine felt ashamed of working in a laundry.

Her social progression from checker to laundress had been rapid and heady. Catherine found herself in a limbo land between respect and respectability. She had earned one. The other, she felt, she did not yet deserve.

The laundry was situated next to the gate-house office and between two parallel hospital blocks. Each red-brick building was four storeys high and cast a permanent shadow over the space below. Attached to the laundry was the sewing room, where sheets and uniforms were repaired.

Although the Hastings laundry produced far inferior work to that she had witnessed at Harton – and demanded at Tendring – the institute's social ranking was governed more by those who worked within its walls than those who sought its relief. The workhouse was still a workhouse and the poor and homeless still needed assistance, but they were no longer part of the scenery.

When Catherine walked through the Frederick Road gate each morning she felt as though she were stepping down. She was in a town where possessing a job carried far less kudos. Rank had replaced simple survival and, for the first time in her life, Catherine found it difficult to come to terms with her own snobbery.

She responded by driving her staff hard. Under her charge were a middle-aged assistant laundress, Mrs Beecham, and ten outside women workers. These were helped each day by as many as twenty-five mentally handicapped patients and five casual men repaying their overnight bed and board. Catherine's inherited belief in hard work and high standards was something new to a workforce which had enjoyed a lax regime and carefree atmosphere. Within earshot she was 'Miss Mac'. Behind her back Catherine was dubbed the 'nigger driver'.

Part of the laundry's duties included washing and ironing the nurses' workwear. Catherine demanded crisply ironed uniforms – any that showed the slightest crease were swiftly rejected. The problem was getting the starch, applied with hot flat irons, to run smoothly. She sought advice from a London-based laundry trade paper.

'They wrote back suggesting we use diluted methylated spirits to help the starch run,' she remembers. 'I got a pint of meths, but it didn't work well so I asked for a second pint. The next thing I knew the board wanted to know what I was doing with it – perhaps they thought I was drinking it.'

Her discipline soon won the respect of the workhouse master and matron. George Moyle Silverlock was a large, bald man who strode around his domain in plus-fours and plaid stockings. Matron Silverlock was a small, quick-smiling woman of French ancestry whose principal concern was the welfare of the inmates. Catherine soon discovered her major fault was that she was a 'disturber of the staff'. The couple had a daughter who was also a member of the institute's thirty-one permanent officers.

To complete her records Mrs Silverlock needed sight of her new laundress's birth certificate. When Catherine explained she did not possess one, the matron made it plain she understood why. Catherine reluctantly confessed. It was a moment she had dreaded. Now it was over she shared her guilt with her mother. In a long letter of reply Kate chastised her daughter for betraying her illegitimacy. Her attempts to protect her daughter had backfired, yet Kate blamed Catherine for not asking sooner. Yes, there was a birth certificate. And yes, it did include the name of Catherine's father.

As Catherine got to know the Silverlocks, she discovered their amiability contributed a great deal to the general atmosphere of the establishment. 'Compared with the institution I had left in South Shields it was like a rest home for the inmates,' she confided to the son of a former colleague nearly fifty years later.

Conditions for the laundry staff were less enjoyable – and far from sanitary. During her interview tour Catherine had failed to notice that the workers' lavatory opened directly into the main washing area. It was unventilated and stank. The matter was soon drawn to Master Silverlock's attention.

The absence of a mess room where her staff could eat and relax during breaks was another omission Catherine was determined to put right. Early in 1932 she began lobbying the master and matron. By May approval had been given for a store immediately below the drying room to be converted to a dining area for the laundry staff.

Catherine did not win every battle. The build-up of heat and steam in the main laundry left the workers dripping and exhausted. In summer the humidity was overpowering. Catherine suggested an electric fan would solve the problem. The borough engineer did not agree. After inspecting the building on a rainy day in April, he concluded the 'proper control of the windows' was all that was needed.

The horrific accident in the Harton laundry – and Catherine's reaction to it – had left her determined to fight for the safety of her staff. She was never slow in enlisting the support of the Factory Inspector. A report following one 1935 visit to the laundry suggests the head laundress 'drew the inspector's attention' to the free access to the back of the laundry machines. Guard rails were swiftly ordered. Far tighter control was demanded under the 1937 Factory Act. Screens to protect the drive belts, hydro extractors and foul washers – previously ruled unnecessary – were now required by law.

*

SEVENTY-EIGHT days after her arrival in Hastings, Catherine received news of John McMullen's death.

In the weeks before her departure Catherine had noticed the emptiness behind the old man's pale eyes. He was losing track of time and interest in life. Late in 1929 Kate had written to say the Father had taken to his bed. Stirred only occasionally to listen to one of Catherine's letters, he spent his days confused by his surroundings and comforted by his memories.

John McMullen died in the early hours of 18 April 1930. It was Good Friday. Dr McHaffie, still the family physician after thirty years, certified the primary cause of death as senility.

John McMullen had inhabited a world far removed from the-day-to-day reality of Catherine's childhood; he was an Irish grotesque wavering between the embarrassments of ignorance and drunkenness. She had longed for his death whenever he pronounced on Ireland; on work; on women; on Protestants, and especially on fellow Catholics.

At home, immersed in the neighbours' fraudulent grief and Kate's sodden hypocrisy, Catherine would have felt immense relief at the Father's going. But here, in Hastings, where her memories were her only protection, Catherine soon discovered her world was suddenly emptier and more tedious than it had ever seemed. In John McMullen's shadow she had learnt a little about love and a lot about life. She had witnessed his first self-conscious signs of compassion and, as she grew older, caught the mischievous twinkle of pride in his eyes.

Catherine decided not to attend the funeral. She added the train fare to the £20 she had saved to pay for her step-grandfather's burial and posted it to No 10 William Black Street. Although not altogether unexpected, the money was a godsend to Kate. That night she mourned the Father – laid out in the same room and upon the same trestles as his wife – with 'a drop of the hard'. Kate remained 'rotten' drunk throughout the funeral and into the next week. There was only enough money left to pay half the undertaker's bill.

The oppressive laundry atmosphere and Catherine's isolation among her staff left her drained. After eight hours she needed reviving. Most nights she walked at least four miles, past Hastings fish market and along the seafront to St Leonards' bathing pool and back. She seldom stopped to speak to anyone.

Loneliness began to erode Catherine's self-confidence. She was, by this time, living in a bed-sit in the West Hill area of the town, not far from the castle. The house had wide stone steps up to the front door. From there she had to struggle up four flights of stairs to reach her attic room.

As Catherine climbed her heart sank. 'I can't stand it,' she said to herself. 'I'm going home, I'm going home.' Before she reached her door Catherine was sobbing bitterly. A continuous stream of blood was flowing from both nostrils. When she woke the next morning, still lying on the bed where she had flung herself, Catherine felt as if she were clinging to life. The bed linen and her clothes were stained and stiff with dry blood.

Her doctor recommended a specialist. His diagnosis was neither confident nor encouraging. After enquiring whether Catherine picked her nose he declared she was suffering from epistaxis – bleeding from the nose. The remedy, he suggested, was an operation. Months later Catherine received the date for her admission to hospital. It was 23 December 1930. She decided the best way of treating 'epistaxis' was by spending Christmas with a friend in Hull.

One rule Catherine had learnt from her superiors at Harton was that senior officers should never make friends with lower staff members or, still worse, the outside workers. It was an edict Catherine had attempted to obey at Tendring, and one she broke at Hastings.

Annie was taken on as a temporary worker during the 1930 influenza epidemic. Her blarney struck an immediate chord with Catherine, who recognised in Annie some of the mischievous charm of John McMullen. Born in Ireland in 1895, Annie was eleven years older than her senior in the laundry. In 1928 or 1929 she had left her husband and mentally handicapped daughter, Maisie, to earn a living in England.

CATHERINE had arrived in Hastings at a time of reform among the Poor Law institutions.

Ninety-five years had elapsed since the passing of the 1834 Poor Law Amendment Act, which had forced the construction of Hastings Union Workhouse in a 'valley called Cackle Street' about a mile from the harbour and town. There was only one voice of dissent. It came from All Saints Vestry, where the clergy complained that the £4,893 workhouse was 'inelegible, inconvenient and unfit for the purpose'.

Cackle Street almost certainly got its name from the large number of hens kept by the rural households and farms. Local legend claims the street – changed to Frederick Road by the time of Catherine's arrival – was so named because of the ceaseless 'cackle' of the vagrants making their way to the workhouse. The eleven miles from nearest workhouse or 'grubber' at Rye was an easy day's walk. Even in the 1930s it was common to see the 'roaders' hiding what money they had in the grass embankments on the outskirts of the town to allow them to arrive in Hastings penniless.

While Catherine had been working at Tendring, Parliament had debated and passed the Local Government Act of 1929. Under the Act, which came into force the following year, the Boards of Guardians set up before Queen Victoria came to the throne were abolished. The network of workhouses across the country were to be renamed Public Assistance Institutions and run by county councils.

The Hastings Workhouse, however, adopted a hybrid hierarchy until the formation of the National Health Service in 1948. Authorities were now obliged to separate responsibility for the sick and non-sick. Wards which had previously catered for the mentally handicapped and destitute infirm were transferred to the administration of local public health committees. The casual wards remaining under county council management. Within days of Catherine taking up her new post, Hastings Union Workhouse was renamed the Municipal Hospital. But, in spite of its title, the medical wards continued to be run under the 1930 Poor Law Act by the county authority.

One man whose job it was to control the late-afternoon arrival of tramps throughout the 1930s was Jim Clarke. Part of his duties as gateman included booking both staff and inmates through the main gate. 'The institution was a grim-looking building surrounded by a high wall and with large iron gates at the entrance,' he recalls. Each morning he watched a 'slim, rather tallish young woman' cross the road outside the workhouse before passing his lodge. 'She usually looked straight ahead and apart from the odd "Good morning" never said a word.'

In April 1931 Catherine was asked to combine her duties as laundress with part of the duties of the workhouse portress. Institute regulations stated that a female portress must be in attendance at the main gate twenty-four hours a day. Rather than return to her West Hill flat Catherine agreed to sleep in the portress's accommodation at the gate house until a replacement could be found.

Searching the individuals for money and alcohol as they queued for admission was a dirty and sometimes dangerous business. After the formalities of admission were completed, the casuals were marched past the hospital church to a long, low building containing the overnight cells. In the morning the labour master would allocate the day's work. The women were told to report to Catherine at the laundry while the men tended the vast vegetable garden or cleaned and fed the pigs.

Six months later the assistant matron, a Miss Clark, became the latest victim of an outbreak of flu. A number of other staff were also off sick. The master turned once again for help to Catherine. Despite, as Moyle Silverlock reported to a hospital sub-committee, her 'working to capacity' Catherine agreed to take on Miss Clark's duties. 'Miss McMullun [sic] is the only officer capable of carrying out her work,' he added.

Catherine moved into the assistant matron's room at the hospital. When she returned to the latest in a series of sparsely furnished rooms she discovered her landlady had been letting the bedsit in her absence, while still demanding the rent. It was time, she decided, to find a flat of her own.

By Christmas, 1931 she had moved into and decorated a flat in West Hill House, less than a mile from the hospital. It consisted of one large room and a combined kitchen and bathroom. To allow her to use the living room as a bedroom, Catherine spent part of her precious savings on a Put-U-Up suite. The rest of the £100 was spent on furniture and decorating. The walls were covered in a dark-blue paper and all the woodwork painted black. Catherine bought a single picture, entitled 'The First Piano Lesson'.

There was another reason why Catherine was hurrying to make the flat look respectable. She wanted to impress Kate.

During August 1931 Catherine had returned to Tyneside for the first time in twenty-seven months. Making her way down Boldon

Lane from Tyne Dock railway station, she found few things had changed. Disillusioned men still crowded menacingly on street corners. Waiting for the tram at the dock gates, she noticed the work queues had grown a little longer, the faces a little grubbier.

Inside No 10 Catherine found her mother happier and more confident than she remembered her being for a long time. David McDermott had been to sea only two or three times since the Father's death. The couple who, for the first time, had the house to themselves had passed the stringent means test and were existing on the little they received from the dole.

Catherine extolled the virtues of Hastings. To Kate it sounded like heaven; a town unscarred by industry and its failures, where the air and the streets were scoured clean every day by the sea breezes. The inevitable holiday invitation was made and Kate was quick to accept.

Early in 1932 Kate stood on the platform at Newcastle Central Station awaiting the arrival of the London train. It was the same station from which her only other adventure had begun. As a teenager in the 1890s she was employed by a family called Patterson. When the household departed for a holiday in the Lake District, they took Kate with them to look after the children. As Catherine caught sight of her mother stepping down on to the platform at Hastings, her weeks of apprehension evaporated. Kate, well dressed and upright, was sober and cheerful. Not once during the next two weeks did she accept, or seek, a drink. 'I think that was the happiest moment of my life,' confesses Catherine in *Our Kate*.

Annie was spending more and more time in Catherine's company, and was quick to befriend Kate. Here was another soul who had endured the rigours of poverty and with whom she could share the heady pleasures of freedom. Annie was as excited by Kate's reaction to the south as if she had paid for her own mother to cross the Irish Sea. They were both, in their own way, discovering a land of plenty.

It was Annie – seeing nothing wrong with a wife living apart from her husband – who first raised the question of Kate moving to Hastings. Annie made sure Catherine was in the room when she asked Kate why she didn't come south to live. Catherine had been skilfully backed into a corner. Under her mother's imploring gaze and with Annie's ill-fated prompting, Catherine had no choice but to give in.

Kate returned north to break the news to David, while Catherine began the search for a larger flat. By chance a five-roomed flat had fallen vacant in Westhill House. It was self-contained and ranged over two floors and the rent was 25s a week.

News that her stepfather had at last found work on a coaster rekindled Catherine's fears. Despite Kate's upright and impressive performance the previous year, Catherine still doubted her mother's resolve to withstand both loneliness and a sudden influx of extra cash. Apprehension welled in Catherine. When she arrived at Hastings station to meet her mother, she found Kate sitting defiantly on her suitcase. The clothes were dishevelled; the face red and bloated; the 'blue eyes almost opaque'. It was obvious Kate had been drunk for several days.

The drinking continued, financed at least partly by £5 contributions posted whenever David McDermott was ashore. The remainder of the money Kate spent on food. What was left from her £3 wage, after Catherine had paid the rent and her insurance policies, went toward decorating and furnishing the flat. To recoup some of the money the pair intended to let the spare rooms to summer holidaymakers.

At first Kate disguised her drinking from the other residents of Westhill House with the same intensity she had originally used on her daughter. By 1933 she had given up any attempt to conceal her daily visit to a public house. The signs were all too obvious. Catherine blamed herself for putting her new life at risk. Each confrontation erupted into accusations and threats, inevitably followed by a guilty silence from Kate, who numbed her self-reproach with another visit to the pub at the bottom of the street. And so the pattern was set.

CATHERINE was approaching her twenty-eighth birthday. She was beautiful, witty and apparently unattached and, because she was older than most single women, fulfilled a certain fantasy for the men who sought her company.

In the four years since her arrival in Hastings Catherine had attracted the attention of five men. One had a passion for classical music. Their evenings together seldom ranged beyond the White

Rock Pavilion, where the couple would sit in the cool twilight and listen to recitals by Hastings Municipal Orchestra. All five relationships ended abruptly. Catherine increasingly feared her qualities were only apparent to married men.

Despite their deceit Catherine remained more at ease in the company of men. Just as when a child she had discovered the power of words, she now exploited her sexuality and growing intellect. It was an ability she would never lose. 'In a room full of people Kitty would make straight for the men,' said a long-time associate many years later. 'Somehow she looks upon men as her equal. She has never really trusted women.'

Catherine also found herself able to hold her own in a strictly male-ordered society. She was a woman earning a man's wage. For that feat alone she demanded respect. 'I have always worked with men and I have always preferred to do so,' she admits in *Catherine Cookson Country*, 'though the men I work with are associates, not bosses. I will not have bosses!'

Some of her early admirers were less brave than others. Among them was a young Prudential Assurance agent called Harold Quilter. Each week Quilter would call at the hospital laundry to collect Catherine's premiums. During quiet moments the pair chatted and, in addition to an interest in books, discovered they shared another secret – both were illegitimate. 'It gave them a special philosophy on life,' explains Quilter's widow, Irene Marshall.

The young insurance agent found the 'articulate and attractive' laundress had experienced many of his own childhood traumas, and was stimulated by her 'fascinating personality'. Only the age difference – Quilter was in his early twenties – prevented him from asking Catherine out for the evening.

Men, Catherine decided, were a disappointment. She would do without them. She would give herself all the things her dreams had promised and the men in her life had denied her. Somewhere she would find the house of her imagination – and buy it.

The Hurst had remained unsold since 1932. Even while occupied it had needed a great deal of money spending on it. After failing to sell the house 'beyond the big red gate' as a private home, the estate agents were trying a new approach. This time the property in Hoads Wood Road was being advertised as a 'gentleman's residence'.

Riddled with woodworm and dry rot, 'It smelled of mould,' Catherine remembers, 'and you could drive a horse and cart around one of the rooms. Yet when the agent led me down a dark corridor into a little room and announced, "This, madam, is the butler's pantry," the house was sold.'

Financing the purchase was no problem. Before Catherine moved south she had insured her life. When she arrived in Hastings she increased the benefit to £1,000. It was a simple enough matter to persuade a building society to take the policy in exchange for the Hurst, especially when Catherine explained she intended to run it as a guest house while keeping her job at the hospital laundry.

Catherine could at last cross the line which separated respect and respectability. Just as the overcrowded kitchen at No 10 had been the centre of her child world, so the Hurst – all fifteen rooms of it – would become the nucleus of her adult existence. Within its walls, through its windows, Catherine could watch the world go by. She could walk around its wooded garden; play tennis on her own court; sit in the domed conservatory; or open the tall windows to let in the sound of summer fancy-dress parties, untouched by poverty, greed or war.

Hoads Wood Road was situated a mile north of Hastings town centre and only yards from the then borough boundary. It was also a considerable distance from the nearest public house.

Money became even tighter. Finally established on her 'square of ground . . . leasehold from God', Catherine was finding it hard to dispose of a more earthly contract. On taking the larger flat, she had signed a three-year lease. All attempts to sub-let the five rooms failed. The twenty-five shillings weekly rent would have to be paid while the flat remained empty. In March 1935 Catherine applied for a pay rise, the first in five years. The borough council's public assistance committee deemed no increase was necessary.

Catherine and Kate set about cleaning the Hurst's cavernous rooms and ridding them of the evidence of neglect. They were soon joined by Annie, who persuaded Catherine to allow her to bring her daughter Maisie to England. When the child arrived she clung to her mother, rushing to her side whenever Annie left the room.

Kate, as devious as ever, soon arranged for a regular delivery of alcohol while her daughter was at work. To Catherine it was the final, public humiliation.

The fights became noiser and more bitter as Kate attempted to disarm Catherine's threats to pack her off to Tyneside with desperate excuses and still more promises. At first Kate blamed Annie's ceaseless chatter, before turning on the hapless Maisie. The child annoyed her. The child got on her nerves. She needed a drink to calm down. In the end Annie could take no more and moved out of the Hurst.

Her departure brought a week or two's respite. Kate had considered Annie's presence a threat to her daughter's loyalty. Her position, she reasoned, had been strengthened. Catherine could never manage the Hurst without her.

By late 1935 Kate was too defensive, and frequently too inebriated, to appreciate the toll the incessant rows were taking on her 29-year-old daughter. Catherine had slipped back into the moody silences of her teens. Her time at the laundry, like her youthful visits to the Maguire household, provided her only escape. But the guilt of her self-inflicted torment was slowly darkening her world and everything in it. Catherine pleaded with Kate to leave the Hurst. She refused. 'One black day' Catherine felt as though she had reached the edge of her sanity. 'It was forced home to her that but for the intervention of Annie she would have had a corpse on her hands,' Catherine admitted many years later in her autobiography.

Kate finally agreed to go. She would move to the still unlet Westhill House flat. To allow her mother to earn her own living by taking in guests, Catherine would furnish the five rooms with items she had purchased for the Hurst. She would also continue to pay the rent. When the three-year lease eventually expired Kate moved to a large house near-by. She would open it, Kate taunted, as a 'select guest house'.

AT the end of July 1936, Michael Jerrom, a teacher at Hastings Grammar School left to take up a senior post at Southend County School. When the staff reconvened for the autumn term they were joined by Jerrom's 23-year-old successor, Thomas Henry Cookson. Within days the pupils had nicknamed him 'Cookie'.

Tom Cookson was the son of an Essex verger, Thomas James Cookson. As a boy he soon developed the analytical mind and rational nature which governed his future life. At school he enjoyed mathematics, although he also achieved his Higher School Certificate in French and Latin. It was a natural progression for him to win a place at Oxford, where he gained a degree in mathematics. Employed primarily to teach his degree subject, Tom Cookson also inherited Jerrom's geography classes.

Staff at the school, founded in 1619 by William Parker, soon came to appreciate Tom's infectious enthusiasm for any form of sport. One of Tom's passions was football, he enjoyed playing and was a 'splendid half-back' according to *The History of Hastings Grammar School*. Here, too, he inherited certain duties from Jerrom. Inter-house matches – and victories – were regarded with pride. Behind Tom's 'cheery countenance lurked a hundred schemes for gingering up the team and outwitting the enemy' adds the school's history. The 'enemy' was any master or boy not a member of Nelson House, to which Tom had been assigned. By 1939 he had been appointed assistant house master.

Another of Tom's initiatives came from his love of boxing. Within months of his arrival he had formed and launched a boxing club. An RAF physical education instructor was recruited as coach and membership swiftly rose to eighty pupils.

Finding lodgings had not been difficult. Jerrom was boarding at a house run by a Mrs McDermott. He suggested that Tom take over his room.

Catherine was out of the country on the August weekend Tom arrived in Hastings. Her enterprise in attracting lodgers had resulted in her first trip abroad – not altogether a pleasant experience.

Like most of the establishments offering accommodation, Catherine wrote out neat little cards for display in seafront shop windows. Hers offered something more. 'Everyone else charged extra for cleaning and polishing guests' shoes,' she said. 'Mine had shoe cleaning included. How I found the time with all my other jobs I don't know.'

Among her earliest guests at the Hurst were a French family. Their friendship with Catherine prompted an invitation to stay with them in Paris.

Catherine travelled to Dover by train one Friday evening after work. Within minutes of the ferry to Calais leaving the dockside she was violently seasick. She recalls the trip with dismay. 'I felt awful. I got to Paris on Friday night still dreadfully ill. On Saturday we went to Versailles and saw the usual sights.' On Sunday she made the return trip in time for work on Monday morning. 'On the way back I was even worse. On the train they had to lay me out on a seat I was feeling so bad.'

She returned to Paris just once more, this time for an extended day trip. Her seasickness has plagued her ever since.

But her French guests did allow her to become acquainted with a number of French writers. She progressed from the translation of Georges Duhamel's *The Pasquier Chronicles* to the short stories of Guy de Maupassant and Voltaire's *Candide*.

OCTOBER 5th, 1936, dawned a bright and sunny day all over England. Catherine left the Hurst as usual to start her day at the hospital laundry. Several hundred miles further north 207 men, a woman, two boys, a dog and a bicycle headed south and into history.

The Jarrow Crusade had been a long while in the planning. Suffering and discontent and poverty had first flowed and then solidified. Now the streets of Jarrow were filled with marchers. Ahead of them went the Crusade bus, a single-decker with seats taken out to make way for a camp kitchen and supplies of bread, meat, tinned food, coal and firewood.

Then came the men – ranging from a nineteen-year-old to a 61-year-old Boer War veteran – four, sometimes six, abreast. The column was lead by the charismatic Ellen Wilkinson, MP for Jarrow. Beside her were the town's mayor and members of the council; and with them the town band. Spirits were high, there was adventure in the air. Thousands lined the pavements. They were making history.

There had been cheering earlier in 1936. The mayor and councillors had guided the Duke and Duchess of York through the same streets they were now walking. Taken to see the derelict slipways of Palmers Yard where, in 1920, she had launched a cruiser, the duchess almost broke down. 'Cannot something be done for the unemployed?' she asked.

In 1923 – a year before Catherine started work at Harton Institute – 41 per cent of those on the register of insured persons were unemployed. It rose to 59 per cent in 1926 and fell to as low as 32 per cent in 1928 and 1929. But by 1934 unemployment had risen to a high of 75 per cent.

As the Jarrow Crusade inched toward London there were fascist riots; seventy people were arrested. The Government was making noises about 'banning political uniforms'.

Catherine knew all about the politics of poverty. Yet she had never heard of Ellen Wilkinson before she left East Jarrow in 1929. Later she read her book, *The Town that Was Murdered* – 'it touched me deeply'.

IT was a Wednesday evening. Catherine was on her way to her shilling-an-hour fencing lesson at St Leonards' seafront swimming pool when she decided to call in and see Kate.

Her visits to the house, less than half-a-mile from the Hurst, had become painful and irregular. Kate was never sober and frequently quite emotional. This time was no exception.

Catherine refused to meet the new boarder. As she was about to leave, Kate swung open the door to the front room. 'This is my daughter,' she informed a rather startled looking young man sitting at a table. Catherine examined 'this good-looking fellow with beautiful hair and in a light tweed coat' before stepping forward. 'Hello,' she said. 'Do you fence?'

Tom informed her he did not. He only admitted much later that he had fallen instantly and hopelessly in love. 'When she said, "Do you fence?" I was never so surprised in my life,' he still remembers. 'Knowing my landlady as I did, I had not expected this woman with the voice that was so vibrant, the voice of someone who had obviously been educated.

'I thought I had been in love before, but this was a different feeling. I wanted to follow her from the first moment onwards – and I still do.'

Tom drifted through the next day with his landlady's thirty-year-old daughter constantly on his mind. On Friday he made up his mind to see her again. All he needed was an excuse.

Catherine arrived back at the Hurst feeling ill and drained. Annie answered a knock at the door. She returned a few seconds later to inform her exhausted friend that a nervous young man was outside with the dubious excuse of bringing Catherine the evening newspaper. Catherine leapt to her feet. Of course she would like to go to the pictures. No, she wasn't too tired.

Almost fifty years later Catherine recalled that first evening together. 'There was ever such a nice manager at the picture house. He used to welcome you as if you were royalty. Tom and I sat in the best seats and then I let him take me home and we had coffee and sandwiches in the study and sat up talking until midnight. I thought he was very young – he was six years younger than me – but even then I knew he was the one for me. We both knew.'

Of course Catherine was beautiful. But the more she spoke, and the more Tom listened, the deeper he fell in love. From Catherine's voice – through it – came a limitless confidence; a will; a certainty to succeed. It was a conviction Tom had never encountered in a woman.

It was also a remarkable voice in its own right. He knew its background. Tom had listened to Kate and expected her daughter to have retained the same Tyneside accent. Instead Catherine's voice was almost cultured, not the privileged plumminess of the gentry, nor the overworked correctness of a social climber, but honest and natural. She articulated correctly. She pronounced accurately. Catherine had not inherited her mother's malapropisms. Yet beneath it all there was a lilt in her voice, the barest thread of her ancestry.

Catherine needed Tom just as she had discovered and sought guidance from Lord Chesterfield. But instead of a teacher, a giver of instructions, she had at last found someone willing to debate the lessons with her. The dam burst. Tom found himself listening to the ideas and opinions trapped for years inside Catherine's head. What did he think of Voltaire's *Candide*? Of Shakespeare's sonnets? Of all the things she had debated in solitude.

The prejudices which once divided Kate and Annie now served to unite them.

Both women – Kate at fifty-two and Annie at forty-one – saw Catherine's growing affection for Tom not only as a threat to their hold over her but, more importantly, as a betrayal of their working-class roots. As a university graduate and schoolmaster he was of a higher social order. It was acceptable and understood for Catherine to better herself. But attempting to change sides by marriage, as Kate well knew, could be painful and degrading.

Tom and Catherine continued to meet: to go for long walks across the clifftops and into the rolling countryside; to go to the cinema; to spend long hours talking. It soon became apparent to Catherine that this was the man she would one day marry. 'I was really in love for the first time in my life,' she admitted in *Our Kate*.

Catherine was a strong, intelligent, life-loving woman in every way equal to the man she was now pursuing. 'Besides the physical attraction I had a strength of purpose. He had what I needed, kindness, a lovely nature, a high sense of moral values, and above all he had what I wanted most – a mind.'

Ever practical, Kate continued to allow Tom to board at her house. No matter what she thought of his relationship with her daughter she was not about to alienate his money.

Tom, aware of Kate's disapproval, continued to tolerate his landlady's addled state of mind and hypocritical lip service.

Annie, too, joined the campaign to separate Tom and Catherine. She had returned to live and work at the Hurst within weeks of Kate's departure. Once again Catherine soon found herself trapped between necessity and friendship. Annie, like Kate before her, knew how finely balanced her employer's resources were. As well as the holidaymakers Catherine had also managed to attract several longer-term guests, epileptics and convalescing tuberculosis patients. None, however, was too ill to haggle over the cost of their board. Without the extra income Catherine would have been in serious financial trouble. From this high ground Annie continued to snipe at Tom.

By 1937 Kate's sole concern was her daily ration of whisky. The spectre of her mother tottering through Hastings, unable even to feed her guests rekindled the shame in Catherine. Her relationship with Tom cooled. Not through any lack of affection – Tom was more attracted and more besotted with Catherine than he had ever been. For her part Catherine was convinced that she and Tom would one day be together. But for the moment she could not stand – even through Tom's forgiving eyes – to be associated with her mother's growing reputation as an alcoholic and gossip.

One by one Kate's boarders deserted her. Other guests, confronted at the front door of the guest house by this overweight and rumpled woman, rapidly changed their mind. Debts began to mount. In the summer of 1937, while Tom was abroad on holiday,

Kate announced she wanted to go home. Ill and alienated and missing her husband, Kate pleaded with Catherine to pay her bills and allow her to return to East Jarrow.

BY the time the new term opened in September Tom had joined the four medical cases and retired Army captain living at the Hurst.

'As soon as Tom entered the door and we looked at each other, it was done again,' recalls Catherine. 'It had never been undone, there had only been a forced separation.'

Catherine's two jobs – as laundry manageress and guest-house proprietor – were occupying at least sixteen hours each day. Her working day began several hours before she left to take charge of the laundry. When she returned soon after five-thirty each evening, Catherine faced another six or seven hours of housework and preparation before she got to bed.

Despite the constant shortage of money and the apparent ease with which the Hurst was crumbling around them, Catherine continued to write. During her lunchbreak at the infirmary, or late at night in bed, she filled notebooks or covered sheets of paper with pencilled short stories and sketches. She was still experimenting with her writing, feeling her way. As each piece was completed, she would store it in a linen cupboard on a stairway landing at the Hurst. Not long after Tom took up residence in 1937 she took him to the cupboard and allowed him to read some of her 'better' stories.

Tom was not the only person from whom Catherine sought approval. Among the guests at Hoads Wood Road was a man in his late thirties dying of tuberculosis. Most of his time was spent reading and writing and Catherine considered him an 'intellectual'. After discussing the merits of various writers, Catherine asked if he would read some of her stories. His opinion was crushing. She returned to the cupboard and burned every scrap of paper.

To help with the day-to-day running of the house and cater for the holiday guests Annie was joined by the irrelative and friendless Mrs Webster. The deaf cook's malicious treatment of food was only matched by her disregard for its cost.

It was soon obvious the guilty release Catherine had experienced with her mother's departure would not last.

Throughout the autumn and winter of 1937 Annie lost no opportunity in pointing out Tom's apparent failings. It was a spite fed by hatred. There was nothing right with him. Tom was not a Catholic. He was too gentle and soft-spoken. He would never make Catherine happy. And when Catherine – tired from work and struggling to control the daily nose bleeds – turned on the subversive Irishwoman she was threatened with desertion.

The price of Catherine's freedom was £1,300. Annie, like Kate, had hopes of running her own guest house. Catherine mortgaged the Hurst for £1,300, enough to pay for a large property not far from the seafront. To this Annie added £100 and moved out of the Hurst for a second time.

KATE walked home from the inquest in a daze of confusion and fear. It was bitterly cold. Outside a Tyne Dock newsagents she caught sight of a *Shields Gazette* billboard: 'East Jarrow Man Drowned on Birthday'.

It was Saturday, 5 February, 1938. In the space of one night her world of relative security and happiness had come to an end. Kate had gone to bed a wife and woken a widow. The state had lost no time on pronouncing the end of her marriage by hearing the evidence of John McDermott's death within eighteen hours.

The couple had given up the three rooms at No 10 William Black Street soon after Kate moved to Hastings in 1932. Since her return six months before, they had been renting a house further up the terrace. When Kate finally reached the sanctuary of her kitchen, she found the courage to read the news story on the front page of the *Gazette*.

> *An East Jarrow ship's donkeyman, David McDermott, of William Black Street, was drowned early today, his 62nd birthday.*
>
> *The South Shields Coroner (Mr W. M. Patterson) recorded a verdict of accidental drowning at the inquest.*
>
> *Catherine McDermott, wife of the deceased, said her husband was employed as a donkeyman on the steamer* Afterglow. *He had been going to sea all his life. Yesterday afternoon he arrived home just after four o'clock in his working clothes and said the ship was sailing about five o'clock. He brought her his wages.*
>
> *He left and returned again about 7.30, stating he was sailing at 11.30.*

They went out shopping together and had a pint of beer and a pie. He had not had anything since breakfast time and said he was very tired.

About 10.30 she left him at Tyne Dock gates. He was sober.

George Watson McConnell, second engineer of the Afterglow, of Sunderland, said the vessel was lying at Bullock Spouts buoys yesterday.

At 11.30 last night he went to the spouts to board the vessel. The wind was howling and he could not hear. Eventually he hailed the night watchman who told him it was too rough to cross to the boat and advised him to wait until slack water, which would be about one o'clock.

Witness went into West Holborn, where he was told that McDermott was waiting on the quay. He returned to the quay and saw McDermott, who was sober. Witness told him he would have to wait until slack water. He answered: 'All right.'

The engineer then left McDermott and returned about midnight. He could not find him and started to search.

'I went on to the Cedarwood, which was lying alongside, and shone a torch and saw something floating in the water.'

Robert Gurney, AB, said he was acting night watchman on the Afterglow last night. McDermott shouted at him at about 11.30 and asked for a boat, but the conditions were bad and he told him to wait until slack water.

Twenty minutes afterwards other members of the crew began shouting and he decided to take a boat over. When he got near the quay he heard someone shouting that the donkeyman was in the water.

He saw McDermott floating in an upright position about four yards from the quay. McDermott was pulled into the boat and landed at Whitehall Point Ferry Landing. The second mate immediately started artificial respiration until the arrival of the police ambulance.

Constable Charles Welsh said he went to the landing at about 12.23. McDermott was unconscious and he tried artificial respiration for quarter of an hour without response and then took him to the Ingham Infirmary. The treatment was continued in the ambulance.

A medical report stated that death was due to heart failure and asphyxia.

Left with just the few pounds David had given her the day before his death, Kate was soon penniless. By the time Catherine arrived from Hastings her mother had moved out of William Black Street to an upstairs flat on Simonside Terrace, overlooking Jarrow Slake.

For two weeks Catherine attempted to console her mother. When sober, Kate gnawed at the injustice of David's death. Each night she would drink herself into oblivion with a bottle of whisky.

Catherine set about persuading the shipping company for whom David had worked that it was morally, if not legally, obliged to make an offer of compensation. The *Afterglow*'s owners denied liability, claiming David had fallen into the water from the quay and not the steamer. Catherine stepped up the pressure. The company finally relented and agreed to pay Kate a little over £200. Convinced such an amount would merely allow Kate to drink herself to death, Catherine insisted the money be paid at the rate of £2 a week.

It was May before the formalities were completed and Kate collected her first payment. With the restriction she had nego-tiated, Catherine was satisfied her mother would at least have the security of an income for the next two years. She had not counted on her mother's cunning. Kate confronted the shipping company with a bogus plan to start a business, for which she would need the balance of her compensation. The business never materialised and the money evaporated equally fast.

By August 1938 Kate was once again destitute. The £200 had been spent on whisky and borrowed by opportunist friends. Kate, fearing her daughter's reaction, turned in secret to Annie. It was two weeks before the Irishwoman confessed to Catherine she had been sending Kate money.

BY the spring of 1939 Catherine knew she would soon have to leave her job at the laundry.

Despite her friendship with the Silverlocks, Catherine had never experienced the satisfaction she had hoped to find in Hastings. In the nine years since her appointment she had seen both her authority and responsibility eroded by the various council com-mittees controlling the Municipal Hospital.

In 1937 it was decided that as each of the four permanent members of the laundry officers left they should be replaced by temporary workers. Two months later, in July, a clash of personalities among the laundry staff forced Catherine to adjust the working hours. Three women appealed over her head to the public assistance committee.

A year later Catherine herself sought the intervention of the committee. Her decision to make use of certain inmates and casual women had angered the labour master, who considered the assignment of work his exclusive domain. While the committee sympathised over the labour master's 'petty attitude' towards Catherine, it declined to support her appeal. The matter, it ruled, was purely administrative.

More annoying was the question of Catherine's salary. Two applications for an increase, in 1935 and 1936, had been refused. She was receiving the same wage and allowances as the day she was first appointed. Her staff, however, had benefited from two rises. The latest, in September 1938, was as a direct result of pressure from the National Union of General and Municipal Workers. Ironers and washing machinists would now receive 8d (3 pence) an hour, taking their wage for a 44-hour week to £1 9s. Washers and calender hands would earn 7½d an hour.

The constant battle to maintain standards and the strain of cajoling an increasingly distracted workforce was too much. In July 1939 Catherine informed the Silverlocks of her decision to leave. Her only source of income would come from Tom's rent and the two remaining patients at the Hurst.

Eight

Time and again I've yelled at the Almighty, the Headmaster of Men, and demanded to know, Why me?

FOR THE SECOND time in twenty-five years Catherine lived through the first day of a war. This time she was convinced she would never see the end of it.

Early in September 1939 Catherine was visited at the Hurst by a relocation officer. Fearing a sudden bombing offensive on Britain's cities, the London County Council began scouring the country for properties into which it could evacuate the hundreds of children and adults in its care. The fifteen-roomed Hurst, occupied by just four people – its owner, one lodger and two patients – was being under-used. Catherine was given the choice of accepting either children or adults. Within days a small convoy of vehicles had delivered twelve blind elderly men from institutions in the East End of London.

Catherine had said no to the children because of the two epileptic patients already at the Hurst. She was dismayed at the condition of the men left in her charge. Most were victims of the First World War. Some were bed-ridden and incontinent. In addition to washing and shaving, the worst cases also had to be hand-fed. Catherine was told she would receive just £12 a week to cover all expenses.

Other disruptions were to follow. At forty-four Annie announced she was joining the Women's Royal Army Corps, apparently content to abandon the boarding house Catherine had helped to purchase. Rather than see the building stand empty, Catherine installed Mrs Webster, the Hurst's deaf and incompetent cook. She now had two large houses to run.

The first winter of the war was a struggle. Catherine's only help at the Hurst was Gladys, a good-tempered woman who somehow never allowed the shortage of food or money to affect the quality of her cooking. In the evenings, or at weekends, Tom demonstrated the practical side of his nature by tackling repairs around the house or mending the apparently irreparable.

By the spring of 1940 Catherine was exhausted. Hardly a day went by without a nose bleed. This time her doctor diagnosed 'nervous debility'.

At least the demands of the Hurst and the general chaos had forced a lull in the personal conflict Catherine had endured in the months before Annie's final departure from Hoads Wood Road. Annie hated Tom with the passion only an Irishwoman could unleash. It was fuelled, almost daily, by Tom's tolerance and kindness toward her. Away from Hastings Annie's hatred smouldered. Each time she returned on leave she could see the hardships Tom and Catherine were now sharing were bringing them still closer together. She was determined to destroy Tom.

On Monday, 27 May the postman delivered a letter to the Hurst. Tom had just left for school and was already out of sight of the house. Catherine ran to the gate and called his name.

Tom stopped and turned to look at her. 'We'll be married on Saturday,' Catherine shouted.

'OK,' he said without hesitation before breaking into a run. Tom always ran when he was happy.

'Everything was suddenly against us,' Catherine once said. 'And I knew if we did not marry soon, we would not be able to marry at all.'

Forty-nine years later – as they approached their fiftieth wedding anniversary – Catherine and Tom agreed to write about their wedding for the *Journal*, Newcastle.

Next I went to the priest and asked him to marry us. He said he wouldn't because Tom was not a Catholic, but I said well, it was the register office for us, then, and he said, oh no it wasn't, so he married us on the Saturday at the Catholic church in Hastings.

It was supposed to be a quiet wedding, at two o'clock it was, but a few people turned up. I'd known I was going to be married sometime so I'd made plans to have my dress made at Plummers in Hastings, which was a lovely shop. Well; when I went to see about it in the few days before the wedding, all the dress makers had left or been evacuated or something, and my dress was still at the cutting stage.

So it didn't matter and I wore a blue dress I had had some time and a lovely fur cape Tom gave me for a wedding present. I loved high hats and very high heels and though I always say Tom and I are the same size, I must have looked a good foot taller than him on the day.

I was given away by Mr Silverlock. He'd always called me his adopted daughter and he wanted to give me away – only the day before the wedding he fell and broke his arm. So he had his arm in a sling.

I had no flowers – I don't think Tom's ever bought me flowers because he knows how I feel – but people said afterwards they had never heard so much laughter in a vestry. I could never understand it. I had this great sadness inside me, not sadness really, more an aloneness, but I always wanted to make people happy and laugh and that's what they remembered on the day.

Then we went back to the house and had some wine and there was a little cake. Oh, it didn't matter. What is all the fuss about a wedding anyway? It's the two people and what they feel about each other that matters. The rest is all show, for other people, I always think. I didn't have an engagement ring though Tom did buy me a ring a few years ago. I've got a brooch he bought me too but I don't go for jewellery. I only wear my wedding ring. It's never been off my finger. Even when I go into hospital they can't get it off and they have to tape over it.

Buy him a wedding present? Why, no. He had me, didn't he. What more did he want?

So we had a one-day honeymoon. We caught the train up to London and stayed in the Charing Cross Hotel. What spoiled it for me was that on the way the train stopped at Tunbridge Wells. It was during Dunkirk and there was another train stopped at the station full of men from France. The Red Cross were there handing them out tea and these men looked so bitter, so angry, so full of despair that I cried all the way from there to London. You could see part of the miracle of Dunkirk on that train and it affected me dreadfully.

On the Saturday night Tom and I went to the theatre to see Ibsen's Ghosts. *There was only about five other people in the audience, I'll always remember it.*

On the Sunday, 2 June, the newlyweds visited Tom's family in Gravesend, south of the River Thames and east of London. They returned to Hastings exhausted and under the weather. Tom had developed influenza and Catherine struggled with a nose bleed all the way home.

The 'My Wedding' feature ends with Tom's recollections of the day. It starts at the same moment.

We lived in the same house for three years before we were married – which people wouldn't understand now – and in the back of my mind I feared we would never get married.

But then there was that marvellous morning when she shouted at me as I walked down the street. I was about 50 yards away but I heard every word of: 'Tom, we'll be married on Saturday.' I was so happy I ran all the way to school.

On that Saturday, June 1, the weather was lovely. There was Saturday school in those days and the school bell went at twenty-to-one. The wedding was at two, so I went home and waited for Kitty to get ready, and then we went to the church in a taxi.

I'm a very sentimental man. Men who say they're not are missing something from their lives, I think. I even found the two tickets from Ghosts, the play we saw on our wedding night, the other day. I remember there was hardly anyone there at the Comedy Theatre –it was their last performance.

The wedding picture is very precious. It was taken by one of the boys from my school in Hastings with his Box Brownie. I used to wear the trousers of that suit for gardening until a couple of years ago.

I never bought Kitty flowers or liked to see her in any form of 'decoration'. I think that's because of the first years I knew her, she kept a book in which she wrote down every half-penny that was spent. It wouldn't have gone down very well if I'd spent extravagantly on her – though when we went to the pictures I always bought her a quarter pound box of Cadbury's Milk Tray.

Each day before the wedding Catherine prayed that her mother would not arrive for the celebration. Childhood shame still haunted her memories: the smell of whisky on Kate's breath and the vulgar, noisy gatherings in the kitchen at No 10. When bride and groom returned to the Hurst after the ceremony a telegram from Kate was waiting. She was celebrating in her own way.

But the legacy of guilt Catherine had inherited from her mother was harder to exorcise. More than anything Catherine wanted to be married, to be Mrs Thomas Cookson. But to do so she would have to compound the lie already locked inside her; Kate's lie.

The church vestry was filled with laughter. Catherine watched as Tom completed the register. Name; Thomas Henry Cookson. Age: Twenty-seven. Condition: Bachelor. Profession: Secondary schoolmaster. Father's name: Thomas James (deceased). Profession: Verger.

Catherine took the pen. Name: Catherine Ann Davies, otherwise McMullen. Age: Thirty-three. Condition: Spinster. Profession: Guest-house proprietress. Father's name: Alexander Davies (deceased). Profession: Commission agent.

Tom knew nothing of his bride's illegitimacy. It is also doubtful whether he knew the reason for Catherine's sudden proposal. The contents of the letter have remained a secret, as has the identity of its writer. The truth will probably never be known.

In the upright society of an English seaside town anyone tainted by immoral conduct, particularly in a public position, was devoured with glee. In their innocence Catherine and Tom had unwittingly provided the perfect climate for gossip. It was common knowledge that Catherine had unknowingly attracted the attention of married men ever since her arrival in Hastings ten years earlier. Now she was living under the same roof as Tom, a teacher at the town's most prestigious school, and with the morals of some of its most cherished sons in his care.

When Catherine had resigned from the workhouse laundry in August 1929, the staff assumed she was planning to marry. With Tom living at the Hurst they could quite easily have been mistaken for a shy, married couple. Just how the governors and staff of the grammar school would have received the news that Tom was 'living with a woman' is open to speculation. It would certainly have cast a shadow across his career.

Catherine needed to act swiftly to side-step the threat. She had always intended to marry Tom and becoming Mrs Cookson would defuse the situation. It would not remove Annie's hatred. Catherine's greatest fear now was that Annie might react by taking more drastic action. Years later, in a television documentary, she hinted: 'Why had I to meet a friend, who was supposed to be a friend, who was so jealous of me that I expected to be shot on my wedding day?'

The blind evacuees were to be transferred before the end of June. Hastings, like every other town overlooking the English Channel, was being turned into a fortress. There were radar installations on the Downs to the west at Beachy Head and eleven miles to the east at Rye. Inland, the town was encircled by a ring of RAF fighter stations. The Cinque Port suddenly found itself in the front line.

It was decided to evacuate the grammar school to the relative safety of St Albans, north of London. A series of vans transported the books and equipment, including 150 desks, while the pupils and masters travelled northward by train. The school would occupy temporary buildings at Spicer Street and the Elms, while games lessons would be held at near-by Beech Bottom. The boys' pocket money was invariably spent at Jack's sweet shop at the corner of Dagnall Street.

Catherine and Tom were allocated official lodgings when they arrived at St Albans' railway station. Within weeks they had found themselves a tiny flat above a barber's shop in Victoria Street, opposite the central library and just around the corner from the eleventh-century cathedral.

The library became Catherine's university. Each day she crossed the road to browse among the shelves or take out a new book. She was still reading *Lord Chesterfield's Letters*, but was desperate to make up for the lost years. Guided by Tom, Catherine drew up a list of 100 books they considered essential to her revived education. The list was in chronological order, starting with Chaucer and ending with 1920s novelists. 'Good plain writing, no hyperbole.' It was a colossal undertaking which typified her approach of tackling the hardest task first.

DESPITE the annoying nose bleeds and the uncertainty of the war Catherine was happier than she had been for many years.

Suddenly the bleeding increased and her periods stopped. Tiredness ruled her life. Each morning she felt sick. In late July Catherine consulted a woman doctor who suggested she might be pregnant – it was another two months before she was certain.

Because of the war most of the younger doctors had been replaced in general practice by older physicians, many persuaded to come out of retirement. The doctor to whom Catherine turned for a second opinion was a former naval surgeon. No, he assured Catherine, she was not pregnant but suffering with a stopped bowel.

Three times a week, until well into September, the doctor called at the Victoria Street flat. Somehow he had managed to acquire a supply of a new drug – 'the last thing to come out of France' – guaranteed to free any malfunctioning bowel. A course of injections proved fruitless. In September the ageing doctor took Catherine's hand in his own and admitted in a whisper she was indeed pregnant. She was thirty-four.

In her childhood fantasies of motherhood Catherine had first wanted a girl and then a boy. She was certain her first child would be a boy. She would call him David.

The newspapers and wireless repeated morale-boosting bulletins issued by the War Office and the Air Ministry. From the streets of St Albans Catherine would often hear the throaty cough of an aircraft engine or make out the white contrails against the cloudless sky. The *History of Hastings Grammar School* records the nights of 1940: 'The raids, the dark solidarity of the cathedral, and the unceasing noise of traffic of war materials and supplies following the historic route which once had heard the tramp of legions.'

To take her mind off the news of the war and the changes which were overtaking her body, Catherine spent the long autumn weeks writing a children's book. It was a collection of simple rhymes, intended for five-year-olds, and 'written' by her unborn son David.

> *He said the clock wanted taking to bits*
> *And when I did it he nearly had fits. Fancy making*
> *such an e . . . nor . . . mous scene!*
> *Why do people never say what they mean?*

Kate, meanwhile, had moved out of the New Buildings and taken a flat above a beer shop in Brinkburn Street, only a few hundred yards from St Peter and Paul's School at Tyne Dock. It was the same beer shop from which Catherine had staggered under the weight of the grey hen twenty-five years earlier.

Kate had tried throughout 1940 to get work as a part-time

housekeeper. Although she managed to conceal the signs of her drinking, her weight and size were offputting. Her habit of using snuff, which by this time had grown into an addiction, also deterred many people from giving her a chance.

Two or three times a week Kate would be waiting outside Tommy Johnson's 'baccy shop' in Frederick Street when it opened at 8.30 pm. Like most tobacconists it stocked as many as thirty-six varieties of snuff, sold by the ounce and dispensed in small triangular paper pockets. Many women who did not want to be seen smoking preferred to take snuff. Kate favoured one of the more expensive brands.

Whatever time of day she visited Tommy Johnson's shop, not once did Kate show signs of drink. To Jenny Johnson, who helped her husband run the business, Kate remained respectable 'Mrs Mac'. 'She was always tidy and nicely turned out,' recalls Mrs Johnson. 'She never let herself go or looked common. Her cheeks were rosy and she was full of good humour.

'Mrs Mac would walk in and say, "How are the Johnsons this morning . . . as if I cared?" It was a sort of catchphrase with her. And then she would stand and chat for hours, all about her wonderful daughter. She thought the world of Catherine. How she had moved south and opened a boarding house and met and married a professor.'

Kate's persistence finally paid off. She was taken on as housekeeper by a Dr and Mrs Carstairs at their Temperley Park home on the corner of Stanhope Road. With her increased income Kate could afford to leave the tiny rooms above the beer shop and move into a larger flat around the corner in Stoddard Street, Tyne Dock.

Throughout the war years Kate would repay the Johnsons' friendship with gifts of cakes and pies and bottles of dried herbs. All were despatched to the dustbin, admits Jenny Johnson. 'I knew she was a good cook, but it was just the thought of someone who took snuff handling the food. They all looked wonderful, but I could never bring myself to taste any of it.'

The kindly doctor and his wife – for whom Kate was to work for the next ten years – turned a blind eye toward her drinking. A friend of the family did not. She wrote to Catherine at St Albans warning that unless she returned north immediately she would never again see her mother alive. The prophecy had an ironic twist.

Five months' pregnant Catherine, shepherded by Tom, made her way to London one Friday evening in November 1940. The couple planned to catch the night train north. It was a journey which once again brought them face to face with the realities of war. The capital had been bombed on every night except one between 7 September and 13 November. Using the Underground to change stations, Catherine and Tom were forced to tiptoe over people sleeping on the platforms to escape the bombing.

When they eventually reached Tyne Dock they found Kate had nothing worse than a cold. Before the end of November it was Catherine who felt she was fighting for her life.

The baby was not due until late February or early March 1941. On Thursday, 28 November Catherine went into premature labour. The midwife, who had been at her bedside almost constantly for nine days and nights finally delivered their first child on Saturday, 7 December. 'An exact, and minute, replica of Tom. Beautiful hands and feet and little features.' The child – three months' premature – was born dead. Seeing the perfectly formed baby shocked Catherine deeply. 'I had imagined a lump of jelly at that stage. We were so ignorant then.'

Catherine, exhausted by the ordeal, sank deeper into despair when she was told they could not bury their son in a grave of his own. Unchristened, the baby would have to be interred in a general grave. He was placed in a coffin with an old woman who had lived for most of her life in the local workhouse.

Years later Catherine admitted that the odd unity her first child had found in death eased her grief. 'Somehow it consoled me, comforted me a lot. I had worked in the workhouse after all, I knew lots of old ladies in the workhouse at Harton. That's where I first learned compassion. And now my little baby was lying in the arms of an old lady. I felt relieved, as though he'd be safe and secure with her.'

Although Catherine was unaware of it at the time, she later discovered she was among the 15 per cent of the population who lacked the Rhesus-factor D in their blood and are Rhesus-negative. Experiments on Rhesus monkeys – which later identified the problem in humans – were being conducted throughout 1940.

In pregnancy, a Rhesus-negative woman who is carrying a child with Rhesus-positive blood inherited from the father, may pick up some of the baby's red-blood cells and produce antibodies against the Rhesus-positive factor. The antibodies then enter the bloodstream of the unborn child and destroy its red-blood cells. Modern treatment can prevent the antibodies forming, but before the results of the 1940 experiments were appreciated it was not uncommon for these babies to be born dead.

Catherine needed a distraction. After Christmas and the New Year she returned to her book of children's poems. But she knew the little volume would have more appeal if it were illustrated.

Not far from the Cooksons' flat, at the other end of Victoria Street, was St Albans' Art School. Catherine, who had originally called to ask if any of the students would be willing to produce the necessary sketches, was persuaded to draw the pictures herself. But first she needed lessons.

The inhibitions of a 34-year-old woman sitting among a class of teenagers were bad enough. Finding she was incapable of drawing anything recognisable was a bigger blow. After three lessons she quit the course.

The urge to draw evaporated. Perhaps, Catherine reasoned, it was one skill she was never meant to master. But it returned, explosively, one day as she walked in the spring sunshine across the Abbey Green. Above her, on a slight rise, stood the red-brick tower of St Albans' Abbey. Catherine hurried back down Chequer Street and into Victoria Street, not to the art school, but the stationer's and art supply shop next door. 'I want to draw stone,' she tried to explain to the assistant.

Equipped with two HB pencils, a carbon crayon, an academy chalk and a pad, Catherine returned to the spot on the green. She found the lines of the abbey, visible through a gap in the trees, came easily. There was little texture to her drawing, but it was clearly identifiable and it was all her own work. Catherine signed the right-hand corner 'C. A. Cookson' and across the bottom in block letters she wrote: 'St Albans, 1941. Very first drawing.'

IN August 1941, after teaching at the relocated grammar school for a full academic year, Tom enlisted in the Royal Air Force. He was twenty-eight.

Tom's degree in mathematics and his interest in wireless would automatically have qualified him for aircrew. Much to Catherine's relief, his natural aptitude as a teacher kept him firmly on the ground.

Catherine carefully packed their possessions from the Victoria Street flat and followed Tom first to Leicester, where he underwent basic training, and then to Sleaford in Lincolnshire.

There were four air bases within ten miles of Sleaford. The closest, RAF Cranwell, housed both No 1 and No 8 Radio Schools, training air and ground wireless operators. The historic airfield – which opened as the Royal Naval Air Service training establishment HMS *Daedalus* in 1916 – was also home to the RAF's No 21 Group, Training Command. Its primary role, however, was as the Royal Air Force College Flying Training School. A year before Tom's arrival, the base had been used as the location for the Twentieth-Century Fox morale-boosting film, *A Yank in the Royal Air Force*.

Because of his rank and married status Tom was billeted in Sleaford, south-east of the base. Catherine, not fully recovered from the loss of her first child, once again discovered she was expecting. This time the pregnancy ended in a miscarriage.

Much to Catherine's dismay, Tom applied for operational duties. Instead, in late 1942, he was posted as an instructor to RAF Madley, south-west of the cathedral city of Hereford.

The RAF found the Cooksons rooms at 31 Ryelands Street, half a mile from the centre of the city. They shared the house with the landlady, Isabel Stinton, and her elderly father George Smith, who had spent his working life on the railway. At the end of the little back garden was a stone wall and beyond it Bulmer's cider factory.

Virtually on the limit of suitable terrain for an airfield because of the hilly country on three sides, RAF Madley was planned and built as a school for wireless operators. No 4 Signals School aimed to train 2,800 ground and 1,200 aircrew wireless operators each year. Tom soon found the repetitive schooling of men – many of whom had no inclination or interest in the subject – deeply frustrating. Once again he applied to be transferred to a tactical squadron. His request was again turned down.

*

CATHERINE produced a drawing of Hereford Cathedral. It was her first sketch since St Albans.

This time she used the academy chalk and carbon crayon to complete a far more detailed study. When the weather was bad she worked indoors, using a photograph. Catherine enquired at a printer's shop about the cost of turning her drawing into Christmas cards.

Encouraged by the printer's assurances that cards with local views would sell well – and his advice to seek out the head of the city's art school – Catherine decided to have the cards made up. A few days later she was showing the cards to the manager of the town's Woolworth store. Several other shops also agreed to stock them. But the venture provided little more than experience. When all the costs had been accounted Catherine showed just a halfpenny profit on each card.

The building stood alongside the River Wye on the Castle Green. It was Regency with a Classical portico and its name displayed on a large notice across the front: Hereford School of Arts and Crafts. Catherine introduced herself to the principal, Thomas Vaughan Milligan.

Milligan had trained at the Royal College of Art. A 'shy, unambitious man', he had moved to the city in 1925 and soon fell in love with Herefordshire, the Wye and its fishing. Catherine produced her slim portfolio of drawings, unaware that architecture and perspective were Milligan's main subjects. He examined the drawings closely for several minutes. Her work, he told Catherine, was capable of passing a third-year examination.

From December 1942 Catherine thought of little else but her art. Magazines and newspapers were filled with Christmas stories and pictures. One carried a front-page illustration of choirboys walking through an arch towards an altar. She carefully copied the picture and on a whim posted it to J. Arthur Dixon, the greetings card publisher based at Shanklin on the Isle of Wight.

She received £5 and a request for more of her work. Catherine's honesty overtook her excitement at having her drawing accepted. She returned the payment with an admission the picture was not an original but a copy.

The editors at the Shanklin Press remained impressed by Catherine's talent, if not a little puzzled by her scruples. Copies were what they wanted. Would she be willing to produce some more? This time they would supply the originals. When they arrived Catherine was dismayed. All the photographs were from Arthur Mee's *King's England*. Some were as small as an inch by a half-inch, others were circular, and all had to be enlarged to eleven inches by nine.

Tom showed his wife how to square a picture and copy each section individually. It was painstaking work. From soon after Tom left on his bicycle for RAF Madley at six-thirty each morning until he returned in the early evening, Catherine would sit at her makeshift desk peering through a magnifying glass. The hours of eyestrain earned her £5 a picture and conjunctivitis.

Catherine was able to reproduce the photographs by instinct. What she lacked was a feeling of perspective. She turned to the books of artist Vicat Cole. It wasn't until many years later she learned that Cole had been the head of Hastings Art School. Cole's advice was to study the works of the Dutch artists, who used doorways and square-tiled flooring as devices to emphasise perspective.

Milligan, who continued to encourage her, was impressed by her growing collection of pencil drawings of other cathedrals. He invited her to hang three of her pictures at an exhibition. They were placed next to a work by Dame Laura Knight.

The momentary acclaim Catherine had received from the exhibition, including a brief mention in the local newspaper, was not sufficient. It was ephemeral; passing; never solid enough for the keepsake achievement she had longed for since childhood.

It was as if she were caught between twin phantoms of her own making. The desire – the need – to attain formal recognition through examinations or tests, yet never controlling her ambition and fear of failure long enough to allow the circumstances to be right. The promise of success was there. 'You are capable of taking a third-year exam,' Milligan had told her. 'And there is no reason why you should not get to SLADE.'

During 1943 Catherine discovered she was expecting her third baby. The pregnancy ended in a miscarriage. Further pregnancies, she was warned, could cost her her life.

This time she turned her energies toward music. Twenty years earlier she had passed her first music examination with honours.

In the empty days when there were no orders for her drawings she would return to play at the piano in the Hereford house three or four times a day.

1944 slid towards a forbidding darkness. What started as a year of hope and encouragement ended as a year of desperation for Catherine.

It was as if the two-way mirror protecting her inner soul from the outside world was wearing thinner each day. Looking in, those around her saw the reflection of a bright, intelligent woman, eager to please and share the humour of any situation. Looking out, the mirror distorted her apparent inadequacies like a grotesque fairground hall of mirrors.

Shame was disfigured into guilt. The secret of her birth. Her daily prayers to keep Tom safe. The guilt of not doing enough for the war effort.

Catherine remained painfully thin. The daily nose bleeds had made her anaemic. Her poor health excluded her from compulsory war work. For the first time she appeared to be one of the few women in Hereford whose days were their own. Not belonging became a burden and she volunteered for work at the Royal Ordnance Factory across the River Wye at Rotherwas.

Each day for five weeks she left the Ryelands Street house and walked past the cider factory, across Greyfriars Bridge to the sprawling site of the ammunition plant. More than 2,700 operatives were employed at Rotherwas, 2,000 of them women. Catherine was given a job packing cordite rods. The mixture of guncotton, nitroglycerine and vaseline produced an allergic reaction and she was forced to leave.

The workforce had just returned from its Whitsun break on Tuesday, 30 May when women filling 2,000 lb bombs and naval mines noticed one of the unsealed bombs was smoking. It was seven o'clock in the evening. As 800 men and women evacuated the cluster of single-storey buildings, works' firemen attempted to damp down the flames with water and sand. The bomb eventually split open and exploded.

During the next four hours thirty-one bombs and mines detonated. Several fire fighters were badly injured as they were blown off their feet or showered with molten explosive and white-hot metal. Miraculously only two people died. Bravery awards were bestowed on thirty-two workers and fire fighters: five George Medals; nine British Empire Medals; an OBE and an MBE, and sixteen King's Commendations.

The Rotherwas filling factory had been working at full stretch. Canteen gossip had sensed the allied offensive. Four days later, on 3 June, Tom witnessed further proof of the imminent D-Day landings when the American General, George S. Patton Junior, flew out of Madley on his way to southern England.

IN a top-floor flat in the older part of Hereford, and almost within sight of the cathedral, lived an engineer called André van der Meersch.

Catherine, who by now felt she knew enough about art to want to paint, had been told of van der Meersch by the printer who produced her Christmas cards. 'Either you can paint or you can't,' the Dutchman told her. 'But you can come and watch me.'

Each Saturday afternoon Catherine climbed the stairs to the flat where van der Meersch lived with his wife and daughter. The walls were covered with paintings of the sea and sea views.

Bludgeoned by chance, van der Meersch somehow remained a 'modest and happy' man. He was a Laureate of the Royal College of Mauritius. During the First World War he had been severely wounded while serving as a bombing instructor with the RAF. In the 1920s he moved to London, where he worked as an assistant on the staff of the London University and ran his own coaching establishment in Chancery Lane. His home was destroyed in the Battle of Britain and he moved to Hereford in September 1940 to become chief physics master at the Cathedral School.

Week by week Catherine watched as van der Meersch painted in oils and water colours, or talked about his two other interests of psychology or music.

The lessons ended abruptly when van der Meersch died of heart failure in September 1944. Catherine bought his paints and brushes and his easel from his widow. She would continue to work on the easel for more than forty years.

IN the autumn Catherine developed phlebitis, a painful inflammation of the veins in her leg. She was ordered to bed by one general practitioner, told by a second to get up and, when the condition failed to improve, was finally confined to bed for six weeks.

Tom departed for Madley each morning leaving his wife alone. A nurse came in once a day to wash Catherine. Suddenly her life seemed as empty and featureless as the brick wall she could see from her bedroom window. She was deeply in love with Tom, but the secret of her birth still separated them. Kate's lie was keeping them apart.

Catherine's deteriorating mental state began to affect her physically. She began to retch, the sound of her heart pumped in her head and her arms and legs twitched violently. Trying to get out of bed a few days later, she discovered her legs were paralysed. A 'foreign, harassed-looking' doctor suggested Catherine needed a change of scene. The hours of solitude, he felt, were not improving her nerves and he admitted her to hospital. The confines of a small ward and the comments of the other patients did nothing to lift the darkness in her life. Catherine returned to Tom and their Ryeland Street rooms.

In the spring of 1945 her doctor announced he could do no more. He would refer Catherine to a psychiatrist. But even before her first consultation Catherine's imagination had embroidered the shame of her nervous disorder into the terror of madness.

It soon became obvious, even to Catherine, that she would need long-term help in conquering her crisis. The psychiatrist hinted she would benefit from treatment as a voluntary patient. Once again Catherine conceded. She was admitted to St Mary's Hospital at Burghill, a village north-west of Hereford. Under different circumstances Catherine would have appreciated the magnificent old country house with its huge, flowing staircase and grand corridors.

The staff treated Catherine kindly. During the day the matron allowed her to sort or tidy the storerooms. As part of her therapy Catherine wove cloth or made gloves. Each evening, after a day's teaching at Madley, Tom pedalled the seven miles from Hereford to Burghill on his old bicycle. His wife's appearance shocked and saddened him.

Catherine could no longer control the creatures of her depression. Through the two-way mirror in her mind she found herself looking out at fears she had previously been able to convince herself only existed inside her head. Ugly, hideous, appalling scenes which at times forced her to the edge of hysteria before she was plunged into the abyss of silent isolation.

And through it all – through the guilt of her religion and the dread of retribution – one face continued to taunt her. A once beautiful face turned sour with drink and bitter with cowardice. Kate was to blame for her life . . . and her pain . . . and her ultimate guilt.

Catherine lashed out, shattering the thin partition which separated reality and nightmare. In rushed the screams and the pathetic gibberish of the other patients and the overpowering smell of urine. Only violence and revenge remained. The object of her hatred was several hundred miles away. Catherine turned on Tom. She told him she no longer loved him, no longer cared what became of him.

The doctors prescribed a course of electric shock treatment. During one session Catherine received a higher voltage than usual; the convulsion was so violent it almost threw her from the couch.

After six weeks Catherine could take no more. She had to get away. Away from Hereford and Tom and find somewhere safe.

Nine

Writing is not only my work, it is my hobby.

THE SUN WAS shining when Catherine returned to the Hurst in July 1945.

She stood in the garden and examined the home she and Tom had left exactly five years earlier. Except for a brief period the house had remained unoccupied. Two separate land-mines had shaken the foundations. The tower was no longer safe and the roof leaked and needed urgent repairs.

Catherine did not know she was pregnant for the fourth time. 'I went to see friends across the road. They let me sleep in the basement, among the boxes. When my mother-in-law came she was furious that they'd put me there, but really they were only being kind. I was actually grateful,' she said.

Desperately lonely she suffered her third miscarriage before Tom was finally demobbed in February 1946. Catherine was distraught, frantically grasping at anything to give her life and five-year-old marriage new meaning. For the first time in almost forty years she needed someone else's strength to help her survive.

There was no one. Catherine once again considered suicide. 'I knew that people who committed suicide needed help. Didn't I?' she confessed several years later. 'I had lots of sleeping pills, three boxes of them, and I just couldn't stop thinking about how nice it would be to go to sleep and never wake up to drag myself through another day.'

Her will to survive – when it came – was again thanks to Tom. 'I thought about Tom and what he'd do without me. The more I thought about him the more I knew I couldn't take the pills,' she said. 'I got up out of bed and flushed them all down the lavatory and when I'd done it I felt such a relief, the like of which I hadn't known for years.

'At last I'd done something positive, I was shouting inside, something to help myself. At last I'd seen some light in the darkness. It didn't last long, that feeling, but at least I'd experienced it. It was good enough to try to recapture.'

Other destructive moods swept over her. Anger and frustration took her to the very edge of disaster. Whenever she saw a baby in a pram outside a shop or left to sleep in the autumn sun she found herself being drawn towards it; to pick it up; to cuddle it; to take it home. A family waiting for Tom's return. Once again her world had turned to black and white, to right and wrong, good and evil. The love – the longing – she felt inside hardened to violent revenge. Catherine forced herself to walk away before she hurled the baby on to the pavement or into the road. When she arrived back at the Hurst she would run to the sink to vomit or hurl herself face down on her bed, beating the evil into exhaustion.

In the weeks after her return to the Hurst Catherine began to examine her childhood in detail, replaying the familiar scenes in her mind. The hatred for Kate compounded with the memory of each broken promise or lost opportunity. She suddenly recalled the £1 Kate still owed Mrs Dalton for the final piano lessons and the examination fee. Twenty-seven years after Catherine took her last lesson in the Hudson Street house she settled the bill in full.

Catherine drew up charts to keep track of the days. Plotting dots above and below a line to record her good and bad days. She still has some of the charts. 'For years I'd go to bed and say, "Tomorrow you'll feel better . . . tomorrow you'll feel better." Sometimes I would, but I never stopped believing.'

She would also confront her anger and her frustrations head on – face to face. This time she used a real mirror. Yet the face she saw looking back at her was always Kate's.

Years before Catherine had promised herself she would never drink and never swear. The obscenities she had heard in the kitchen of No 10 and on the streets of Tyne Dock and East Jarrow had petrified her. She dreaded the possibility her mind could produce the same loathsome sounds. The foul, polluting words would never leave her brain. They had to be driven from her life.

'What does a soldier do? What does somebody do when they're in battle? They don't turn and run away. The only thing to do is to face your fear and go towards it,' she explained. 'So I learnt a trick;

if I have a fear coming on, I go to the mirror and swear at myself. Aloud. I would shout: "You're bloody well not going to get the better of me this time."

'People would think I was barmy. They would think the breakdown had really caught up with me. I could conquer it just by going for myself.'

Kate's subconscious approval only served to fan Catherine's anger. 'It always appeared that the person standing in that mirror was Kate. I never saw my reflection, it was always Kate saying, "Yes, that's right Hinny, have a damn good swear at yourself and you'll feel better." '

Looking back Catherine admits she learned to view the tragic end of her four pregnancies and her near suicide philosophically. 'Now I realise that had I had a baby or babies they would have all likely been haemophiliacs because of my hereditary blood disease. And that would have been terrible to have passed on without realising it.

'If I had had children then I would not have written a word. I would have spent my time raising them and caring for my family.'

But in the late 1940s Tom and Catherine never gave up hope of a family of their own. They tried various organisations in a bid to adopt a child. One society willingly accepted them as prospective parents, only to announce they were 100th on the waiting list. Catherine approached a Catholic adoption society. When she admitted she was no longer a practising Catholic, they refused to consider her.

Her world, once again, turned from grey to a suffocating black. The exhausted peace Catherine achieved each day by filling her hours with manual labour around the house and in the garden appeared out of reach. Even with the aid of pills she was sleeping fewer than four hours each night. She could not recall a single good incident in her life. Tom was pushed aside. Her friends were ignored. There was nothing nice. Nothing worthwhile. Everything was bad and black.

Until the years of the mid-1950s – through the early years of her success as a writer – Catherine learned to live a dual existence. A façade of quiet normality, hiding the screams from within.

'The hardest thing was to try to stand on my own two feet,' she confides. 'Outwardly everything was fine and I'd laugh and carry on just as usual. But underneath I was writhing in fear. The shadows never leave you.'

More than forty years later in *Let Me Make Myself Plain* she described her breakdown in a different way. 'A breakdown is like the eruption of a volcano. Your mind is boiling with the most terrifying thoughts, all negative, fear, aggressiveness, hate, self-pity; they come spewing up, spilling over, overpowering you for a time. But just as a volcano gradually wears itself out, so your mind settles, at least on the surface.'

In *The Invisible Cord* – written in the 1970s – one of her characters passes his own judgment on the experience: 'I once heard someone say that they wouldn't wish the devil in hell to have a breakdown and I can endorse that.'

Catherine returned to filling every hour of every day. She meticulously wrote out schedules of routine jobs to be done or special tasks completed. She dug the ever-demanding garden; chopped down trees; sawed the branches into logs. In the evenings she returned to her writing. She had started writing a play but the characters, she soon realised, were false and populated a world at odds with her own turmoil. She attempted two more plays before abandoning the form altogether.

TOM'S return brought with it an end to the years of apprehension. He was back at the Hurst for good. The circle was complete.

The staff and pupils of Hastings Grammar School had ended their four years' relocation in late October 1944, when the Cooksons were still in Hereford. Tom lost no time in applying for his old post as maths master. He was immediately appointed master of Norman House.

A number of the staff had remained with the school throughout the war, among them fellow maths master Bill Barnett, who had joined Hastings Grammar in 1921 after losing a leg in the First World War. He was never a favourite with the pupils.

Sharing the same subject, he befriended Tom on his appointment in the 1930s, a friendship which was to last until Barnett's retirement in 1960. At the end of Tom's first post-war academic year he and Catherine invited Barnett, his wife Primrose, son John – then a pupil at the school – and two cousins on a boating holiday. For two weeks during the summer holiday the group explored the Norfolk Broads on a motor cruiser.

The holidays afloat were to become a regular feature of the Cooksons' life. Tom, Catherine soon discovered, was 'boat mad'. To please her husband, Catherine smothered her fear of water and the memories of the two horrendous Channel crossings. The boats never sank. The fact that Catherine never tumbled overboard amazed her even more.

But when the new school year started in September 1946, one new pupil instantly fell foul of Barnett's bad temper. He was eventually to owe his future career to 'Cookie'.

'Tommy Cookson was a capable "hands on" technologist,' recalls John Ridd, who attended Hastings Grammar until 1951. 'One of his greatest achievements was to light a fire under me. I developed a keen interest in his subject and gained a good qualification in mathematics.' When Tom discovered Ridd was interested in radio engineering, he presented the teenager with a book on the subject. Ridd went on to become a Post Office Radio Service investigator.

In 1948 Tom was appointed form master of class 2A. As a housemaster he had the right to cane boys, a duty he saw as a last resort. Tom was frequently at odds with his fellow masters. Although he regarded himself as a disciplinarian, he also considered the pupils his equals.

Tom volunteered to referee the final of the school's annual six-a-side football competition. Held on the Flat, the school name for the playground, it was watched by the entire school. 'During the match one of the players indicated he disagreed with a decision,' recalls a former member of Norman House. 'Mr Cookson saw this and came over and told the boy that a referee's decision is final and should always be accepted without argument.

'None of us thought anything more about the incident. However, a day or two later Mr Cookson came into the classroom and apologised to the boy in front of the whole class. None of the other masters would have done that.'

Another post-war pupil, Terry Jones, remembers Tom as 'a short man with fair wavy hair, red cheeks and always smiling'. Jones's mother had worked under Catherine in the institute laundry. In 1940 she had refused to allow her son to be evacuated to St Albans with the grammar school because she considered it 'too dangerous'.

'I was back at the grammar school when Tom Cookson rejoined the staff,' adds Jones. 'The first thing that struck me was that here was a man who appeared to know his log tables by heart.'

There were other connections between the Frederick Road Infirmary and Hastings Grammar School. Within days of Catherine's arrival in 1930 a young mother, taken into the workhouse, gave birth to a son. Sixteen years later Derick Rainton was a sixth-form grammar school pupil. His maths master was Tom Cookson. 'I remember him as a very enthusiastic teacher,' says Rainton, 'but also as a good friend.

'On one occasion, just before I was due to sit my final exams, I became very depressed and felt like giving up. Tom gave me some very sound advice and put me back on the right track.'

Rainton kept in touch with his former teacher. In 1953 Tom and Catherine gave him a hand-painted fruit plate as a wedding gift.

But Tom's gentle approach to teaching was far from the norm. Other masters, particularly the older members of staff, relied on various forms of corporal punishment to maintain discipline. One geography lesson included a series of slides on tropical forests, the teacher was reading the slide captions as they appeared on the screen. 'This is the land of Ma Hogan,' he said pronouncing it as Maah-Hogaan, in the style of a red indian chief. 'Please sir, it's mahogany,' said one pupil. His correction earned him six of the best.

Soon afer rejoining the staff in 1946, Tom volunteered to help run the school scout troop. In 1948, when the 24th Hastings scouts departed for their summer camp at Fritham on the edge of the New Forest, Catherine went too.

Tom and Catherine travelled to the camp site by car, towing a caravan. Although Catherine spent the fortnight sleeping in the caravan, it didn't stop her taking part in camp life. In the evenings she would join scouts and masters for a sing-song around a huge fire. Her party piece was an arm-waving version of the 'Blaydon Races'.

ALTHOUGH much of the war damage had been repaired, the Hurst was still making great demands on the Cooksons' time and money.

Catherine had already proved the worth of keeping a tight rein on money. She never slackened her grip. Every penny was recorded. Each item of shopping was dutifully listed in a small cash book. A quarter of sweets, still rationed until 4 February 1953; a jar of Gales' honey, the Cooksons' favourite; a trip to the pictures.

By the time Tom returned from the RAF Catherine's savings had reached £500, enough to pay off the mortgage on the Hurst. The first – and only time – the couple signed a hire purchase agreement was in 1957 when they bought a new fridge. For years Catherine insisted on doing the washing by hand rather than spend money on a washing machine.

But if work on the house was a necessity, Tom and Catherine enjoyed every minute they spent in the rambling garden. Tom, more than anyone, knew that the physical stamina Catherine had inherited from her mother was one way of beating her depression. Just as Catherine had needed a rigid timetable of work, Tom used a more subtle approach to keep his wife busy.

Encouraged by Tom, Catherine gradually spent more time on writing. She took to composing poetry. 'Prose on short lines . . . I have my own standards of poetry.'

> Lord, beckon me to joy:
> My mind is weary
> My body sick:
> Who can I employ
> To ease my spirit
> And lift my heart
> And give me strength
> To combat this strife
> And the energy
> To work at life?
> Lord, beckon me to joy.
>
> I have no hobbies:
> No more do I knit,
> Play the piano or paint:
> My mind abhors the needle,
> My fingers irritate the keys

I see no colour, no trees,
Then what do I do
With my days?
I write,
And part of the night.
O Lord, beckon me to joy.

The poem, one of dozens she wrote in the 1940s and 1950s, remained among her papers until it was published for the first time in 1986 in *Catherine Cookson Country*.

Tom's gentle company revived other achievements. Her drawing was dead. Alone at the Hurst, even the sound of a piano had annoyed her. Now, with Tom ever-present, Catherine began to compose tunes and melodies. The sounds of the chords – the control she had over them – was both pleasing and therapeutic. Many of the tunes were lost. To some she gave lyrics. The words of one Catherine used in her first novel.

Let the beauty linger in my soul
Of a rose just bursting into bloom,
Of a bird in flight,
Of the moon, new born in the night,
Reflecting on a sea of gentle ripples.
Let the beauty linger in my soul
Of a winter morn draped in patterned frost,
Of air like wine,
On sunlit snow on limbs of trees,
Of black, brown trunks bare to the winds that sweep the woods.
Of drifts of crisp brown leaves,
Swept, now here, now there, with the breeze.
Let the beauty linger in my soul
Of firelight in a darkened room,
Of kindly words,
Of lovers' laughter coming through the night,
Until, at last, I know no greater peace nor ease But to remember
these.

Kate Hannigan

THE little woman sitting at the top of the table closed her eyes and drifted into a trance.

Suddenly, as if someone standing near her chair had whispered her name, the woman opened her eyes and listened. 'There is someone trying to find out who has lost a friend by his own hand,' she said, examining the men and women seated around the table. Catherine shook her head. 'He has a message for this person.'

The seance continued. Catherine listened to each new message. The medium broke off in the middle of a sentence and, lifting her hand, pointed at Catherine. 'He's standing behind you. He says you are not to worry any more about him. It was done on the spur of the moment.' Still the message meant nothing to Catherine. 'His name is John.'

John had been a friend of the Cooksons. Depressed by money worries, he had shot himself.

The woman had not finished with Catherine. 'There is someone else with him, and he's very old. He says you are to return to your way of working.'

The apparent accuracy of both messages startled Catherine. For months after her return to Hastings a friend had been trying to persuade her to sit in on a seance at the resort's House of Healing. There was no way the medium could have known about John's suicide. The second message also meant something only to Catherine.

Guided by Tom over her reading list, she had accepted his suggestion she should also attempt to improve her grammar. Catherine had always written her stories as she saw and heard them. She watched her characters and described them. She heard them speak and she wrote down the words.

When Tom heard the sound of a word his logical, analytical mind projected nothing more than the letters it contained – always spelled correctly. Inaccurate grammar or sloppy punctuation perpetually irritated him.

Armed with a copy of Fowler's *Modern English Usage* Catherine attempted to homogenise her stories. Each evening Tom would read and correct her day's work. His criticism was often harsh and ungiving, frequently reducing his wife to tears. The result of this imposed formality on Catherine's English was that her characters lost their identity and her prose lost its guts.

Catherine had gained a universal language, but lost her regional accent.

She had not heard the old man's spiritual voice. She didn't need to . . . *go on, go on, don't stop, for begod it will get you some place* . . .

For over a year Catherine had been suffering from a pain just below her eye. The antrum – the space in her cheekbone – had become infected, making it painful even to wash her face. The only cure would be an antrostomy, an operation to drain the pus and relieve the pressure.

The pain in her cheek was becoming unbearable. Catherine returned to the House of Healing, this time persuaded by her friend to allow herself to undergo spiritual healing. As Catherine lay flat on a table, the woman who had conducted the seance gently pressed and rubbed her face. On the way home the pain was so intense she began to cry. Three days later, on the Monday morning, Catherine hesitantly began to wash her face. The pain had gone. The infection never returned.

Although Catherine no longer attended Mass she found it difficult to irrevocably break with her religion. *She* no longer held any faith, *it* held *her*, and it was a faith once more under attack. The rigidity of the Catholic Church seemed at odds with her own experiences. In Hereford she had been advised against further pregnancies. When she sought guidance from a priest over the question of contraception, he told her, 'Let your husband do the sinning'. A few days later an envelope arrived containing a book entitled *A Letter to a Lapsed Catholic*. It warned: 'You will go to hell possibly through refusing the appeal of this letter.'

The realisation she must finally break with her Church – after two previous lapses – no longer troubled her. As a child the damnation had seemed all too real; she could touch the gates of hell and feel the eternal heat. Her breakdown had shown her – was showing her – there were very few material manifestations of the God she had trusted and the Devil she had feared.

Through her visits to the House of Healing, Catherine was learning to trust in a new force. A power which, turned inward by personal guilt, became destructive and negative. Set free through nature, it appeared to offer only peace.

Tom was at school. Catherine was overcome by a particularly

black mood. She was walking in the small wood adjacent to the Hurst. She still remembers the exact words in her head. 'Oh God! What am I going to do? I can't go on any longer like this.' Stopping in front of a mature oak, she turned and pressed her back against the bark, holding the trunk with her hands. A new and unfamiliar voice inside her head commanded her to breathe deeply. With each breath the tension seemed to flow down her arms and out of her body.

FOR days a new picture inside Catherine's head had been pestering her. It was of a small girl with 'long, nut-brown ringlets and round blinking eyes'. Catherine put out her hand and the frightened child disappeared. But the apparition refused to leave her. Catherine used the little girl in a short story. As she did so the image became sharper; she could see the upturned nose and the small mouth and spindle-straight legs below the pinafore dress.

Catherine called the story, intended as the first in a collection of short stories, 'She Had No Da'. It describes how the child is taunted by her friends because she has no father. The shame drives her to the Church where she confesses she would rather be dead than fatherless.

Other short stories – about other Northern children – followed. But, like the characters in her plays, Catherine could not believe in them. Only the little girl with 'no Da' seemed real. It was the first time Catherine had subconsciously ignored her imagination and transported an image direct from her memory. The young girl's personality and physical appearance had been drawn from her own past. Catherine had discovered Mary Ann Shaughnessy, a character she would use in no less than eight books.

Hastings Writers' Circle met in the basement of the Rougemont Hotel overlooking the seafront. In 1948 Catherine had forced herself to join. Within a year she had been elected secretary. The meetings, usually good-natured affairs at which members offered up their latest work for group criticism, were frequently adjourned to Dimarco's, a near-by cafeteria famed for its hot chocolate.

Searching for something to take to one of the regular Friday meetings, Catherine decided on 'She Had No Da'.

Catherine sat at a table with the chairman and other members of the committee, their backs to the sea. Too nervous to stand and read the story aloud, she blamed the rheumatism in her legs. As she finished, the room fell silent before erupting in applause. On her way home to Hoads Wood Road the façade finally crumbled and she burst into tears.

'Catherine was a brilliant critic and a good reader,' recalls Joan Moules, a member who benefited from Catherine's advice. 'She really acted out the stories. She often read mine and made them sound far better than they actually were.'

Joan Longfellow, as she then was, had been given the name of the Writers' Circle secretary by the fiction editor of magazine publishers' George Newmans and C. Arthur Pearson. The nineteen-year-old – who went on to establish her own career as a novelist and to teach creative writing – found Catherine could be ruthless when necessary.

'Her remarks were constructive, but always very much to the point,' says Moules. 'She was tremendously enthusiastic and very much a no-nonsense person. Yet she could put over her comments with sensitivity too.' After a particularly fierce criticism of one of the teenager's stories, Catherine took her aside and told her: 'You took that well. I came down hard because I believe you can write – if I didn't think you had it in you I wouldn't have bothered.'

Other writing skills Moules attributes directly to Catherine. 'She taught me the value of writing a tight story. Cutting is difficult when you begin, but she always made me see it was necessary.'

Catherine put the short stories aside and started work on something fresh. Her sessions in front of the mirror were supplanted by a new therapy.

'It's the greatest psychiatrist's treatment in the world because you're your own judge, and I knew that unless I faced up to my early beginnings, unless I could throw this pseudo lady and pseudo gentleman out of my life and admit to my beginnings, admit to these two terrifying words, which upset me even when I read "bastard" or "illegitimate".

'Unless I could look in the mirror and say, "Well, yes, that's what you are. You're a bastard," I knew I would never get any peace. And I had to have this long session with myself, and I said: "All right, I'll write it down. I'll write the background of my early beginnings."

'I didn't think I'm going to write a novel, or I'm going to do fiction, or romance, nothing like that. I just wanted to put down the background of my mother and my grandmother, from what I felt in the kitchen, from the surroundings of the New Buildings,' she said.

'And so I wrote this story called *Kate Hannigan*. And I thought, "That's it!" But it wasn't. The breakdown was still with me.'

Catherine only briefly owned a typewriter, preferring instead to write in longhand. Her writing became the opposite of the destructive electro-shock treatment she had received at St Mary's Hospital at Burghill. Instead of obliterating the memory of her past, Catherine was now reliving it line by line. It would not bring her peace, but for a part of each day it numbed the raw nerves of her memory.

She made little effort to disguise the incidents and characters. She described many scenes exactly as they had happened – as they were happening – hiding her own life under the thinnest of washes.

It is not hard to imagine Catherine reading the initial section of *Kate Hannigan* to the members of the Writers' Circle, unaware that they were listening to the opening pages of her own life.

The story begins with Kate Hannigan in labour, about to give birth to a bastard child – Catherine's mother was also called Kate; she is attended by a young physician, Dr Rodney Prince, as was Kate McMullen by Dr McHaffie; both doctors drove cars; below, Tim and Sarah Hannigan wait out the delivery in the kitchen, 'Tim Hannigan sitting in his chair by the fireside, wearing his look of sullen anger' and Sarah with 'her weary face', exactly as John and Rose McMullen must have waited. The child Catherine calls Annie, her own middle name.

Catherine uses the clever device of confining the chapters to a single day each year, Christmas Eve. It enabled her to span the years from Annie's birth to the day Kate Hannigan is finally united with Dr Prince, a crippled victim of the First World War.

The majority of the story takes place within the narrow environment of Catherine's own early years, from the fictitious Fifteen Streets at East Jarrow – only yards from the New Buildings – to the luxury of Westoe. The only exception is the final chapter, which opens in a boarding house at St Leonards, near Hastings, where Kate and Annie have fled.

There are no less than sixty-two instances in the novel that can be directly related to Catherine's own life: Kate's kindly neighbour is called Mullen, instead of McMullen; Dr Prince's assistant is called Swinburn, the name of the girl who had so unceremoniously ended Catherine's career as a bully; the picture of Lord Roberts is smashed in a domestic fight . . .

But if Catherine endowed Kate with her own dreams of refinement, she saved her bitterest condemnation for her step-grandfather.

There is no doubt Tim Hannigan and John McMullen are one and the same, both men 'lost on the empty plain of silence and ignorance'. Forced to return from service to nurse her dying mother through the final months of dropsy, Kate Hannigan endures the same physical beatings and sexual fears as Catherine's mother. There is one brief respite, when Hannigan injures his leg. In the end the old man dies, not through the injuries he suffers when knocked down by a tram, but through the shock and humiliation at finding himself in the workhouse infirmary.

Harton! . . That's what he was always feared of, having to end his days in the workhouse . . . It's the only thing that ever worried him; he was mortally afraid of the workhouse . . . He died of fright . . .

Catherine's attendances at Writers' Circle meetings were interrupted by two operations on her womb in 1948 and 1949. She was to undergo a third in 1950. Yet she always returned as forceful as ever. Even the rejection of fifty short stories in a single year failed to curb her enthusiasm.

In addition to reading new work, it was also a custom for members to announce their successes. Surprisingly, Catherine's first triumph was a piece of non-fiction written for the radio.

Early in 1949 Catherine had overheard a woman's remark about the carrying power of her voice. She decided to show the woman how far her voice would carry – all over Britain.

Within days Catherine had written the script for a talk on discovering artistic talent later in life. But it took three months of morning 'rehearsals' after Tom had left for school before she considered she was good enough to overcome her nerves and read it in person. She sent the script to the BBC, where it was passed to the producer of *Woman's Hour*. Launched in 1946 as a means of helping to rebuild family life and the home after the war, *Woman's*

Hour regularly attracted 6 million listeners a day. Catherine was called to London for a voice test. On Monday, 15 August 1949 she read her talk – 'I Learned to Draw at Thirty' – live from Broadcasting House.

In the autumn Catherine wrote a second script; this one entitled 'Making Dreams Come True'. Once again it was accepted for *Woman's Hour* and broadcast live on 30 January 1950.

But even before *Kate Hannigan* had been accepted, Catherine had started work on a second novel. Her new book would be a sequel. It would continue to allow her to exorcise her own childhood through the eyes of 'Kate's daughter'. Catherine called it *Annie Hannigan*.

CATHERINE was half-way through writing *Kate Hannigan* when she spotted the poster advertising a lecture by Major Christopher Bush. The talk was entitled: 'How to Write a Novel'.

The winter of 1948–9 was bitterly cold. She arrived at Hastings Library on the dark evening to find only twelve other people, all women, had braved the weather to sit through a lecture.

Bush, whose real name was Charlie Christmas Bush, was born in East Anglia in the late 1880s. He had combined Army service in both world wars with a prolific writing career. His first thriller – *The Plumley Inheritance* – was published in 1926 and introduced Ludovic 'Kim' Travers, the detective he was to use in the majority of his novels. By the time of his death in September 1973, he had published eighty murder mysteries and thrillers under the pen names of Major Christopher Bush and Michael Home.

Any woman who could write a laundry list, claimed the Major, could write a novel. Having disagreed vociferously during question time, Catherine sought out Bush to apologise. She left with the name and address of the Major's literary agent.

Catherine lost no time in writing to Christy & Moore and outlining *Kate Hannigan*. A few days later she received a reply from John Smith, asking to see the manuscript as soon as it was completed.

'I read four chapters and told my managing director we just had to take her on,' recalls Smith, then thirty-three.

His enthusiasm for *Kate Hannigan* was not shared by Murray Thompson at Macdonald & Co, the first publisher Smith approached. His initial verdict on the story was that it was 'too deep'. He passed it back to his secretary to be returned. Instead, she took the manuscript home and sat up most of the night reading it. The next morning she persuaded her employer to reconsider publication.

Macdonald's offer to publish *Kate Hannigan* hit Catherine like a whirlwind. After forty years she had at last found someone – and not just anyone – who was prepared to listen to her fantasies. And not just listen. She was going to be paid to tell stories.

No money had been mentioned. Catherine believed Smith when he told her he would get the best advance he could. The Hurst was in urgent need of repair, and a regular gardener would give her extra time to write. If there was anything left, maybe a car, or a fur coat.

To the editors at Macdonald, Catherine Cookson was just one of the outside runners publishers backed every year. First novels rarely sold well. Most bookshops would never take more than three copies, and those on sale or return. Smith haggled. Macdonalds gave ground and offered a £100 advance. Catherine, for once, was speechless.

First off the top was her agent's fee; then £10 she had paid Peggy Storey, also a member of Hastings Writers' Circle, to type the handwritten manuscript. In all less than £8 10s a month for a year's work.

There remained one publishing formality. Catherine would have to travel up to London to meet Murray Thompson and sign the contract.

Arriving at Macdonald's city office, Catherine discovered her agent had given her the wrong date for the meeting. Instead she was treated to lunch with Thompson's secretary. Over the meal the woman confessed her part in Catherine's success.

Smith, whose initial faith in Catherine was never betrayed, went on to negotiate the sale of the majority of her books. 'She has never changed,' he admits. 'She is warm-hearted and immensely professional. That's quite a combination.

'She matured, of course, but the most marvellous thing is that she's still little Kitty inside. She's a very wise person and a very good person, too.'

THE postman knocked at the door of the Hurst. When Catherine opened it she was handed a small parcel with a London postmark. Inside were her six free copies of *Kate Hannigan*.

Catherine studied the cover. Ran her fingers slowly down the spine. Fanned the pages before stopping to read sentences and paragraphs as they caught her eye. 'I was floating,' she recalled many years later. 'When you have your first book published your head swells. When it arrives, when you have it in your hands, it is pure joy.'

Catherine desperetely needed to talk to someone – anyone – about her book. Tom had already left for school. His sister, who was staying at the Hurst, had gone out.

At twelve-thirty the kitchen door opened and Tom arrived back from school for his lunch. Catherine watched him getting more and more excited as he too examined each book in turn. Ouside, in the garden or the street, Tom would have jogged or run to burn off his emotion. Indoors, at home or at school, he rocked lightly from foot to foot.

Someone knocked at the door. Tom grabbed a copy of *Kate Hannigan*. 'I'll show the baker,' he said, ignoring Catherine's look of horror.

Framed in the doorway was a tall, military-looking man holding a wicker basket. 'Look, baker,' said Tom, waving the book triumphantly above his head. 'My wife's first novel.'

The man's face was frozen with a superior kind of indifference. His eyes lifted to the book and then he turned to Catherine.

'White or brown?'

Part Three

'Write It All Down, Hinny'

Ten

I have my writing and I sell a few books.

ON 14 JUNE 1950 – six days before Catherine's forty-fourth birthday – the Newcastle *Journal* reported the arrival of a 'new author'.

> *I am sure my readers will join me in welcoming another Tyneside name on the list of English novelists – Catherine Cookson.*
> *Her first novel, entitled* Kate Hannigan, *which is to appear next week, is, I am told, a 'deeply emotional, powerfully told human document of life in Newcastle'.*

A few days after its publication Catherine was passing a book shop in the centre of Hastings. An assistant tapped on the window and waved her in. 'I've sold one,' the woman said with excitement.

The same thing happened the next day, and the day after that. As Catherine passed the woman would hold up a finger to indicate how many copies of *Kate Hannigan* she had sold.

Then one morning she rushed out of the shop and announced: 'I've sold them all!'

'What, all six?' asked Catherine.

Catherine's contract with Macdonald bound her to offering them first option on her new book. She posted the typed manuscript, convinced her readers would want to hear more of *Annie Hannigan*. Before the end of the week she received a letter from the publisher regretting her second attempt was not as good as her first. Catherine burst into tears.

Two hours later she was on the telephone to Macdonald's London office demanding the return of the manuscript. It was, she considers, one of the bravest and wisest things she ever did. She still has the original and unpublished typescript in her files.

Catherine badly needed a new story. 'I was alone and I thought and thought but didn't have an idea in my head,' she explained.

'I'd given up God at that time and I was still fighting my breakdown, but as I sat in the room I suddenly had this feeling that I wanted to talk to something – someone. I can remember looking up at the ceiling and saying, "Well, if there's anything there, then give me a story." It sounds phony now, but that's what happened. Within an hour I had the complete story for my second novel, *The Fifteen Streets*.

'I never had to alter a word of it and I still think it's a good story. It's never happened to me again, but I took it as a sign that I was meant to go on writing.'

The producer of *Woman's Hour* also wanted Catherine to continue writing – and speaking.

On Monday, 1 January 1950 – even before the publication of *Kate Hannigan* – she was back in London to read another of her talks. This time entitled: 'Making Dreams Come True'. Thoughts on a third radio talk had to be postponed while she worked on *The Fifteen Streets* and plotted her next book. It wasn't until the beginning of May 1951 that *Woman's Hour* listeners heard her voice again. Catherine had chosen a subject she had enjoyed for many years: 'Buying Secondhand Furniture'.

The breakdown was far from over, but at last Catherine had found something to keep her away from the darkness in her dreams. The dots on her charts were slowly climbing above the dividing line. On the bad days, when nothing seemed to go right, she would tremble with fear and ache with retching.

It was time, she thought, to conquer her nerves with knowledge. Catherine read every book – both for the professional and layman – she could find on nerves and nervous disorders. It soon became apparent she would have to change her way of thinking. The conviction in her own future was adapted into a crude form of self-hypnosis – '*The word IMPOSSIBLE is black . . . I CAN is like a flame of gold.*'

But telling herself – persuading herself – was one thing. No matter how hard Catherine willed herself she could still not find the courage to stand and talk at the same time.

On 21 March 1952 she went to London to read a *Woman's Hour* talk entitled 'Getting Your Nerves Under Control'. It was her fourth broadcast. Catherine knew she could find solid comfort in the studio furniture. Being invited to talk to a meeting of business and professional women or the Women's Institute was another matter. She fell back on the ruse she employed at Writers' Circle meetings. Rheumatism, she claimed, forced her to sit.

After each meeting Catherine was invariably approached by a member of the audience who shared a memory or experience. Her latest radio talk produced dozens of letters from listeners struggling to come to terms with mental breakdowns or offering advice. Catherine replied to each one personally.

The same month Macdonald published *The Fifteen Streets*. In it she included a contrasting thread that was to run through many of her early works. Catherine held the rigidity of the Catholic faith and its unbending priests at least partly responsible for her breakdown. Father Bradley's uncompromising devotion conflicted as much with the younger Father O'Keefe's kindness and generosity as the good and evil they both preached.

It was a powerful message which Catherine used as effectively as any symbolised by the other real-life characters who peopled her books. In *Kate Hannigan* and *The Fifteen Streets* Father O'Malley and Father Bailey cast light and shade – fear and hope – across their parish, just as Father Bradley and Father O'Keefe had forced the young Catherine to face the nightmare of a black and white world.

The priests reappear in her third book – *Colour Blind* – once again administering to the inhabitants of the fifteen streets, this time the undisciplined and extravagant O'Briens.

Following the death of her cousin Mary in 1924 Catherine had lost touch with Aunt Sarah's family. The separation had been fuelled by a dislike Catherine felt for the hard manners and hard attitudes of miners and the way they treated their families. All four of Sarah Lavelle's sons had gone down the pits.

In 1952 Catherine returned to Tyneside and met her cousins for the first time in almost thirty years. Tempers flared, sparked by a complaint about the high price of coal in the south of England. She did not see why she should have to pay £7 a ton for coal in Hastings while in the North-East they were getting it for 'next to nothing'. Catherine found herself not only facing four irate miners – but also a challenge to descend a pit and discover the real 'cost' of coal.

Peter Lavelle was deputy at the Betty Pit at Birtley. He and his three brothers had spent their entire working life at the twin Ann and Betty pits. The thought of going underground 'petrified' Catherine, coming as it did at the time when she was still struggling to overcome her depression. The reality was little better. Her tour of the workings lasted three hours.

Catherine returned to Hastings and abandoned the 40,000 words she had already written of her new novel. She reworked the characters, only this time giving the story a mining background.

Maggie Rowan – which opens in the shadow of the Depression in the 1930s – is partly set in the fictitious County Durham mining town of Fellburn, a location Catherine was to use in future novels. Uncouth and unloved, Maggie is terrifying in the intensity of her two great ambitions – to have a child and to escape the inevitability of life in a pit cottage. She achieves both when she bribes the slow-thinking, deformed Chris Taggart to marry her. Chris gains comparative prosperity and even independence in the wartime boom in scrap metal, but trouble is never far away.

Catherine dedicated the book to Peter and Michael Lavelle and Jimmy Tiplady, 'whose descriptive reminiscences lent colour to my thinking'. Her admiration extended to the anonymous miners 'whom I saw working in the bowels of the earth and who evoked so much of my admiration that my fear became lost under it'.

It wasn't right somehow ... Never having tried to reason things beyond her ken, she could not explain why it wasn't right; she had only her feelings to go by and they kept telling her that to spend most of a life-time down here to get money for food to enable you to live in the light for a short while wasn't right ...

Maggie Rowan

The fascination – the horror – of Catherine's visit down the Betty pit was compounded a few years later when she was writing her second mining novel, *The Menagerie*, also set in Fellburn. As part of the research Catherine wrote to the Ministry of Mines. The accident reports they sent her included detailed maps and diagrams of pit disasters; inch-accurate records of where pieces of a man's personal equipment had landed or where a miner's head or hand had been ripped off in an explosion.

But if British readers had found a new source of writing talent – and with it a working-class area full of gossip and scandal – so had its tax collectors.

Catherine's first tax bill for her income as a writer was for £2 10s. She was so indignant that she went in person to the Inland Revenue office in Hastings to complain. An inspector suggested she find herself an accountant. She did. Forty-one years later, and still her accountant, she dedicated her latest novel to Bill McBrien, who tactfully sorted out the tax demand of an 'irate and raw beginner'.

The euphoria over her successes did not last long. Her early menopause had weakened her resistance. For weeks Catherine had been losing blood, both internally and through nose bleeds. Yet another operation was suggested and Catherine found herself once more recovering in St Helen's Hospital.

WHEN Kate paid her first post-war visit to the Hurst in 1947 she found Catherine 'thin and pale'.

The holiday lasted two weeks. Kate returned to her flat in Stoddard Street, Tyne Dock, and her job cooking and cleaning for Dr Carstairs.

The visits continued and with them Catherine's awareness that the drink was once again drawing them inevitably together. In 1950, at the age of sixty-five, Kate could no longer manage the housework and retired. Her days were spent idling and drinking. When she was too ill to leave her flat she got a friend to bring in her whisky.

The prospect of even a few weeks in Hastings, a place she still enjoyed, gave Kate more cause for celebration. Each year until 1952 Catherine met her mother at Hastings railway station fearful of what she might find. Kate kept her pride. She was always smartly dressed. But she could do little to hide the damage the whisky was doing.

Nursed by Catherine and mellowed by Tom's forgiving kindness, Kate's visits became longer and longer. Once she appeared to suffer a mild stroke and lost the use of an arm. She remained at the Hurst for three months.

By 1953 Dr Carstairs, who continued to treat his former housekeeper, could ignore her drinking no longer. He secretly contacted Catherine to inform her he had diagnosed stomach cancer. Kate had only a few months to live. Tom insisted she should not suffer the indignity of dying alone.

When Catherine arrived at the Tyne Dock flat to bring her mother home she found Kate in a 'deplorable state'. Bloated with dropsy and her breath shortened by a heart condition, Kate was a hideous caricature of her early self. Her blue eyes had faded almost to white, her nose was bulbous and red – 'there was no beauty left, not even the beauty of age'.

Hatred swept through Catherine – 'I wished she would die. She had been the plague of my life for years' – only to be replaced by a new compassion. Catherine desperately needed to prolong her mother's life. The moments of love they had shared when their eyes met in the William Black Street kitchen had never died.

Catherine's third novel – *Colour Blind* – produced a surprising admission from Kate, and demonstrated how much hidden material was buried in her daughter's memory.

Bridget McQueen commits the grave social error of marrying a negro sailor. Her daughter, Rose Angela, suffers the inevitable torments of her mixed heritage. At school she is sneered at. The girls tell her that when she dies she won't be admitted to the 'White heaven'. It is Father Bailey who finally reassures her. 'God,' he says gently, 'is colour blind. It's the truth – one of the great truths.'

Throughout the story works the evil genius of Rose's Uncle Matt. It is Matt, his face 'narrow and overhung by a thick mop of sandy hair' who has driven her father away with his insane jealousy. And Matt who transfers his hatred from father to daughter.

When the proofs of *Colour Blind* arrived from Macdonald Catherine let her mother read them. Kate was shocked to discover the story described a brother's lust for his sister. The incident, which Catherine believed was imaginary, described in detail Jack McMullen's attempts to rape his half-sister more than forty years earlier.

In February 1954 Catherine and Tom left Kate in the care of friends. Catherine's reputation as a chronicler of Tyneside had earned her an invitation to address the South Shields Lecture and Literary Society.

AT first Catherine had resisted the idea of leaving the Hurst and its demanding garden. She had travelled more than three hundred miles to find the house in which her childhood dreams could mature and grow old. Now Tom was asking her to make another journey.

By the summer of 1954 it was becoming obvious that attempting to maintain a fifteen-roomed home for just three people was not only a waste of time, it was a waste of money. They began to look for a smaller house.

Loreto was situated at the end of St Helen's Park Road, an unmade road less than a mile from the Hurst. The house was one of a matching pair given to his two daughters by a shipping magnate. Although smaller it was no less majestic than the Hurst. Built of red brick, the second floor was clad in black and white mock-Tudor beams. The front door was protected by a tiled porch and led to a hall and polished wood staircase. And the kitchen, still the hub of Catherine's home, was warmed by an Aga cooker.

'When we came to look over the house,' recalls Catherine, 'the nurse of the owner said to us: "I would like you to have it because I think that Miss Harrison would like you to have it." '

They moved in November and from the first Catherine wasn't happy. Soon after Tom was decorating and standing on a ladder. The Cookson's first dog, a brindle Staffordshire cross-terrier called Bill, was near-by. 'Bill suddenly started to bark and his bristles were standing up,' said Catherine.

'He wouldn't budge off the stairs. He just refused to move. He growled at something at the bottom of the stairs and suddenly he acted as if someone was stroking him. But there was nobody there.'

The sensation of not being alone in the house continued until Christmas Eve. 'I had a strong feeling of a presence,' Catherine continues. 'I sat down in front of the fire then suddenly turned around and said aloud, "It's all right Miss Harrison, I will look after your house for you." Gradually the presence went away.'

Catherine was also troubled by more earthly imaginings. Tom had decorated the drawing room with some very expensive wallpaper. A few days later Catherine telephoned Peggy Storey, the Writers' Circle friend who had typed her first three handwritten manuscripts, to complain about the paper – 'I don't like it, there are savage-looking bull frogs glaring down at me all day.'

Kate, settled in a downstairs room overlooking the garden, seemed content and happy with her new 'home'.

MACDONALD'S Christmas list for 1954 included a new novel by Catherine Cookson, *A Grand Man*. 'It is not,' she confided, 'my usual type. It is made up entirely of humour and pathos.'

But much more had gone into the tale of an impish little girl with green eyes and ringlets. Catherine was still attempting to use the therapy of exhausting work and non-stop writing as an escape from her depression. She had used the ragged edges of her guilt in *Kate Hannigan*, jotting down memories or passages on scraps of paper after – and frequently during – the housework or gardening. The breakdown continued.

'I wrote *The Fifteen Streets* and brought more in,' she recalls. 'I brought the docks in, I brought the mines in and I brought the men out of work and everything I'd been brought up with. Still the breakdown was with me.

'I should have been rid of these fears. Everything should be clear, it should be marvellous. It wasn't.' Catherine was an orphan to her own memory. 'I couldn't remember one happy incident that had happened in my life. Nothing. Everything I looked back on was black. There was no humour, there was nothing.

'And then I thought well, there was humour. Katie laughed. Katie joked. Katie played. And so I wrote the first of the Mary Ann stories. And I thought "This'll do it." It didn't.'

In May 1954 John Smith had sent a proof copy of the book to Group Film Productions, a J. Arthur Rank company based at Pinewood Studios in the Buckinghamshire countryside west of London. Within days the company had signed a six-month option on the film rights. A decision to proceed with the project was made in August. Filming would begin early in 1955.

The part of Mary Ann Shaughnessy would go to twelve-year-old Jacqueline Ryan, a Dublin convent schoolgirl and daughter of former actress Phyllis Ryan. Her alcoholic father would be played by John Gregson. And Father Owen, the parish priest, would be played by Noel Purcell an Irish character actor. Although

One of Tom's favourite photographs of his wife.
It was taken at Bristol Lodge in 1985 (picture: University of Newcastle)

Straker Street, East Jarrow: Where the chemical fumes burned the McMullen's throats and clogged their lungs

The Ravensworth Arms, Lamesley: Here Kate worked for two years and met her "gentleman" lover. All the female staff shared the cramped attic room (centre)

Leam Lane End – the junction of Leam Lane and the Jarrow Road. On the left is the "Twenty-Seven" public house. The two men have just passed No 5 Leam Lane where Catherine was born

The Jarrow-South Shields tram which Catherine used to take her to school, to the pawn shop – and finally to escape the "squalor and grime" of Tyneside. In the background is the first of the massive Tyne Dock arches

Right: Catherine's grand-mother and step-grandfather, John and Rose McMullen, with their only son, Jack

Jessie Eckford in the doorway of her Phillipson Street shop – recalled as "Cissie Affleck's" in *Our Kate*. Catherine has always refused to acknowledge the existence of the Eckford family

James Eckford's allotment: Here Catherine would often play with Belle Eckford and attend Guy Fawkes night parties. In the background is the rear of Simonside Terrace, on the left Phillipson Street

Harton Workhouse: Feared by John McMullen but where Catherine enjoyed her own room, four meals a day and earned £2 a month

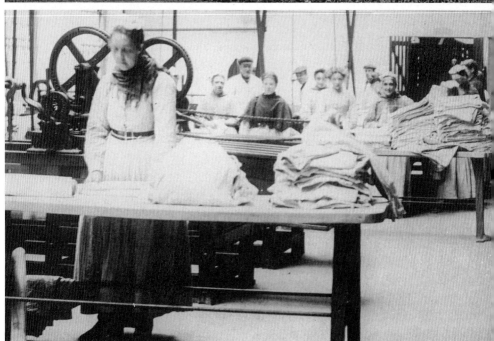

Workhouse inmates in the laundry at Harton: Conditions had changed little since Victorian times. At the back on the right is the glass booth where Catherine was employed as a checker

Catherine aged nineteen: "From the start I noticed how smart
and tidy she was. Her hair and skin were beautiful"

Above: The Clifton Road, Hastings, shop where Catherine rented a first floor bedroom (left). In the doorway is George Morris who shared her interest in books

Right: The Hurst, Hoads Wood Road: The fifteen-roomed mansion beyond the "big red gate" Catherine struggled to turn into a gentleman's residence

One of Tom's pupils snatches a wedding photograph on his Box Brownie
camera as Mr and Mrs Cookson emerge from the church on June 1, 1940.
In the doorway is George Moyle Silverlock, the Hastings workhouse master,
who gave Catherine away

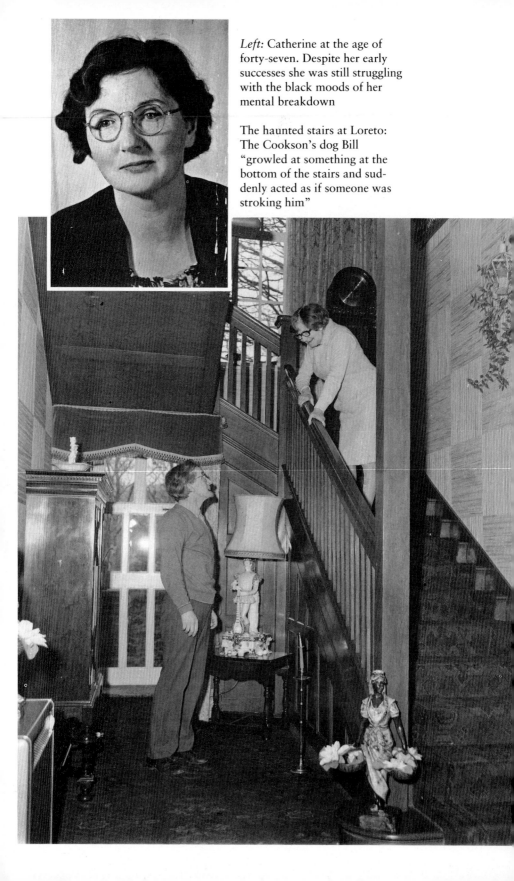

Left: Catherine at the age of forty-seven. Despite her early successes she was still struggling with the black moods of her mental breakdown

The haunted stairs at Loreto: The Cookson's dog Bill "growled at something at the bottom of the stairs and suddenly acted as if someone was stroking him"

Left: The Cooksons, and their dog Simon, at Loreto in Hoads Wood Road. On September 23, 1956, Kate died in her downstairs bedroom – before "the roses had withered" Catherine began work on *Our Kate*

Below: After nearly drowning as a child Catherine bought High Barns at Corbridge because of its heated pool. Her daily swim helped ease the pain in her back and hip (picture: *The Journal*, Newcastle)

Below left: While Catherine worked on her books Tom answered the 3,000 letters and parcels that arrived at High Barns each year. All received a personal reply (picture: *The Journal*, Newcastle)

Melvyn Bragg interviewed Catherine for a South Bank Show documentary. She hoped it would help shed her romantic novelist image, instead "she hated it" (picture: *The Journal*, Newcastle)

Below: In 1984 Catherine agreed to allow a new rose to be named after her – but only if a proportion of the profits went to help children and the disabled (picture: *The Journal*, Newcastle)

Above: Malay-born Prue Clarke was chosen to play Catherine's Tyneside heroine Katie Mulholland. By the end of the 28 Newcastle Playhouse performances all 2,572 tickets had been sold (picture: *The Journal*, Newcastle)

Above: On June 20, 1986, Catherine celebrated her 80th birthday with a special lunch at Corbridge. Her personal guest of honour was Tom – "He has given me his life in order that I have the time to write" (picture: *The Journal*, Newcastle)

In royal company: Catherine holds her god-daughter Elisabette Karina de Roumanie Medforth-Mills. Looking on is King Michael of Romania and the baby's mother, Princess Helen (picture: *The Journal*, Newcastle)

In 1991 Catherine was presented with an honorary doctorate by the Council for National Academic Awards. She had already received an honorary MA degree from Newcastle University (picture: *The Journal*, Newcastle)

January 1, 1993: Dame Catherine Cookson (picture: *The Journal*, Newcastle)

Catherine had no quarrel with the cast, she was unhappy about two of Rank's other decisions.

It was rumoured that pressure from the child star's agent and famous mother was behind a decision to call the film *Jacqueline* instead of *A Grand Man*. Rank also announced it would be setting the film in Belfast instead of Tyneside. Roy Baker, the film's director, explained that with so many Irish actors and actresses among the cast it would have been 'confusing' to stay with the original location.

Catherine worked hard to distil the book into a film script. She also flew to Belfast with production staff to 'get the feel of the place' and made a series of visits to Pinewood where, by March 1955, the last scenes of the film were being shot before editing.

News of the film contract also put Catherine in the firing line as far as newspapers were concerned. Ironically her first mauling at the hands of the press came from the Newcastle-based *Journal*.

The telephone rang. It was John Smith warning her a reporter from the Newcastle *Journal* had attempted to pressure him into giving away how much Catherine had received from Rank for *A Grand Man*. Smith had refused, only to be told the journalist would ask Catherine direct.

'A few minutes later the telephone rang,' recalls Catherine. 'I took John's advice and refused to tell him the amount. Anyway the *Journal* carried a story claiming I had received £5,000, which was a ridiculous figure. You could retire on £5,000 in those days.'

The cheque from J. Arthur Rank had actually been for £750, of which Macdonald was entitled to 25 per cent and her agent 10 per cent of the remainder. For little over £500 Catherine produced the first draft of the script which consisted largely of dialogue lines; a second revised version, and travelled to Belfast to help with the selection of locations.

Catherine remained unhappy about the choice of Jacqueline Ryan to play the title role. She still saw life through Mary Ann Shaughnessy's eyes as very much her own. 'That girl was all wrong,' Catherine admitted years later. 'She was a pudding and I was thin, very thin. She had a mop of hair and I had ringlets.'

Jacqueline was released in the summer of 1956. As the curtain fell on the film's première in London's Leicester Square, Catherine began to think of John McMullen – '*Go on, go on. Either into the clink or into the money'.* 'I suddenly thought that perhaps his prophecy was coming true,' she said.

Unknown to Catherine her growing circle of admirers now included Queen Elizabeth the Queen Mother. During Ascot Week the Queen – prompted by her mother – arranged for a special screening of *Jacqueline* for her guests at Windsor Castle.

A friendship which blossomed from the film was with the 37-year-old John Gregson. A diffident actor with dark curly hair, he had been chosen for the male lead because of his Irish accent. 'He was a lovely man,' remembers Catherine. 'I learned so much from him.' One lesson came during a 'glamour day' shoot for a British women's magazine. During the dinner which followed, Gregson insisted the waiter keep his and Catherine's drinks' bill separate from the rest of the party.

Catherine's books had always prompted a regular supply of letters from her readers. The release of *Jacqueline* brought a new kind of feed-back – not all of it approving. Charles Hardy – who as a child had attended St Peter and Paul's Church at Tyne Dock – wrote to Catherine complaining about the film's change of location. 'I expected her either to ignore my letter, or send me back one just as heated,' he recalled. 'Instead she sent me a very nice note and explained why the alterations had to be made.'

No matter what their opinion of her work, Catherine insisted on replying to every letter in person; a rule she was to obey all her life. It would not be many years before she was forced to curb the invitations to call. But in August 1957, when Hardy and his wife arrived at Loreto, they were treated to a tour of the house and tea in the garden.

In the spring of 1956 Rank expressed an interest in a second Cookson story, *Rooney*. George Brown, who had produced *Jacqueline*, claimed in a newspaper interview that he and Catherine were firm friends. It was to prove a prophetic assumption.

'I bought *A Grand Man* because I was captivated by its warmth and humanity,' said Brown. 'Catherine Cookson writes from the heart. She is one of the few people who can write about working people without being patronising. Her characters are real human beings.' John Gregson once again agreed to play the lead and filming began in the late summer of 1957.

The book was inspired by the scavengers whose long-handled shovels had unseated anyone making use of the backyard toilets at East Jarrow and later the dustmen who emptied the bins at Catherine's Hastings home. 'I thought to myself surely they are entitled to one day of love. One day of happiness. Every working man is entitled to that.'

During filming at Pinewood Studios Barry Fitzgerald – an Irish-American actor visiting Britain – persuaded the producer and director that he should step into the role of 'the father'. It had already been cast with another actor. Catherine was asked to rewrite the script. Despite being ill at the time and committed to other work she agreed. 'It was a hard slog,' she said. 'I worked at it non-stop for three or four days, with Tom feeding me endless cups of coffee.'

Several weeks later John Smith telephoned to ask Catherine if she had received a cheque from the film company. Traditionally all payments were made through her agent. When Smith contacted Rank to find out why Catherine had not been paid for the additional work, he was told they had assumed she 'would do it for nothing' as part of the original deal. 'All I got from them was a bunch of flowers.'

Rank also apparently took Catherine for granted when *Rooney* was released. Instead of the VIP treatment offered to the Cooksons for the première of *Jacqueline*, the couple found themselves sitting with the critics at the second film's London première. In Ireland all mention of Catherine and the original book was dropped from the publicity material.

At the time Catherine diplomatically said she had 'enjoyed' the film. Years later she admitted, 'The film was very disappointing. It was not my story.'

Artistically *Rooney* was a flop. For Rank it became a financial disaster. Only one or two copies of the film still exist and television companies consider it so bad it has been refused even an off-peak screening.

The experience left Catherine bitter. 'The way they treated me was scandalous,' she said. 'I vowed then that I would never deal with J. Arthur Rank again and I never have. I would not let them film one of my books even if I was starving.'

The film adaptation of *Rooney* produced one beneficial spin-off. John Smith managed to persuade Corgi to take the book, the first time the paperback rights of a Cookson novel had been sold. For *Rooney*, Corgi paid an advance of £150 against royalties of one and seven eighths (old) pence on home sales and one and a quarter pence on export sales. It would be another eleven years before the appearance of a second Cookson paperback.

After *Rooney*, Group Films quietly allowed its option on a third Cookson book, *The Menagerie*, to lapse.

The suggestion that Catherine had received £5,000 for the film rights and work she did in adapting *A Grand Man* rankled for a second reason – it was exactly the sum Catherine had set her heart on saving to allow Tom to retire from teaching.

Since the late 1920s Tom had suffered from severe migraine. The attacks – which sometimes started while he was asleep in the early hours of the morning – usually consisted of a series of blinding peaks clustered together over three or four days. Work was impossible. All Tom could do until the pain eased was to sit upright in a darkened room, unable to lie down or rest, his eyes streaming with tears. The slightest movement of his head would trigger a fresh attack.

Although the Cooksons enjoyed the exercise and achievement gardening gave them, Catherine could never fully appreciate her husband's enthusiasm for the open countryside. She once conceded: 'Tom wants to stop the car if he sees wild roses. I get much more excited crossing the ferry or seeing cranes and gantries.'

For nine years Tom had been helping to run the 24th Hastings troop as an assistant scoutmaster. When the 1955–6 school year started he agreed to take over as scoutmaster. His enthusiasm and obvious pleasure at working with youngsters kept the troop near strength. The summer camps continued. In 1956 the troop spent a fortnight at Petworth. The Cotswolds, the Wye Valley, Exmoor and the Dorset coast all followed. Tom also inherited the troop's annual pantomime – 'a kind of January saturnalia' – for which he acted as stage manager.

BY June 1952, one million letters had arrived at the Surrey home and sanctuary of spiritualist Harry Edwards, asking for advice and guidance.

Catherine first wrote to Edwards several years earlier when she failed to trace the woman 'healer' who had so successfully treated her for the antrum infection. A short, round, silver-haired man, Edwards was an accomplished medium and writer and the country's leading spiritualist. His letters, as ever, were strong and calm and promised unseen help.

Edwards first became aware of his healing powers with the Army in the Middle East. Born in 1893, he served in the First World War and eventually found himself in Persia. When a Muslim priest brought his son to Edwards with an abscess, he could do nothing more than cut open the boy's foot with his razor and clean the wound. The boy felt no pain and quickly recovered. More patients followed, among them a shiekh's mother. Edwards, equipped only with bandages, castor oil and iodine, was amazed at how innocent faith in their new-found Hakim – or healer – could apparently cure the most painful conditions.

In 1946 Edwards purchased Burrows Lea – not dissimilar in appearance to the Hurst – situated in the Surrey stockbroker belt and surrounded by fourteen acres of grassland and trees. Working from the quiet of the Healing Sanctuary at the house, Edwards began a remarkable career of delivering hope and strength to thousands in physical and mental pain.

He filled the next thirty years with public demonstrations of healing in almost every town and village in Britain. Towards the end of 1948 he took part in the world's largest healing demonstration at the King's Hall in Belle Vue, Manchester. The press were not convinced. The majority of the 6,000 who attended needed no further persuasion of his powers.

On the one occasion Catherine attended a Sunday afternoon healing session in the theatre at Hastings Pier, Edwards's touch and confident words failed to bring any lasting relief. The experience did release a conviction that he was far more than a simple faith healer. Edwards, Catherine remains convinced, acted as a lightning rod for a far greater force. His was not the original power, but an ability to make things happen, to 'open doors'. She hesitates to call that force God. In *Let Me Make Myself Plain* Catherine asks: 'As I am an agnostic to Christianity so I am an agnostic to Spiritualism; yet can I say I am an agnostic to what is called Spiritual Healing?'

The conviction that certain people can help channel this mystic power has remained with Catherine for the rest of her life. Two episodes during the 1950s convinced her that faith was more potent than prayers.

In 1953 Catherine decided Kate should live at the Hurst. She was concerned about the practicalities of the journey south and the prospect of her mother once again dominating her life. Catherine sought Edwards's advice. His reply was characteristically simple – 'You will be helped.'

The task, which involved two separate train journeys and a connecting ride across London, was accomplished with ease. Ambulances were waiting at each station. Railway staff cheerfully helped to manoeuvre the overweight patient in and out of carriages. Even Kate appeared to enjoy the extra attention.

The second episode took place on a Sunday afternoon in 1955. Catherine, dressed in her nightgown, was lying on the living-room couch watching Tom through the window as he cut the grass. Unwell before the trip to Ulster for Rank, she was admitted to hospital soon after her return. She considered she had let Tom down and blamed herself for not giving him the children he rightly deserved. Their oldest son, had he survived, would have been thirteen, old enough to be helping Tom in the garden. On Wednesday Catherine was due to be admitted to hospital once more, this time to have a hysterectomy – 'to be finished as a woman'. She had written to Harry Edwards, but had not yet received a reply.

From within a voice ordered her to 'Get up and go into the garden and put your hands into the earth.' Catherine obeyed. Tom, apparently powerless to stop his wife, brought her a cushion to kneel on. Catherine continued to weed the border and touch the soil for an hour. On Monday the urge overcame her a second time.

Edwards's reply from Burrows Lea arrived in the first post on Tuesday morning. He told Catherine not to worry and reassured her that she was already being helped. The bleeding had stopped. Catherine cancelled the operaton.

A YEAR later – on 16 March 1956 – Mary Ann Shaughnessy made her second appearance in *The Lord and Mary Ann*, this time set on a farm in some indeterminate county between Jarrow and Newcastle. Away from the temptations of the town Mary Ann's father must surely turn into the angelic being she knows him to be.

Catherine wove into Mary Ann many of her own experiences, and many of the sensations, feelings and fears she could not yet admit to. 'As a small child Mary Ann is me,' Catherine admitted to one journalist many years later. 'Her ingenious way of working things round to involve God is very much me. Her fear and reaction to drink is very much how I used to feel.'

Catherine, much like Mary Ann, was not averse to teasing her readers. At the beginning of *A Grand Man* she states:

> *Everthing in this story is fictitious,*
> *except that which you yourself know to be true.*

And, carrying the joke through to the end of the second Mary Ann book, she concludes:

> *Well, it'll serve you right if nothing nice ever happens to you; it will so.*

John Smith was quick to exploit the universal appeal of his client's books. *The Fifteen Streets* had already been translated into French and *A Grand Man* was published in America six months after it appeared in Britain. By 1958 both Mary Ann books had also appeared in Italy and Germany.

Smith did not neglect the British market. In 1955, as *Jacqueline* was being edited at Pinewood Studios, he persuaded *Woman's Hour* to use a two-week serialisation of *A Grand Man*. The following year millions of listeners were treated to *The Lord and Mary Ann*.

Catherine and Tom desperately needed a break. Three years of nursing Kate, while keeping secret her stomach cancer, had made their patience brittle, as had Kate's stoic attempts to earn her keep. With Tom as the 'breadwinner' and her conviction that Catherine should now spend all her time writing, Kate saw it as her duty to help around the house.

Catherine and Tom were now convinced a person's health and energy could be enhanced by the food they ate. They had, for several years, followed the advice of American nutritionist and vegetarian writer Gaylord Hauser, in many ways a man thirty years ahead of his time. It was a philosophy alien to Kate, who still believed a meal wasn't adequate unless it included meat and was smothered in thick gravy.

Kate had also begun to cling to her daughter. It was as if her fears of dying unloved and alone in the Stoddard Street flat had returned to haunt her. She fretted when Catherine left Loreto to do the shopping or call at the library. Even being left in her downstairs room for too long prompted a sarcastic remark. The Cooksons booked a week's boating holiday on the River Cam between Cambridge and the small cathedral city of Ely. A family of friends were to move in to look after Kate.

In the days before their departure Catherine endured her mother's irrational fears and tearful pleas. Kate's qualms finally turned to defiance. Catherine and Tom were barely out of sight before she had telephoned and ordered a delivery of whisky. When they arrived home the following Saturday – Kate's seventy-second birthday – it was obvious that the free supply of alcohol had taken its toll.

The following day Kate looked unwell. She was scratchy and could not settle. On Wednesday she got up and insisted she would do the ironing. Within minutes she was sick, the vomit stained with blood. Catherine's regular doctor was away. When another local doctor arrived – a large-framed, bearded man – Kate took to him immediately. He held her hand and laughed at her jokes and prescribed ice with a little brandy.

Catherine and Tom sat beside the bed in the corner of the room throughout Thursday night. Kate continued to vomit. On Friday she slipped in and out of consciousness. In one brief period of lucidity, 'she held my hand', Catherine recalls in her auto-biography, 'and said that she had been a wicked woman'.

Kate never regained consciousness. She died at one o'clock on Sunday, 23 September.

Catherine's guilt overwhelmed her. She felt she had failed her promise to keep her mother alive and had misused their final years together.

'She was with me and I wanted her to die,' said Catherine. 'But once I got her back to the Hurst I thought, "No, she mustn't die. She must live and we must get to know each other." And I had given up God, the Catholic Church, but I prayed and I said, "Give me a chance, too."'

'I needed to find myself as much as I needed to understand her, because she had had one hell of a life. A really terrible life. I don't know how she even suffered it. And so, for three years, we lived together and we had peace and we laughed and we joked.'

There were still so many unanswered questions, so many things Catherine wanted to know about her father, but Kate was gone and she was free. The downstairs room her mother had occupied was empty. The last of the autumn roses were tapping at the window. Yet Catherine could still see Kate around the house, hear her voice. It was as if Kate were telling her, 'Write all down Hinny, write it all down.'

Before the roses had withered Catherine moved her Victorian davenport writing desk into the room. Each day she remembered –and watched – and attempted to lay Kate's guilty and humiliating ghost to rest. She poured it all out. And with the resentment came the tears. 'When I read the first draft I felt relieved, but I thought I could never publish this. It was full of bitterness. The bitterness came up off the page.' She put the manuscript aside.

In May 1958 Catherine and Tom were back on Tyneside – this time in response to a spur-of-the-moment telephone call. The South Shields Branch of the Infantile Paralysis Fellowship had needed a star to open its fate at Hedworth Hall. The request, at seven days' notice, coincided with a Hastings Grammar School holiday.

Catherine had taken a Pygmalion theme for her third Mary Ann novel. Delivered to Macdonald earlier in the year, it appeared on the bookshop shelves in time for the Christmas rush. Mary Ann is growing up. Attempts by well-meaning helpers to turn her into a lady only succeed in uniting *The Devil and Mary Ann*.

Once again John Smith approached the BBC. In October *Woman's Hour* continued the adventures of Mary Ann Shaughnessy. In eight years the BBC had serialised four of Catherine's books.

VARIOUS attempts to cauterise the blood vessels in Catherine's nose had failed to cure the bleeding. As she grew older she frequently sensed the metallic taste of blood in her mouth, and her tongue had also begun to seep blood.

It wasn't until after the war, when Catherine returned to the

Hurst, that she noticed a tiny red mark about an eighth-of-an-inch across below her left eye. Within three years she had developed several more, on the left side of her face, her lip and even on her tongue. When another appeared on her neck, Catherine went to her doctor. He dismissed them as 'age creeping on'.

It was becoming increasingly difficult to hide the blemishes under her make-up. Shortly after Kate's death Catherine decided it was time to consult a doctor again. She had still not connected her bleeding with the red marks. This time she was referred to a hospital specialist, who instantly diagnosed the cause as hereditary haemorrhagic telangiectasia.

First identified in 1901 by one of the century's leading physicians, William Osler, telangiectasia involves bleeding problems caused by abnormal blood vessels. Although rare, it is a well-recognised 'dominant' genetic disease which can be dangerous if a blood vessel breaks in a vital place, such as the brain.

Two, or even three, years earlier the news would have pushed Catherine back toward the edge. It was eleven years since the onset of her breakdown. In that time she had undergone repeated surgery; endured a premature menopause; contracted neuritis, a disease of the nervous system which produces muscle weakness and loss of sensation in the skin; developed mastitis after a gardening accident, and caught mange from her dog. She was in almost constant pain from the childhood leg injury. But above all she had survived Kate's death and the guilt of her passing. Catherine decided that putting a name to a condition she had lived with since her late teens was not going to make her give back the ground she had fought so hard to win.

TOM had spent the afternoon watching a football match. He returned to Loreto to find Catherine weeping uncontrollably.

'What's the matter?' Tom asked his wife, fearing the worst.

'I've just killed Fanny off,' Catherine stammered through her sobs.

For twelve months she had been working on *Fanny McBride*, the story of a large and indomitable Jarrow widow with an equally large and cheerful family.

Catherine never hesitated to use a character in more than one novel. In the tight, back-to-back communities she wrote about it offered her readers a sense of scandal, of catching up on the latest gossip.

Fanny McBride first appeared in *A Grand Man*. She lived below the Shaughnessys' attic flat in Mulhattan's Hall and won Mary Ann's heart when she dismissed Mike Shaughnessy's drinking and announced 'apart from that there's not a better fellow living'. Catherine had used the character – one of her favourites – in *The Lord and Mary Ann* and *The Devil and Mary Ann*. It was time, she decided, to give Fanny a book of her own.

The Shaughnessys have moved out of Mulhattan's Hall and 'she missed them in more ways than one'. Fanny turns fifty and, for the first time, begins to feel a little lonely. With all but one of her children married and gone from home she has time on her hands, too much even for the long-standing feud with Nellie Flannagan. Fanny takes a job at the local 'Ladies' – only to find it a surprisingly stimulating experience.

Catherine had never tried to pigeon-hole her writing. She was simply attempting to write about an area and the people she knew best. While out shopping in St Leonards one day she suddenly noticed a woman in tweeds and brogues and wearing a collar and tie striding toward her. 'Ah!' said the woman, deliberately blocking her path, 'Mrs Cookson, the regional writer.'

The woman demanded to know why all of Catherine's novels were set in the North-East. 'Can't you write about any other place than the North-East?' After a few minutes' heated discussion the pair headed in opposite directions up London Road. Before she reached home Catherine was determined to show the woman she could give her stories any location she wished.

For weeks Catherine gathered material for a story about the Hastings fishing fleet. She made contact with the fishermen and clambered over their vessels. She watched the early morning unloading of the catches and talked to the men who bought and sold the fish. And she spent hours browsing in the cluster of chandlers' stores near the harbour.

Six months later Catherine abandoned the idea. 'The only thing in the story that had any guts was the fish,' she admitted years later. 'I was a regional writer. I couldn't write about any other place but the dirty, backward North-East.'

But it was Tom's insistence on spending their summer holidays afloat which finally produced his wife's only book set entirely outside the region.

John Smith had been asked if Catherine would consider writing a romantic novel. The advance on offer was £150 and the book was to be serialised before publication. They both agreed any lighter work should be kept separate from her Catherine Cookson stories; which left the question of a suitable pen name. 'I couldn't think of a name so John said he would find me one,' explained Catherine. 'In the end he came up with Marchant. I thought it was terrible. I hated it. I still do.'

Attempts to drain the trackless fens of eastern England several centuries earlier had been harassed by independent and solitary men who inhabited the windswept wastelands. They employed cunning and craftiness to halt the excavation of their domain and frequently resorted to murder. These early environmental guerrillas had earned the name 'Fen Tigers'.

The legend fascinated Catherine as she and Tom cruised the Fenland waterways for their summer holiday. Transposing the character of these rough, crude individuals to the present day, she created Michael Bradshaw, the *Fen Tiger* of the title.

The story appeared as a serial in *Woman's Own*. It was published in 1963 by Macdonald as a Catherine Marchant novel.

Writing the story at least took Catherine's mind off her fear of water. The sheltered fens were calmer than her pre-war Channel crossings, but she still closed her eyes each evening amazed she had not fallen overboard and awoke the next morning thankful to find the boat still afloat.

In 1958 – at the age of fifty-two – Catherine decided that if the boating holidays were to continue she should at last learn to swim. After twenty lessons she finally overcame her lifelong fear of water and swam away from the edge of the pool at Hastings Baths. Swimming became her daily exercise. 'My body became stronger,' said Catherine, 'even the blood disease wasn't such a problem. I felt invigorated, a younger woman.'

The swimming also eased the chronic osteoarthritis in her leg and spine. The disease had classically first shown itself during her menopause. At times the pain was so severe Catherine could not even go shopping without Tom having to lift her legs in and out of the car.

While on holiday in Norfolk, something else caught Catherine's eye. Sitting on their hired cabin cruiser or walking the banks in the summer sunshine she and Tom had often noticed the flash of an eel in the shallow water. The Fen locals had a name for them – Slinky Janes.

The name fascinated her. In April 1959 she introduced her readers to her own *Slinky Jane*. From the very first paragraph Catherine sets a new tone of voice.

> *The village of Battenbun lies on a hillside in Northumberland. The village proper is shaped like a half moon, with its back closely wooded, and houses two-thirds of the population of a hundred and seventy-four; which number includes Tilly Boyle's son, Tony the half-wit, seven children of Mamie Spragg, each of whom just fails to qualify for the pseudonym of Tony Boyle, sixty women over fifty, fourteen men over sixty, eight over seventy and one coming up to ninety.*

Her characters still share the prejudices and weaknesses of her earlier books, but the story is light-hearted and teasing. It also allows the 'clown' inside her the chance to do what Catherine has always wanted – 'to make people laugh'.

The story centres around a giant eel found in the lake behind the village, where no eel has ever been seen before, and the sudden arrival of a slim, attractive woman in an ailing Alvis car. The mysterious traveller decides to stay until her car is repaired. Her attraction is as magnetic as the eel's, prompting the women of the village to speculate whether Slinky Jane is fish or female.

In many ways Catherine had inadvertently captured the first faint spirit of the impending Sixties. When *Slinky Jane* was published as a paperback in 1967 Tandem made full use of its suggestive title. By the time it had reached its seventh reprint in 1975 – three during 1971 alone – the demure front cover had been replaced by the photograph of a young couple in a sexual embrace and a *Sunday Express* quotation in praise of 'a comic, rumbustious novel'.

But the new decade – and the influx of younger, less traditional decision-makers – ended Catherine's attempts to break into television. Her treatment by J. Arthur Rank had left her embittered, but it also left her with a taste for screenwriting. More than ten years after she had turned her back on the stilted characters of her stage plays, Catherine was exploring a new way of bringing her stories to the screen.

Using the experience she had gained writing the screenplays for *Jacqueline* and *Rooney*, Catherine started work on the first of two plays for television. Both scripts initially found favour. 'The producer, who liked them very much, intended to use them,' said Catherine. 'But with a change of producer they were put "on one side" and I never afterwards bothered about them.'

There was another reason for their ultimate rejection. The public, it was deemed, wanted reality not nostalgia. If they were to be made to feel guilty, they should at least get a thrill from the experience. A young television executive at the time recalls: 'They [the scripts] were certainly well written – but there wasn't enough sex in them.'

Eleven

This morning I don't feel any joy but I have an idea for a story, which is the next best thing.

THE 1960S WAS to prove a decade of pain for Catherine. It would also become one of her most successful.

Although Catherine had vowed never to allow Rank to turn another of her stories into a film her agent, John Smith, was still attempting to sell *The Fifteen Streets* to a different company. It would be another twenty-nine years before the novel was eventually adapted, this time for television and not cinema audiences.

Her own attempts to make use of her film-industry experiences were abandoned – on doctor's orders. Catherine had accepted an invitation from the South Shields Lecture and Literary Society to speak after its annual meeting in late March. The title of her speech was to have been 'From Paupers to Pinewood'. Instead Catherine spent the week in bed at Loreto.

Since the completion of the first draft during 1957, Catherine had periodically returned to work on her autobiographical manuscript. She was already calling it *Our Kate*. The book's subject was also influencing her fiction. *Fenwick Houses* – published on 5 October 1960 – is the first novel in which aspects of Kate's character and experiences can clearly be identified.

Christine Winter lives in a row of pit cottages somewhere on Tyneside. She is the daughter of respectable parents who struggle to prevent her from coming into contact with the unsavoury side of life.

Christine fights off the amorous attentions of one of the boys next door, the rough and uncouth Don Dowling, while treating with deep affection the devotion of his gentle brother Sam. She becomes the victim of her misguided love when she gives birth to a child, whose father, a youth of breeding and education, deserts her.

After the untimely death of her mother, Christine drifts from one difficulty to another. With the war come the soldiers, and in her desire to escape her unhappy past and the memory of the man she should have married she seeks solace in the 'bottle'. Finally Christine becomes enmeshed in the fruits of her own weaknesses.

Not long after the publication of *Fenwick Houses* Catherine developed a cold. Bed rest failed to ease the symptoms. She continued to write despite a high temperature and a painful chest.

Tom finally persuaded his wife to see a doctor. When he arrived it was obvious Catherine had more than a simple cold – she had been fighting pneumonia. Her blood condition also produced a reaction to the antibiotics. Catherine felt as though she were dying.

Seven days later she forced herself into Hastings to deliver a promised speech at a Conservative luncheon. On 11 November – still weak and desperately tired – she was back on Tyneside.

Unknown to Catherine, the April meeting of the South Shields Lecture and Literary Society had elected her president in her absence. Instead of a post-meeting speech the members now expected a presidential address. Catherine gave them 'Child of the Tyne', delivered in her best dialect.

It was the distance between her childhood and her adult home, she told the society members, which helped her focus her memories while writing. And in an interview with the Newcastle *Journal* she conceded: 'I think one sees Tyneside better at a distance. One uses the imagination. I have no difficulty seeing my characters.'

Indeed they were all around her. 'When I was last in Jarrow,' she admitted to another newspaper, 'I walked about the old places and I thought the old days and the old characters had gone. Suddenly I saw a woman coming out of a shop and she was the image of Fanny McBride.'

Arriving at the New Buildings, Catherine discovered the cornfield opposite William Black Street had disappeared and the pubs near the dock had been demolished. She felt that 'gradually the old, intimate community spirit is breaking up'.

In the same interview she made her readers a promise she was to keep for more than thirty years. 'I have more stories in me than I have years to write.'

Forcing herself to keep that promise – and hoping she would be strong enough – produced a unique and final anger in Catherine she would never forget.

Illness and injury had dogged her throughout 1960. Despite the material success there had been very few good days. Beneath it all she could feel the panic of her years of depression. The endless blackness of the late 1940s might have gone, but the self-doubts remained. Why bother? Where was it all leading? What was it for? It was as though she was being cheated of the inner calm her daily writing sessions gave her.

Catherine was standing at a window, watching the garden and the trees she loved. Suddenly, from within, she became aware of an angry presence; fighting back; demanding peace; refusing to listen to the angry voices. A new strength had taken control. 'I had left the bottom,' Catherine accepted many years later. 'I had left the bottom.'

Part of that new confidence came from a surge in her output. Her first sixteen books, including the rejected *Annie Hannigan*, were all written in longhand. Each story would take twelve months from beginning to publication. In May 1961 she was to suffer from a minor ailment which would force a major change to the practical side of her writing.

Catherine had harnessed the energy and endurance she had inherited from Kate to drive herself relentlessly through the days of her breakdown. She thought nothing of mowing the lawn in the evening before returning to the kitchen to prepare supper for her husband, while her mind relentlessly formed and reformed the next chapter of her latest book. Marriage, Catherine believed, was a partnership, yet there were parts of it her working-class upbringing refused to relinquish. 'My husband expects me to run the house and quite rightly too,' she said.

Her workload was intense. *Love and Mary Ann* was in the final stages of publication; she was literally writing *Life and Mary Ann*; accepting numerous speaking engagements, and still finding time to produce pieces for a woman's magazine. For the first time in her life the act of writing was proving painful. Suddenly, and without warning, the muscles in her wrist and hand would tighten and contract. Catherine had developed writer's cramp, an affliction already recognised as an industrial disease. More serious was the discomfort in her shoulder. Despite being prescribed pain-killers, the interruptions to her daily output grew steadily longer. Catherine began to imagine her writing career was over.

After a month of growing frustration, Tom suggested a possible solution. Catherine, he said, should return to basics. She should 'write' her stories in the most natural way possible – by speaking them. She acquired a bulky, reel-to-reel tape recorder. At first Catherine was hesitant. 'I didn't know then that a new world was opening up for me,' she explained later in *Catherine Cookson Country*.

For many years Catherine had read her stories aloud, 'to get the flavour of them'. Instead of seeing them – hearing them – she was at last able to live them. 'I could feel through my voice their emotions, their laughter, their humour, their sorrows, their joys . . .'

Altough her regular typist now transcribed the tape recording as the first draft, the new technique did nothing to hold back Catherine's productivity. When she was in what she described as 'grand fettle' she continued until exhaustion drove her to bed. 'The most I ever dictated in one day was 15,000 words, but I was completely exhausted at the end of it.'

The clumsy tape recorder – later exchanged for a modern dictating machine – only made the initial creation faster. Once the tapes had been transcribed she would go back, slowly and carefully, correcting and redrafting. 'I never do fewer than four corrections.'

To relax Catherine spent many hours in the garden, where the scent of wild flowers allowed to grow on the grassy bank opposite the side of the house mingled with the crisp, sea air. The Cooksons had extended Loreto's garden since they moved in to almost two acres by taking over adjacent plots. Their latest project was the construction of a rambling walk through the trees between the road and the house. By the early 1970s they had cultivated more than 2,000 azaleas and planted 10,000 daffodil bulbs.

Catherine had also found another way to relax. She had a full-size billiard table installed in a first-floor room and regularly challenged Tom. 'I love billiards,' she said. 'It was a great thrill when I made a break of twenty-seven. I completely relax during a game.'

ONE Christmas, early in the 1960s, saw the arrival of all of Tom's family at Loreto – unaware they were about to be bugged.

The couple had decided to make the festival something special. Tom cut the top from one of the garden's pine trees for the house and decorated the rest of the trees near the house with coloured lights. Catherine busied herself preparing the accommodation and food for her twelve guests.

Tom's family sat down to Christmas dinner unaware he had hidden Catherine's tape recorder under the table and placed the microphones around the room. 'When we played it back later everyone fell about laughing,' said Catherine. 'They were with us for four days and it was a wonderful time.'

The next Christmas Tom's relatives arrived once again. This time the magic was shattered by Catherine's lingering nightmare of her lost babies.

Tom, who had also suffered badly before the holiday with his recurrent migraine, had been unable to decorate the garden.

During the year his half-sister had married and had a baby, whom she brought with her. In the excitement and fuss someone attempted to pass the baby to Catherine. She backed away. The more the family pressed the child on her the more Catherine panicked. Only Tom understood the rejection which shocked his relatives.

Catherine recalled the incident: 'They just seemed to think I was being silly and hard, not wanting to take the baby, but I just couldn't. For years after that I couldn't hold a baby. It took a long time for Tom's family to forgive me.'

CATHERINE and her stories became regular features of BBC radio broadcasts.

In 1961 *Woman's Hour* serialised *Fanny McBride*. It was followed six months later by a two-week reading of *Love and Mary Ann*. Catherine herself made two broadcasts in 1962: "The first in March as *Woman's Hour* guest of the week, and then in June, when it broadcast her reading of 'The Day of the Party', taken from her still unpublished autobiography.

At the beginning of December 1962, *Woman's Hour* began an eight-part reading of *Life and Mary Ann*. The actress chosen to narrate the book was Isla Cameron, a Scots-born adopted Geordie.

Almost thirty years later, Catherine finds it hard to recall all her work for the BBC. Despite the corporation's daily records, two 1963 items – listed as 'romance' – escape her: a *Woman's Hour* broadcast entitled 'The Train to South Shields' and a similar recording, later repeated, for a programme called *Home for the Day*.

In September 1963 Catherine made use of more material from the autobiography she was still revising. This time listeners to the hour-long woman's programme were treated to 'Me Granda'. Six months later they heard 'Up the Creek'. North-East listeners also heard a review of her latest book – *The Blind Miller* – on the regional programme *Voice of the North*.

After a gap of almost a year Catherine once again persuaded the producer of *Woman's Hour* to take one of her talks. Unlike her early contributions her latest – 'Thursday's Child Has Far to Go – was pre-recorded. 'Playgrounds' was broadcast twice in 1965, once on *Woman's Hour* and a month later on the morning edition of *Home for the Day*.

THROUGHOUT 1960 Catherine had been working on her most ambitious novel.

She had not yet been afflicted by the painful wrist and shoulder which forced her to give up writing by hand. *The Garment* – her fourteenth book – was eventually published in April 1962.

It received immediate acclaim. One national reviewer compared its 'eruption of natural forces' with the plays of Sophocles and the stories and novels of D. H. Lawrence. Another said, 'It is a tragedy full of foreboding from the beginning, which still leaves the reader wondering, "What could anyone have done to prevent it?" '

The Garment came as a deep shock to those who judged Catherine's work on the light charm and bubbling enthusiasm of her recent books. It is the study of a complete egotist, blind to his own selfishness and, at the same time, clever enough to get away with it.

The time of the story is the years before, during and after the Second World War. The setting is a small Northumberland village. The character who dominates the novel is the parson Donald Rouse.

Growing contempt for her husband's impotence and her own

need for children propels Grace Rouse into a passionate love affair with Andrew MacIntyre, a man who has neither the charm nor education of her husband. What he does possess is the warmth and natural human intelligence the parson lacks. Separation is impossible. When Grace has children Donald Rouse gives them his name but, at the same time, attempts to alienate them from their mother.

He is a man who will not – and cannot – stand criticism. He hates his wife not for her infidelity, but because she knows the truth about him. Rouse is also able to manipulate the forces of a society too ready to support him.

With the physical restrictions lifted from her writing, Catherine's output was slowed only by the bottleneck of publication. The six months between November 1963 and May 1964 saw the appearance of three new Cookson stories.

In *The Blind Miller* Catherine returns to the mythical Fifteen Streets. The main character is equally familiar. Sarah, a staunch Catholic, reaches womanhood in the hard years between the two World Wars. Born at the lower end of the streets, and dominated by a brutish stepfather, she marries a kind and gentle man.

House of Men – published four months later in February 1964 – was her third Catherine Marchant story.

May saw the publication of *Hannah Massey*, the story of a family head who is proud and crafty, ignorant and intensely ambitious, a born ruler of her working-class County Durham household who demands blind family loyalty in the face of unreasonable demands.

To Catherine's surprise, her Mary Ann stories were more popular abroad than they were at home. Even before its publication in Britain late in 1964 John Smith had negotiated the translation into German of *Marriage and Mary Ann*. All five previous Mary Ann titles had been bestsellers in West Germany where, unlike Britain, they had been taken up by book clubs and issued in omnibus editions.

In 1965 Catherine – writing as Catherine Marchant – published *Evil at Roger's Cross* in the United States. Lighter and more romantic than the bulk of her work, it nevertheless used traditional themes of conflicting personalities and a legacy of old wrongs. The story – set in the English Lake District – was eventually published in Britain twelve years later as *The Iron Façade*.

Her writing had kept her away from the North-East. It was time, Macdonald's publicity department reasoned, for a tour of the region in which her books were most popular.

In July 1965 Catherine returned to Tyneside for the first time in five years. Between visits to relatives and old friends, the Cooksons were scheduled for what seemed an endless round of interviews and book-signing sessions.

Among her titles targeted for promotion was *Matty Doolin*, Catherine's first attempt at a story for younger readers, which had been published the previous month. Matty is a fifteen-year-old boy who lives in Brinkburn Street, Tyne Dock, and who passionately wants to train as a vet. His father has other ideas – 'at fifteen he should be earning good money in the docks'.

Despite brisk initial sales *The Long Corridor* – published in April – proved a disappointment to many of Catherine's regular readers. The story is only lightly set in the North-East, with a brief reference to Newcastle. Most felt that after the success of *The Garment* further examination of a contemptuous egotist and the darker side of human nature was unnecessary.

Once again the Cooksons stayed with Dr Mannie Anderson and his wife, Rita, at their South Shields home. Anderson, a hospital doctor, had first met Catherine in the early 1950s. He had impressed her with his dedication to his patients, unhesitatingly answering calls at any hour of the day or night. Catherine had repaid the couple's friendship by dedicating *Fanny McBride* to them. Anderson had also been chairman of the town's Lecture and Literary Society during Catherine's presidency.

She also found time to visit Lily Bulloch with whom, forty-five years earlier as Lily Maguire, she had shared the bicycle rides around the County Durham countryside. It was Lily's sister Maisie who had laboured over the 16,520 words of Catherine's first complete story.

Catherine was not impressed by the bore of revitalisation which was sweeping away the narrow streets and grubby alleys. The 'mucky North' was awash with reform and Sixties vision.

The rolling, sooty landscape was now punctuated with tower blocks – 'thousand-eyed monsters', a sky-line a nation would soon recognise as the back-drop to the television comedy series *The Likely Lads*. 'But older Tynesiders,' said Catherine fearfully, 'I just can't see them living there somehow. I can't fit them into these masses of concrete. These places are just like ant heaps.'

Catherine gratefully returned to her St Helen's Park Road home, Simon her golden labrador and her sixteen-hour working day.

Other parts of old Tyneside were also disappearing. In 1966 a blaze swept through St Peter and Paul's School at Tyne Dock. It left the building so badly damaged it had to be demolished. Only weeks later William McAnany, who had approached Catherine at the instigation of her parish priest, was also dead.

Catherine had decided on a higher social stratum for her next book, completed before her new look at Tyneside. Set in a northern town, somewhere near Newcastle, *The Unbaited Trap* was published in June 1966.

It centres on the life and loneliness of a solicitor, loneliness which is the direct result of a wife who, deprived of one form of emotional outlet, concentrates her affection on their only son and on being the perfect hostess within their small circle of friends. The underlying reason for this marital discontent is known only to the solicitor and his wife.

IT was a bitterly cold day. Tom and Catherine were working in the garden at Loreto. As she cleared the summer debris, Catherine's mind repeatedly returned to the 'big story' playing again and again inside her head.

Part of her Tyneside heritage had included lessons and stories about Hadrian's Wall. Constructed by the Romans to keep out the marauding Picts, its easternmost end had been discovered in Swan Hunter's shipyard at Wallsend across the river from Jarrow and Tyne Dock. Catherine wanted to open her new story among the Roman inhabitants of the wall and ending it in the early years of the twentieth century. She had consulted her agent John Smith and John Foster White, her editor at Macdonald. They differed in their opinions of a story with such a vast time-scale.

Tom and Catherine retreated to Loreto's kitchen, warmed by the Aga cooker. As Tom lifted a hot-plate cover to put on the kettle for a cup of tea, his wife shared her misgivings about her new book.

Never doubting Catherine's ability as a story-teller, Tom had his own idea of where the saga should begin. 'You're always talking about Palmer's shipyard in Jarrow,' he said. 'Why don't you just bring the story to the last century and start it there?' Catherine instantly knew he was right.

The exploits – and hardships – of the workers who funnelled down Jarrow's Ellison Street and into Palmer's shipyard and iron works each day had been woven into the fabric of Catherine's early years as tightly as those of the dockers. In many ways the yard's decline paralled her own disillusionment with Tyneside.

Catherine plunged herself into research. She needed to discover the missing years and the secret of Palmer's success. She contacted Sir Charles Palmer's grandson and read Jarrow MP Ellen Wilkinson's *Politics* and its condemnation of the yard's management and misrule and final bankruptcy in 1934.

Eighteen months of research were followed by the relentless slog of dictating 1,500 words each day followed by re-reading and polishing. 'After ten writings, re-writings, editings and cuttings, I was throughly sick of it,' she openly admitted.

The completed manuscript was 275,000 words long, the equivalent of 750 printed pages. Set in Jarrow and South Shields and spanning the vast social revolution between 1860 and 1944.

But the depth of research brought with it problems as well as praise. Twenty years later, in *Catherine Cookson Country*, the writer admitted, 'It had been the most difficult story to write in the first place . . . in the end I felt I could speak for the working man – and also make pig iron.'

As she worked her way through the story, Catherine discovered, quite involuntarily, her characters were taking over the plot: 'Katie absolutely dominated the book, which turned out to be six books representing six different periods of her life.'

She chose to give her heroine, Katie, the same name as her mother. The opening sequences are located on the high ground around Simonside where Catherine went to school and overlooking the New Buildings and Jarrow Slake. There are other, more private, similarities.

It is 1860 and Katie Mulholland is a fifteen-year-old scullery maid at Greenall Manor, the home of a rich Tyneside mine owner. From the manor can be seen 'the silver thread of the River Don hurrying towards the Tyne'.

Katie is ravished by the son of the house and turned off from her job, forced to live with her family in a makeshift tent on the moors. When she can stand it no longer she marries the pit's hated master weighman, the man who checks each miner's tally of coal and had the power to cut a man's wages by half.

His cruelty to Katie leads to his murder and the wrongful hanging of her father. During her lifetime Katie Mulholland becomes a legend in the area. But it is really the hatred she carries all her life for the son of the mine owner which has repercussions throughout the coming generations.

In a perverse way Catherine literally wrote her way back into the paperback market. Following the 1958 publication in paperback of *Rooney*, John Smith had twice approached Corgi, the US-based paperback publisher, about signing Catherine. On both occasions his advances were declined. Offered *Katie Mulholland* by the persistent Smith, management at Corgi could, at last, see the potential of her work – with one condition. The story would have to be cut by one-third.

Macdonald, too, had doubts about the book's length. Catherine was advised to trim the industrial scenes. They wanted 50,000 words cut from the manuscript. She spent another six months painstakingly editing the book. 'I tried,' Catherine confessed, 'but could only knock out about 40,000.'

Although Catherine had already been published in hardback in America the hesitation in offering some of her best stories as paperbacks – both at home and abroad – continues to puzzle Smith. 'I could never understand why it took that long,' he later admitted.

In March 1967 – with the publicity bandwagon for her biggest-ever book already rolling – Catherine was back on Tyneside to address South Shields Lecture and Literary Society.

She had accepted an invitation to attend a literary lunch at Harrogate, after which she and Tom would continue on to Newcastle for the 25 May publication of *Katie Mulholland*. An attack of phlebitis forced her to cancel the trip.

TOM had always appeared the silent partner in the Cookson marriage.

An educated thinker with boundless drive of his own, he had

been attracted by Catherine's energy and had drawn on it ever since. On the few occasions his jealousy was aroused, it surfaced as white hot anger. Travelling on a train a man made a rather crude and obvious pass, unaware who the woman in her sixties was or that her husband was sitting near-by. Tom exploded. Catherine 'never spoke to him for a week'.

Tom's soft voice and almost frail figure belittled the vitality within. A group picture of pupils and staff of Hastings Grammar School taken in May 1964 shows Tom well below the head-line of the other masters. Frequently dwarfed by many of the older boys –Tom was just five-foot four-and-a-half – he nevertheless used his size as an effective teaching aid.

'One of his "lessons" to us was that he would try to touch the top of the blackboard,' recalls Peter Bolwell, one of Tom's third-year pupils during the 1968–9 academic year. 'He couldn't, and he would explain to us that he couldn't touch the top and had never done so yet, but he would keep on trying and one day, he assured us, he would succeed.'

In theory Tom's classes were scheduled as maths lessons. In practice they covered 'more important things', Bolwell remembers. 'We felt at the time that it would have been beneficial to have periods timetabled with him, not for any particular subject, but just to listen to his wisdom and advice as he talked to us in an endless series of digressions.'

Tom paid particular attention to pupils who appeared to be shy or timid. On one occasion a first year knocked on the classroom door during a lesson to ask permission to collect something. The knock was apologetic, hardly audible. Tom called the young boy in and told him to go back outside and knock more loudly, 'to make everyone aware of his arrival'.

'One of the things he told us, and something I have never forgotten, is not to believe anyone who told you that a certain thing was impossible and could never be done,' adds Bolwell. 'Because all that meant was that "he" couldn't do it.'

Tom had already decided it was time he took a less active – although equally involved – role in out-of-school activities. In 1963 he retired after seventeen years with the scout troop, eight as scout master. He was rewarded with a medal of merit. The scouts' place was taken by the school model club. Tom busied himself planning and helping to build railway lay-outs, stage exhibitions and arrange talks and outings.

His interest in scale models has never left him. Nor did he turn his back on sport. He remained a member of Hastings Wanderers Cricket Club, rising from a player to be elected treasurer and ultimately a vice-president.

Tom's teaching career at Hastings Grammar had, by the late 1960s, spanned thirty years. He was made head of the lower school. But the migraine attacks, which forced him to sit motionless in a darkened room, still plagued him. During the 1950s Catherine had strived to save enough money to allow her husband to retire from teaching. Tom had returned to the classroom each day during the 1960s, not through any financial necessity, but because of his sheer joy in teaching. As the summer of 1970 approached Tom, supported by Catherine, announced he would not be returning to Hastings Grammar at the start of the next academic year. He was fifty-eight.

Although she had lived in the south for almost four decades, Catherine's life was still dominated by the twenty-three years she had spent on Tyneside. Her memories were as real to her as the stories she had made up as a little girl. Every word. Every flicker of an eyelid. Early in 1968 when a Newcastle bowls team was playing at Hastings, she made a point of going down and introducing herself – 'just to hear a Geordie talk again'. For the next two days members of the team and their wives were treated to afternoon tea at Loreto.

Two of her books published in 1968 attracted considerable acclaim.

The Round Tower – her thirty-sixth book – was chosen by the Royal Society of Literature as the best regional novel of 1968.

Although set entirely in the present, the theme is little different from Catherine's historical works. *The Round Tower* revolves around class barriers: the contrast between the posh Brampton Hill and dismal Ryder's Row and the clash between the high-falutin' manager of an engineering works and the up-and-coming foreman from a working-class home.

The idea for the book came from a Tennyson poem called 'Children's Hour'. Catherine explained: 'I remembered reading it at school and how it used to frighten me, especially the lines, "I have you fast in the round tower, the round tower of my heart."

'So the heroine of the book is made to remember this poem, the only thing she does remember from school, and from this the story builds up.'

On hearing the news she was to be awarded the Royal Society of Literature's prestigious Winifred Holtby Prize – the first professional recognition of her work – Catherine burst into uncontrollable tears, a reaction which followed news of all her subsequent successes.

At the same time BBC television announced it was turning her children's novel, *Joe and the Gladiator* into a three-part series. The adventures of Joe Darling, who meets a rag-and-bone man, Mr Prodhurst, and his intelligent horse, the Gladiator, were to be filmed on Tyneside. It took two years for the BBC crew to arrive in Newcastle, but only after Catherine had spent hours pouring over local maps to pinpoint locations with the story's adaptor, Anna Howe.

BY April 1969, Catherine was at last ready for the final exorcism of her guilt.

Our Kate – the book Catherine had written in the same room at Loreto in which her mother had died – was an immediate success. Within weeks Macdonald had ordered a reprint, the first of fifteen covering three separate editions.

Unlike many of her novels, *Our Kate* was not just a vivid reconstruction of poverty and material suffering. It also gives an inkling of the hellfire of confused Catholicism, which remains a mystery to those outside the faith.

Part of its original attraction was not that it simply fed the growing public demand for social nostalgia – a genre Catherine had played a major part in creating – but that it invited the public to witness the destruction of a public image, an act more traditionally reserved for the media.

Catherine had not only flung open the door to the confessional, she had lifted her head and delivered the sins of her birth openly and honestly and, for the first time in her life, without shame. At sixty-three years old she had entered the confessional with a cherished public reputation. A 'highly educated and intelligent' woman, seemingly confident of both herself and her success, she emerged as the child of an alcoholic mother, who had given her the yoke of illegitimacy and spent a lifetime stoking the fires of love and hate and shame.

However many times Catherine had wished her mother dead and however strong the final bond had grown, Kate's death had extinguished the one source of true information about the man who haunted both their lives. 'I should have talked to her more about this man,' Catherine confessed to a television audience in the 1980s. 'I should have brought it into the open. So many things I should've asked and so many things I should've done.'

Kate was at rest. But sitting in the far corner – with her mother's presence still heavy in the room – the unanswered anger continued to rise from the pages on which Catherine was writing. Why should this child have to go through this? Why had I this terrible childhood? Why had I been scorned? Why had I to come and start this awful life again in Hastings? Why, why, had I to lose four babies? Why had all this happened to me?

'It was all out in that first draft,' said Catherine. 'I should have thought of all the nice things that did happen, but it didn't come like that. When I finished the first draft it was full of bitterness. And when I read it I thought "no". I felt relieved, but I thought I could never publish this.

'And so I left it – I was still writing other books – and I left it lying for a time and I started it again and thought I mustn't say that about her there. I must describe her as I know she was, as I know the beautiful character, the kind character, the humorous character, the loving character. The woman who was worked to the ground, I must see her like that.

'But in the second draft she didn't come like that. There was still the bitterness. I poured it out, all these things that had happened to me. I thought I can't do it. So I did it again, and again.'

But Catherine knew absolution could only come from within. She begged no forgiveness from her readers. It was a brave decision which she had not taken lightly.

In the foreword to the 1974 Corgi paperback edition of *Our Kate*, she wrote:

Although the book took twelve years to complete and I rewrote it eight times, each attempt became more and more therapeutic as I deleted the bitterness from it. But when, at last, in 1969 it was ready

*for publication, I was in two minds whether or not to withdraw it.
Yet I knew that my cure would never be complete unless I could
openly associate myself with two words, two words that had been
my secret shame for so long, namely, 'illegitimate' and 'bastard'.*

But the cure was only partly successful. Catherine never
absolved Belle Eckford for using a piece of adult gossip and
turning it into a cold and cutting weapon. She erased their
friendship from her autobiography and everything associated with
it.

Not once in *Our Kate* does Catherine acknowledge the
existence of Belle or the Eckford family. She lists almost all the
other girls she played and grew up with – Flori Harding, Janie
Robson, Olive Swinburne, Joan and Lottie Woodcock – but never
Belle. Even Yvette Feret the French girl living in Morgan's Hall
who walked to school with Catherine, is expunged for her
friendship with young Jim Eckford.

Jessie Eckford, whose shop Catherine must have visited almost
daily from the age of ten, is supplanted by its previous owner
Cissie Affleck. When Catherine describes her attempts to gain
access to Belle's birthday party she dismisses Jessie as 'Mrs X'. And
Jim Eckford, whose allotment dominated the wasteland at the
centre of the new Buildings and whose Bonfire Night parties
Catherine always attended, is equally ignored.

The friendship between the Eckford children and Catherine
continued at least until she started working at Harton Workhouse.
Belle has long claimed it was she, and not 'a girl at the church
whose father had been a sea captain', who introduced Catherine to
Gladys Cooper the art teacher. And young Jim Eckford met
Catherine regularly at the tennis club behind the Tyne Dock
Church, at least until her twenty-first birthday.

A BRIEF visit to Jersey – surprisingly without Tom – also served to
underscore something which had remained with Catherine since
those early years – her abhorrence of alcohol.

As her earnings rose, Bill McBrien, her accountant, urged her to
take steps to cut back her liability. One way was to become a tax
exile. The problem was where.

Catherine had left England just four times. She had been to Paris twice in the 1930s and twice to Northern Ireland for the filming of *Jacqueline* and *Rooney*. She had no intention of travelling further than necessary. There were just two choices, Jersey or the Isle of Man. McBrien persuaded her to take a closer look at Jersey and he and his wife agreed to show her around the Bailiwick. Tom remained at Loreto.

They soon found a house Catherine liked. 'It had everything, thick carpets and all the luxury and they said I'd be silly not to buy it.' She telephoned Tom. He agreed that if Catherine liked it she should close the sale.

But something was wrong. From the minute she arrived Catherine had sensed a reserve towards potential new residents. The island was cliquey and she disliked cliques of any kind. There was also a mystery. No one would tell her what was being built at the bottom of the road only yards from the house.

'It was awful,' she remembers. 'Like a pigeon coop.' She telephoned Tom again, this time to tell him she did not want to live on Jersey and would be cutting short her four-day visit.

Depressed, and missing Tom, she went for a walk. 'I saw a woman walking in the opposite direction,' Catherine recalled. 'I asked her if she could tell me what they were building. "Oh, yes," she told me. "That's the new prison . . ." I couldn't get off the island quick enough.'

The flight home turned into another nightmare. Several passengers were returning from a wedding and were still celebrating. One drunk stood at the front and shouted, 'I'm a hijacker. All the ladies take their knickers off.'

Catherine was repulsed. 'I felt sick. I could feel myself go stiff with disgust. My accountant's wife, who was next to me, understood but then, when we came to get off the plane, worse was to come. There was this same man standing next to the stewardess saying goodbye to everyone, shaking them all by the hand.

'There was no way I could avoid him. I had to get by. I told him he was disgusting . . . I couldn't help myself. Do you know what he did? He got hold of me, pulled me towards him, said he knew he was, knew all the names I was thinking, but that I was nice and then kissed me. I ran away so fast people wondered what was wrong.'

A visit to Derbyshire in August 1969 proved more enjoyable. Catherine had been invited to deliver the last-night talk at a writers' summer school. 'She had the 300 writers and would-be writers in the palm of her hand,' recalled one student. 'As soon as she had us crying with laughter she would turn on the pathos and have us sobbing real tears.' Catherine's standing ovation lasted longer and louder than any previous speaker's.

The speed at which she was now producing books was also causing problems for Macdonald's. Catherine's latest manuscript described the fortunes of one family from 1933 to 1973. The future date was just as well – the novel was not scheduled for publication until 1972. A log-jam of books was piling up. *The Glass Virgin* was ready for publication in January 1970, with *The Invitation* to appear later in the year. The manuscript of *The Dwelling Place* was already being edited at Macdonald's and had been allocated a place in the summer 1971 list. Catherine was writing faster than her publishers were willing to release her new stories.

Macdonald had no such misgivings about re-issuing her previous titles. To coincide with the July 1969 publication of *The Nice Bloke*, it also issued new editions of *Fanny McBride*, *Colour Blind*, *The Garment*, *The Menagerie* and *The Unbaited Trap*.

'A 'nice bloke' was the assessment of Harry Blenheim's family and colleagues. Unromantically married with two sons and a daughter, he was an ordinary 38-year-old with respectable principles – until he escorted a typist home from the office party.

This innocently intended event results in the ruin of his career and the break-up of his family. When it became embarrassing for his friends and relatives to recognise their connection with Harry, after his imprisonment for an assault on his father-in-law, the 'nice bloke' image abruptly fades.

Corgi had published *Katie Mulholland* in January 1969. In October it followed the belated return of Catherine Cookson to its list with the paperback publication of her first novel, *Kate Hannigan*. It was to prove one of her most popular and profitable books. During the next decade Corgi would issue no less than thirteen reprints.

Her success at Corgi was not immediate or expected. Michael Legat, editorial director at Corgi's parent company Transworld, was lobbied several times by his friend John Foster White at Macdonald's before he agreed to sign Catherine. Legat now admits his enthusiasm for his new writer was only 'moderate'. He explains: 'I had read several Cookson books and thought they were entertaining and I recognised that Catherine could tell a good story, but there was nothing in her past history as an author to suggest she would achieve more than a modest sale. As a hardcover author she was no more than steady.'

The initial Corgi print runs were less than 30,000 copies, a sale Legat only just expected Catherine to reach. When demand pushed print orders, first to 40,000 and then 50,000 he conceded Catherine had moved into the bestseller class.

CATHERINE spent most of the 1969 Christmas holiday in bed with flu. She did not send for the doctor. At the end of the second week – the first weekend of the new year – she attempted to shake off a growing depression. She had been sleeping badly. Her dreams were beginning to invade her waking life. Fresh air and gardening were what she needed.

Tom had already spent most of the day tidying the garden of its winter debris. As Catherine put her weight on the blade of a spade, a searing pain shot through her foot and leg.

The next twenty-four hours were agony. It took two weeks of medication and daily treatment by a physiotherapist before Catherine could stand or lie flat. Sitting was still impossible without pain. And it was another six weeks, the end of February, before she felt confident enough to venture out shopping.

Hastings town centre was bitterly cold. Two hours after the couple arrived home Catherine began to feel faint. She asked for a glass of wine. Tom gave her a glass of port and watched in surprise as his wife swallowed it in one go. By three in the afternoon Catherine felt ill. An hour later she was bleeding internally.

Tom's attempts to make contact with their doctor failed. In desperation he bundled his wife into the car and carried her up the path of their doctor's home. He finally agreed to examine Catherine. The diagnosis was that she was either bleeding from the bladder, had acute cystitis or the telangiectasia had erupted again. But, said the doctor, there was nothing he could do. Catherine needed to see a specialist. He sent her home.

For four days, until the Wednesday, Catherine drifted in and out of reality. She was bleeding continually. The thought occurred to her that she might actually be dying. Two fears took over her mind; how would Tom cope without her and what would happen to the story she just started?

On the Wednesday afternoon, after yet another telephone call by Tom, the specialist finally arrived. He needed only the briefest examination before ordering Catherine into hospital for an emergency operation.

The Cooksons' crumbling faith in the medical profession was restored a few months later when Catherine met a St Leonards' doctor called Dr Gabb, himself dying of cancer. Through his referral Catherine consulted a surgeon at the Middlesex Hospital in London. She accepted his suggestion that the bleeding, particularly from her nose, could be eased if skin from her hip was grafted into her right nostril. He also cut a small wedge out of her tongue.

It was the first time anything positive had been done to alleviate the effects of her blood disorder.

Twelve

Isn't it strange that from the wider world into which I escaped I have to return, like the eel to the Sargasso Sea.

IN A ROOM on the first floor of her Helen's Park Road home Catherine had collected the typescripts of thirty of her books.

Stacked in neat piles across the green baize of the full-size billiard table was the original working copy of *Kate Hannigan*, next to it the thicker manuscript of *Katie Mulholland*. The most recent was *The Glass Virgin*, published the previous year. Some were neatly bound, others tied into loose-leaf bundles. All thirty – weighing 220 lbs – were destined for the austere library of Boston University.

'They just sent and asked if they could have them. Out of the blue,' she explains. 'I had dumped them in the attic and often wondered what on earth I was going to do with them all. I thought maybe I should make a bonfire of them now or let someone do the job when I was dead.'

After weeks of sorting the thousands of sheets into order, they were finally ready to ship.

By the early 1970s her correspondence had become almost as time-consuming as her novels. One woman wrote to Catherine as 'Lady Chesterfield-Cookson', a reference to her lifelong mentor. Letters from overseas would regularly arrive addressed to 'Catherine Cookson, England'. Other readers, aware she had turned her back on the Catholic faith, attempted to enrol her in theirs.

To cope Catherine was rising early and at her desk by seven each morning, a result of mental alertness more than rigid timekeeping.

With anything up to fifty letters arriving each week, she could still not bring herself to sign copies of a standard, duplicated reply. Until the 1960s she, or sometimes Tom, would answer every letter in longhand. The neuritis in Catherine's shoulder and the pain in her hand now forced her to dictate the messages. She still insisted on keeping them personal. Tom, who typed most of her correspondence, maintained an exhaustive card index of every letter, cross-referenced, and including coded comments: 'VWL' – very warm letter; 'VNP' – very nice person.

Some letters were highly emotional, thanking Catherine for stories which had guided a reader through a personal trauma or grief. Others, quite openly, told her: 'You have saved my life.' This she appreciated. In the early 1950s, during her own crisis, she had written to Leslie Weatherhead, the Methodist minister and writer. In 1951 he published *Psychology, Religion and Healing*, a book Catherine found strangely in tune with her own thinking at that time. The book, she felt, had gone a long way to giving her own life new direction. She was warmed to get a reply from Weatherhead saying that her letter had also helped him.

Most days Catherine also found time to telephone her Aunt Sarah, still living at Birtley. She would make the calls early in the morning, sometimes before breakfast, while her energy was at its highest. It was a habit she would continue throughout her life.

But from 1969, when *Our Kate* was published, Catherine began to receive a different kind of letter – from people claiming to know the identity of her father. At first the letters disturbed her. The majority were from men and women wanting a share of her growing wealth, some little short of confidence tricks. Others were simply sincere in their belief they were related to the writer. Catherine has learned to live with the 'paternal' letters which still arrive almost weekly.

'I've had that many Das you wouldn't believe it,' she says. 'Since *Our Kate* I've never been without a father.'

In some cases people have gone to extraordinary lengths to research and prove their claim: tracing their relatives' movements, checking dates, pointing out physical similarities. Knowing how much Catherine's illegitimacy meant to her, Tom would painstakingly double-check each claim; cross-checking dates and places and examining every detail. One family were positive they shared the same father – until Tom discovered Kate's lover would have been ten years' old when Catherine was born.

AT first Tom found it difficult to settle into the regime of retirement. His teaching career – including his years as an RAF instructor – had spanned almost four decades. Yet he was never idle. The large garden at Loreto needed constant attention. The Cooksons' latest dog, a golden labrador called Simon which invariably greeted visitors to the house with a rubber ball in its mouth, kept him exercised. But it was Catherine who provided her husband with a new 'career'.

Freed from the constraints of the school calendar and her understandable reluctance to be separated from Tom, Catherine was now able to consider far more of the growing number of invitations she received each week. During the 1950s and 1960s most acceptances to speak at lunches or society gatherings had been confined to events in the south of England within easy driving distance of Hastings. Any which demanded an overnight stay were restricted to school holidays. Throughout the winter of 1970 and the following spring Tom slipped happily into his new role as his wife's road manager, chauffeur and travelling companion.

In April 1970, a ten-man BBC film crew descended on the village of Westoe where, as a teenager, Catherine had turned her back on the chance of a trip to Italy because of her religion. As part of her consent to the adaptation of her children's story *Joe and the Gladiator*, Catherine had insisted all the exterior sequences of the film should be shot in and around South Shields. It was the first time a Cookson story would be seen by television viewers.

Not only were the locations authentic – South Shields beach and terraced houses about to be demolished – but many of the cast were also Geordies. The part of Joe was given to nineteen-year-old Dennis Lingard from Wallsend, Newcastle. Even the Gladiator was played by Peggy, a thirteen-year-old mare who, in real life, had just been bought by a retired miner for his part-time rag-and-bone business.

Originally published in 1968 by Macdonald, *Joe and the Gladiator* was due to appear as a Puffin paperback in 1971. Its sales would demand eight reprints within the next nine years.

For the second time in her career Catherine was compared with many of the writers whose names had appeared on her 1940s reading list. One review pleased her more than most. It so closely reflected her own view of her work she might have written the critique herself. '*The Glass Virgin* is a work of high romance, and yet it is also a piece of fictionalised social history,' said the reviewer. 'Romance is a shockingly debased word; I am using it in the old sense – I am thinking of the Brontës and Scott and George Eliot and Robert Louis Stevenson, no less.'

In contrast her second book that year – *The Invitation* – underlined Macdonald's apparent intent to contrast Catherine's novels of social history with lighter, more modern stories. She returns once more to 'the best end of Fellburn, which was not Brampton Hill anymore but further out in the district known generally as the rise'. It was a location she had first used in 1954 in *Maggie Rowan*.

In her latest novel Maggie Gallacher is a woman with big bosoms and blue eyes and a belly laugh that attracts the young builder Rodney Gallacher. The invitation of the title is from the Duke of Moorshire to attend his musical evening. When Rodney gets Maggie pregnant he is forced to marry her. Five more children follow and Maggie is immersed in their troubles – among them a whip-wielding sex maniac; a should-have-been priest, now living in monastic severity writing snide poems about his siblings; and her youngest daughter, full of religious fervour to become a nun.

The following May Catherine journeyed to Northumberland to speak at Ashington's sixteen-day annual festival. All 400 tickets for her talk – entitled 'Granda' – sold within hours.

In line with its light–heavy marketing policy Macdonald and Catherine agreed her next book should be *The Dwelling Place*. Published in August 1971, it is a story in the classic Cookson mould.

The book tells of the bleak survival on the Northumberland fells of a young girl striving to raise her orphaned brothers and sisters in nineteenth-century poverty. Young Cissie struggles to keep the family together and out of the workhouse and the boys from being sold into the darkness of the pit or to sweep the flues of endless chimneys. But Cissie falls prey to the son of a nobleman – and incurs the wrath of the young lord's violent sister – only to bring another mouth to feed into the dwelling place.

The inspiration for *The Dwelling Place* had come originally from her *Katie Mulholland* research, as did the background for *The Glass Virgin*.

'I discovered that a family by the name of Cookson had once owned quite a lot of land in Shields, besides which they were very important glass manufacturers,' she recalls. 'I was also horrified by the plight of the nineteenth-century mine workers, particularly the children.'

Her latest novel – *Feathers in the Fire*, published in November 1971 – also made use of the windswept Northumberland fells. Its chain of tragic and violent events begins in 1881 when Molly Geary, a hand at Cock Shield Farm, is found to be pregnant and suffers a flogging from the master rather than disclose the name of the father. Slowly the other occupants are drawn into her plight: the master, supposedly a staunch pillar of the church; his wife, Delia, who sees through his hypocrisy; his daughter Jane, and young David Armstrong, a farmhand.

The remoteness of the Northumberland countryside attracted Tom, whose own curiosity and imagination thrived on the bare landscape. It may also have been the increasing number of appointments around the country which triggered a spark of restlessness in the Cooksons.

During the summer of 1971 they began to talk more and more about finding a new home. The Cooksons had lived at Loreto for almost seventeen years. There was no longer any need for Tom to live near Hastings Grammar School. He now had the urge to live near a river.

The house-hunting was forced into second place when Catherine began what she already envisaged as three separate novels relating the story of a violent and passionate family dogged by a malicious curse. Catherine discussed the outline of the story with Tom – 'to fix it in my head'. She finished all three books in fourteen months. The exertion left her drained and 'poorly'. To recuperate the Cooksons once again returned to Northumberland, to spend most of the autumn of 1972 in the remote Allendale area.

During her tight writing schedule Catherine and Tom took time off in March 1972 for a 'duty visit' to the North-East to sign copies of her books. The tour of bookshops was organised by Corgi, which was producing a new Cookson paperback every two months. The manager of Binns department store in South Shields took the precaution of ordering an extra 1,000 Cookson paperbacks – every copy was sold during Catherine's hour-long appearance.

To save time in the busy schedule the Cooksons agreed to be interviewed over lunch at the Royal Station Hotel, adjoining Newcastle's Central Station. The conversation turned to the inevitable sex in her books and Catherine turned to Tom, gently stroking his hair. 'You know, Tom, I've never told you this but I've always wanted to be some man's mistress,' she admitted, more for her lunch guest than her husband. 'But it's too late now and you'll have to do.' Tom smiled a scholarly smile and went back to his meal.

As 1972 ended Catherine looked forward to a new year and a new publisher – she was already under the guidance of a new agent.

In the early 1970s John Smith had announced his intention to retire. He agreed to sell his client list, which in addition to Catherine included the novelist Muriel Spark and the astronomer Patrick Moore, to Anthony Sheil. Catherine agreed to the transfer. She was also aware of the intense debt she owed Smith. It was at her insistence Sheil consented to retain Smith on a freelance basis to advise on the handling of her books.

Catherine's hardback contract with Macdonald had expired. Anthony Sheil knew that if the publishing house wanted to hang on to its best-selling author it would have to reconsider and rethink the advances and royalties it was offering. Sheil promised Catherine he would get the 'best deal possible'.

Sheil turned up the pressure by approaching several other publishers. News that one of Britain's best-selling authors was once again on the open market produced a flurry of in-house calculations and out-of-hours gossip. To keep in touch with developments Catherine spoke by telephone to her agent almost daily.

One publisher, Heinemann, had approached Catherine even before her contract with Macdonald had expired. Tim Manderson, Heinemann's sales director at the time, recalled, 'When I first read Catherine Cookson I wanted her to come to Heinemann and persuaded Charles Pick to make overtures to her.'

With the Mallen trilogy at stake – and the prospect of sales well into the millions – Pick was even more determined Heinemann should outbid its rivals. He was also willing to compromise. Since

Kate Hannigan Catherine's books had been edited at Macdonald by John Foster White. She was concerned a new publisher and new editor would sever the intuitive feel Foster White had developed for her stories. Pick agreed Foster White should be included in the new deal 'as a kind of extra-mural editor' at Heinemann.

'Catherine knows exactly what she wants, is extremely on the ball and incisive, but is also a very good listener,' said Manderson. 'She's a remarkable person to work with.'

Advances, both for hardback and paperback editions, saw a comparable increase.

For the 1958 paperback rights to *Rooney*, Corgi paid an advance of £150. By the time *The Glass Virgin* was published, in December 1971, the advance on a Cookson book was up to £1,000. In May 1972 *Rooney* was republished with a new advance of £1,000. Other paperback publishers became interested, and competitive bidding in May 1973 obliged Corgi to pay an advance of £15,000 for *The Dwelling Place*.

On 21 January 1973 – the eve of publication of her fiftieth novel, *The Mallen Streak* – Catherine appeared on the Tyne Tees Television programme, 'Challenge'. Her unscheduled interview was arranged at the last minute after the original guest, the actress Moira Shearer, was injured in a car accident.

Catherine's answers were honest and forthright. 'My illegitimacy created a sense of shame and rejection which ended in my nervous breakdown,' she said. 'I wanted to get away from everybody who knew about the circumstances of my birth – I wanted to get away from the shame.'

She also admitted to the programme's presenter, Fred Dinenage, that she now received at least 2,000 letters each year from illegitimate men and women who had read *Our Kate*. 'They tell me they have carried the burden of being illegitimate for years and, because I have spoken out about it, they thank me.'

When Dinenage asked Catherine whether she would ever return to live in the North-East she replied: 'Everything I possess is in the south. But if I am cremated when I die I would like my ashes to be scattered here because it is here where my heart is.'

Her thousands of readers who snapped up the copies of *The Mallen Streak* next morning found illegitimacy also played a major part in the first book of the trilogy. Just as Catherine had inherited the blood disorder from her father, so the Mallen bastards are also heir to a genetic quirk – this time an unmistakable streak of white hair.

Set in the mid-nineteenth century, the tempestuous Mallens – already facing financial ruin – live in High Banks Hall in the far west of Northumberland. Most of the action takes place in the small but empty triangle of upland between Ninebanks, Carr Shield and Alston, the district in which Catherine had convalesced. The Mallens' rakish behaviour was remarkably similar to the Gay Delavals, a real-life family who had already earned their place in Northumberland legend.

Within a month *The Mallen Streak* had been named as the *Daily Express* Book of the Month. In time it was to be Catherine's best-selling novel. By 1993 an estimated 1,027,000 copies had been sold in Britain alone.

The second book in the trilogy, *The Mallen Girl* was listed for publication late in 1973. Heinemann, hoping to prolong sales on the first book, delayed publication until January 1974.

The Mallen Girl follows the life of Barbara, the beautiful but proud illegitimate daughter of old Thomas Mallen, who shot himself after raping his niece in the first book. She, however, has one restraint on her adolescent passion: she is going deaf. This disability enables the starchy governess, Miss Brigmore – the main linking character of the first two novels – to protect her from her sordid origins. But Barbara has her eyes set on her cousin, Michael, another bastard unaware of his status. This conflict comes to a head in a violent incident on the fells, when Barbara betrays her Mallen traits by savagely injuring a rival. The shock causes her to recover her hearing and, when she discovers the secret of her birth, she runs away to die on the moors.

The *Mallen* trilogy has constantly remained among Catherine's best-selling books, both at home and abroad. Of her six top-selling novels in the UK three places are taken by the *Mallen* books. Combined sales to 1993 had reached an estimated 2,876,000.

But the stories of bastards and betrayal did not produce universal approval. One story, circulating in the book trade at the time, told of a woman who picked up one of Catherine's novels. She was about to take it to the counter when another woman, standing next to her, snatched the book away. 'I don't think you would like that,' said the stranger. 'After all, she is rather coarse.'

The undercurrent was not typical, and certainly had little effect on the sale of Catherine's books. Having changed the way the world saw the industrial blackland of the North-East, Catherine was now rewriting publishing history.

During 1974 she would sell between 1.5 and 2 million paperbacks, half a million in North America. In just five years, sales of *Our Kate* had topped 400,000 in Britain alone. The initial print run of a new Cookson novel was 15,000 with a 5,000 reprint within days. By August a set of twelve Cookson books had been sold for translation into Turkish and three more books were about to be bought by American publishers. Her stories of suffering and survival on Tyneside were already being read in Swedish, Norwegian, Dutch, Danish, Italian, French, Spanish, German, Japanese and even Hebrew.

Perhaps recalling how difficult it had been for her to realise her teenage ambition to become a writer, Catherine was now only too eager to do anything she could to encourage young authors – especially from South Shields. In January 1973 she agreed to donate a £50 prize for a short-story competition which was open to under-eighteens. Six months later young writers and poets throughout County Durham were offered the chance to compete for the Catherine Cookson prize in their own competition.

Her home town was also anxious to honour one of Britain's leading writers whose childhood ambition was to 'taalk proper'.

About to disappear under the 1974 local government re-organisation, South Shields Council voted to award Catherine the Freedom of the Borough. The four other recipients were a councillor, the authority's last town clerk, a union official and a veteran Labour party member.

Catherine's nomination had been sponsored by her long-time friend, Dr Mannie Anderson. He told the freedom-making ceremony: 'What she has to say is something universal. She made the Tyneside dialect universal.'

CHRISTMAS Day 1974 was a Wednesday. Catherine and Tom decided to take the day off.

The last few weeks had been hectic, with Catherine working

long hours on her writing and Tom attempting to keep pace with the mail arriving from every corner of the world. As the holiday approached, the continuous stream of letters turned into the annual flood of presents. Catherine proved she had done a remarkable job of spinning a public image for herself. Most of her readers saw her as a successful and respected woman of letters. Others refused to forget her roots. With the silver eggcups and spoons came the toilet-roll covers and dishcloths.

Early in 1975 Catherine reluctantly gave permission for a semi-documentary film based on *Our Kate*. The £900 film was to be produced by a nine-strong student film crew from Harrow College of Technology and Art. Its director and editor, John Cheyne, had decided to focus on Catherine's life between the ages of eight and eleven.

The final book in the Mallen trilogy, *The Mallen Litter*, had appeared in 1974. While it resolutely held its place in the top ten of Britain's bestsellers, her latest novel, *The Invisible Cord*, proved Catherine could deal equally well with the fine detail of the 1960s as she could the broad sweep of Victorian life. It also showed she had not lost contact with the back streets of South Shields – and their current notoriety as a centre for drug dealing.

The saga Catherine unfolds in *The Invisible Cord* spans a quarter century from 1943 onwards. The theme which bonds the story is a mother's love.

The mother is Annie. Her shotgun wedding to a rather dim RAF cook – stationed 'in some god-forsaken place called Madley' –dismays her family and friends. But iron-willed Annie is determined to make the best of a bad job. Surviving a disastrous start – an air raid takes a heavy toll of the wedding guests – she buckles down to the task of turning her husband into a success, first as a small coal merchant, then as a garage owner. The main threat to their peace and prosperity is their elder son, Rance. As he grows up, she alone is blind to the vicious flaws in his character, even covering up for him when he kicks his father downstairs. Family tensions finally explode in tragedy.

Alan Earney, whose association with Catherine began in the late 1960s, was asked what impressed him most about working with Catherine Cookson. The Corgi editorial director replied, 'I have never known her to be other than co-operative (even though she can be forthright, particularly when she is described as a "romantic novelist"). Over the years I have become increasingly conscious of her warmth and generosity and her determination to carry on writing in the face of debilitating health problems.'

Only Tom knew the true toll that 'determination' was demanding from his wife. In her diary for 18 January 1975 Catherine confided:

I felt very ill yesterday. The feeling continued into the night; I couldn't sleep. My Siamese twin self-pity was in charge. This was a real bout of self-exhaustion. For months now it has been a fourteen hour day, seven days a week, up at half-past six in the morning trying to get through my ever growing mail; the day allotted to the phone, visits from agents, editors, photographers, interviewers and, just recently, the BBC unit. I tell myself it can't go on, but it does.

Catherine had also written another book under the Marchant pseudonym. In July 1975 Heinemann published *Miss Martha Mary Crawford*.

Early in October she accepted a second invitation to appear on a Tyne Tees Television programme. Catherine pulled no punches about her childhood, describing herself as 'the best-paid bastard in the business'. With review copies of her latest book, *The Gambling Man*, about to go out to newspapers around the country the phrase was a godsend to critics and feature writers. 'The best-paid bastard in the business, as she likes to call herself,' said one reviewer, 'obliges her legion of devotees just in time for the seasonal spending spree . . .'

Catherine had been just as truthful when writing her new novel. Its opening page is pure memory, she could equally have used it to begin a second autobiography. It was all there, just as her mind's eye remembered it. *The Gambling Man* opens in 1875, more than three decades before Catherine would set off to discover the world surrounding Leam Lane End, yet the terrain was already fixed. The five dock arches with 'streaks of dull green water running down from their domes' and, in the opposite direction, the grim and desolate Jarrow Road bordered by the 'great open stretch of mud'. Even before her schooldays Catherine knew there was something special – something hopeful – to be gained from climbing the hill overlooking her birthplace.

There was nothing grim about the road to Simonside, for as soon as you mounted the bank Tyne Dock and East Jarrow were forgotten, and you were in the country. Up and up the hill you went and there to the left, lying back in the well-tended gardens, were large houses; past the farm, and now you were among green fields and open land as far as the eye could see. Of course, if you looked back you would glimpse the masts of the ships lying along the river, but looking ahead even in the falling twilight you knew this was a pleasant place, a place different from Tyne Dock, or East Jarrow, or Jarrow itself.

The Gambling Man tells the story of Rory Connor, a South Shields slumland rent collector with a talent for gambling. A little spot of fiddling the takings, plus a bad beating at a card game, conspire to wreck his marriage. His wife is conveniently lost at sea. Rory marries his boss's plain daughter and develops a taste for luxury – then his luck really turns sour.

John Smith, who had originally invented the name Catherine Marchant, now felt it was time to end the writer's career. Catherine had produced her last novel under the pen name. *The Slow Awakening* was published early in 1976. It would be followed a year later by the appearance of *The Iron Façade*, originally published in 1965 in the United States as *Evil at Roger's Cross*.

TOM had long felt that if his wife was going to die she should die in her own part of the world, although he was not convinced the move – any move – was a good idea. Catherine, quite simply, felt she had been away long enough.

Forty-six years after she turned her back on the 'grim, grimy, dock-bound river towns' of Tyneside, Catherine decided she must at least make the effort to return. She was not sure she could readjust to life in the north, or worse still, what effect it would have on her writing.

There was only one answer – they would commute the 350 miles between Hastings and Newcastle. But first they needed to find a northern home.

The house the couple settled on was at 39 Eslington Terrace in the better-class Newcastle suburb of Jesmond. Tempted to view the four-bedroomed property by an advertisement, written entirely in verse, they completed the purchase while on a trip north. It was not a typical Cookson home.

Eslington Terrace was a busy residential street within walking distance of Newcastle city centre. Accustomed to privacy and solitude, first at the Hurst and then at Loreto, Catherine and Tom looked upon their new semi-detached home as a stepping-stone on the way to a more permanent residence. It was certainly luxurious, if not always to Catherine's own taste. Deep-piled shaggy carpets covered every inch of floor, Annigoni prints – a legacy from the previous owner – lined the dining-room wall and a stone-clad bar, complete with draught beer on pump from the cellar, dominated the largest of the three reception rooms. The garden was non-existent compared with the two-and-a-half acres at Loreto. And Catherine would miss her daily swim in her heated indoor pool.

'I want to see if I can resettle in the north,' admitted Catherine in November 1975, 'but it is a matter of the weather and my health. I am slightly bronchial and I've got to be reassured that I could stand the weather.'

If she was unsure after the harsh winters, she had already made her mind up about the warmth of the welcome she would receive. 'It is a different atmosphere than in the south. I understand the people. They are my own folk.'

Tom's doubts, too, were soon dispelled. Ten years later, in 1985, he finally admitted he was not 100 per cent behind the move. 'When Catherine wanted to come back, I didn't fully understand why. But the north is so much her home, her people. And if I have any regret in my life it's that I wasn't born here too.'

In the meantime Catherine had work to do. The Cooksons installed a 'caretaker' at Eslington Terrace and returned to Hastings. They intended to return every six weeks or so. If they eventually decided to remain in the south they would keep the Jesmond house for visits.

Catherine found she needed the north and the stimulation it gave her more than ever. Its people were also reluctant to lose her, even for a few weeks. No sooner had Catherine returned to Hastings than a new flood of invitations would arrive from Tyneside.

Throughout the winter and spring appeals to open fêtes, make speeches, present prizes and talk to the media, both on and off screen, had poured in. Newcastle City Council unanimously agreed to invite Catherine to open the city's Tyneside Summer Exhibition. She agreed. Catherine Cookson was on everyone's wanted list.

During one period in occupation at Eslington Terrace in April 1976, Catherine was booked to conclude Durham City Technical College's lecture season with a talk entitled 'Old John McMullen versus Lord Chesterfield'. The event was a sell-out with Cookson fans outnumbering the students twenty to one.

But with every acceptance she insisted on one over-riding condition – whatever the event the organisers must have a stand-by guest. She was still suffering three or four severe nose bleeds a week, some of them severe enough to confine her to bed. 'I hate letting people down,' explained Catherine. 'But I may suddenly be whisked off to hospital.'

For the first time in more than a quarter of a century Catherine discovered she could not write to order.

'I find I have a tremendous amount of calls on my time,' she said. 'I don't mind it at all – what author would – especially as they are my own folk, but I find it difficult to do any work. Writing is not only my work, it is my hobby. Back home in Hastings I never wanted to go out. Life is so exciting here. I want to go out all the time.'

Six months after buying the Eslington Terrace house – and spending a total of three months in occupation – Catherine knew her return would have to be permanent. It also needed to be on her terms. She needed to keep the world at arms' length.

Loreto, the house in which the majority of her novels had been written, would be sold. Many years later she admitted, 'I did not want to leave my home – it took twenty-two years to make the garden – but the time came when we were sort of galloping towards the end. And, except for my blood condition, I really do feel better in all ways since I came North.'

The Eslington Terrace property was also put on the market. The agents handling the sale were quick to capitalise on its literary connection – 'We are privileged to offer for sale the home of one of the North-East's most delightful personalities and a leading British authoress.'

In May 1976 – with her seventieth birthday rapidly approaching – Catherine returned north to a converted church near Morpeth in Northumberland.

But the Morpeth cottage had one disadvantage, it had no swimming pool. Catherine had swum every day at Loreto to keep her spine supple and her body fit. While on a visit to the historic Northumberland village of Corbridge, to arrange for the construction of a pool at their new home, the Cooksons discovered – and bought – yet another house, this time one that already included a heated pool.

All that remained was to sell the three other houses the Cooksons had acquired.

TOM's dream of living near a river had finally come true. From the gently sloping garden he could watch the Tyne shimmer through the trees. It was the same river, sixty years before and thirty miles away, in which Catherine had almost drowned.

The Northumberland countryside around Corbridge intrigued and excited him. It was greener and gentler and promised more secrets than the open windswept fells. Each day, no matter what the weather, Tom would spend hours exploring the paths and lanes around the village.

Meanwhile, Catherine set about redecorating High Barns. She filled the fourteen-room, stone-built house with her antiques, carefully packed and shipped north. But the main focal point – as with all the Cookson homes – was the large, airy, office-cum-study. A photograph taken soon after their arrival shows Catherine reading mail while seated at a wide, modern desk. Tom, looking relaxed and wearing a turtle-neck sweater, is busy typing on an electric typewriter nearby. Between them are the rotary files recording details of every letter received and every reply sent.

Catherine soon regained her writing stride, although it would be almost fifteen months before a new Cookson story for adult readers would be published. Her final book of 1975 had been a Catherine Marchant story, *Miss Martha Mary Crawford*. It would be followed during 1976 by *The Tide of Life*, later to be re-issued as a Catherine Cookson original; *The Slow Awakening;* and *The Iron Façade* first published in the United States in 1965 as *Evil at Roger's Cross*. The unique run of four Marchant novels was the last time she would use the pen name. Her only other book that year was a children's story, *Mrs Flannagan's Trumpet*.

The worldwide enthusiasm for Catherine's books was also spreading, although sometimes in some odd directions. In the summer of 1976 she heard *Katie Mulholland* was being produced as a booklet for use as a Puerto Rican educational aid.

It also brought the world to the door of her Northumberland home.

One such guest was American Oscar Dystil, president of Bantam Books. After flying 3,000 miles across the Atlantic, he flew from Heathrow to Newcastle airport in a private jet and was then driven to Corbridge. An hour later he was on his way back.

But the appearance of Mr Dystil – looking more like a London barrister in a blue pin-stripe suit than a North American publisher – was deceptive. He had seen the destructive as well as the constructive side of publishing. During the Second World War Dystil was in charge of printed psychological warfare in the Mediterranean area. He was now president of the largest paperback publishing company in the world. Corgi, which had published Catherine in paperback since 1969, was expecting to sell millions of Cookson books well into the next century. As shrewd as ever, Dystil had made the 6,000 mile round trip to meet 'this remarkable woman' who was helping to make his company even more profitable.

Catherine had, for many years, received her own invitations to cross the Atlantic. 'I don't like travelling,' she confesses. 'I don't want to go anywhere. I just want to write. I've had carrots as long as a room held out to me from America. I promise to go, but I make something happen so I can't.'

In the late nineteenth century the residents of the isolated farms and cottages around Allendale had relied for medical treatment on a Dr Arnison. His library had included a book on Allendale and Whitefield written by George Dickinson Junior and published locally in 1884. Dr Arnison's grand-daughter passed the book on to Catherine, whom she had got to know during one of the Cooksons' many holidays in the area.

The book fascinated Catherine and inspired *The Girl*, a novel published in September 1977, and her only story to appear that year. She named the doctor in the story Arnison, although she took great pains to point out the village of Elmholm – set in the foothills of the Pennines where the three counties of Northumberland, Cumbria and County Durham meet – was fictitious.

The novel opens in 1850 and tells the story of Hannah Boyle, the daughter of a prostitute from the Newcastle slums. When she is eight, her dying mother's last act is to take her to a lead-mining village, arriving on the doorstep of Matthew Thornton, a respectable engineer, to claim the child was fathered by him during a business trip. Thornton's prim and proper wife treats Hannah with extreme cruelty, and in turn is horse-whipped by her husband in her own bed. He seeks sexual solace elsewhere and this leads to his murder, leaving Hannah – now a beautiful teenager – without a protector.

The following spring the woman whom many regarded as the 'Voice of the North-East' spoke her mind once too often. Catherine had agreed to launch a Northumberland Health Authority campaign to encourage people to dump or hand in unwanted drugs. She arrived at the authority's Morpeth headquarters as arranged. Her brief speech, however, included a revelation the local Labour councillors did not want to hear.

'Doctors' surgeries are more than half-full of people who should not be there,' Catherine told the assembled press. 'They go out of habit. I have six friends who go out of habit. One goes out of loneliness.'

Worse was to come. She went on to say she was proud to be a private patient and how the year before, in addition to paying to see a doctor, she had also cheerfully paid up £11.50 for a bronchitis drug.

Her innocent side-swipe at the Health Service brought a swift rebuke from Labour councillors and socialists across the region. Some branded her comments 'rubbish'. Others condemned her for turning her back on the poverty of her childhood. The debate rumbled on.

Two days later Catherine wrote to the Newcastle *Journal* claiming she had been misreported. 'Your reporter states that the Labour Party members were stunned,' her letter said. 'I, too, am stunned to realise that my short address was taken as being political.

'I have never dabbled in politics; but calling myself a political agnostic, I have, over the years, performed services for all three parties.

'The further implication that I have risen from a working girl – at seventy-two I am still a hard-working girl – to become a successful author and so can now afford to be a private patient, thereby separating from my own folk is entirely unwarranted.' She had always paid her own way, Catherine's letter went on, and paying for her own medical treatment was just the same.

What many of her accusers did not know was that Catherine had indeed recently returned to the streets where she grew up. She made the pilgrimage to record scenes for a television *Life Style* documentary about her childhood years and later fame.

The site appeared little different to any other neglected and vandalised area dotted along the banks of the Tyne between South Shields and Jarrow. Catherine arrived dressed in trousers and a caped jacket and hat. Only the houses in Phillipson Street – whose backyards had been opposite those of William Black Street – remained. Everything else was gone. Catherine stumbled on the grass covered rubble as she tried to locate the exact position of No 10 and its kitchen. Watching from behind the camera, Tom could see the effect the interview was having on his wife. When it was over the tears began to trickle down Catherine's face. Recovering in her car she found a scrap of paper and wrote:

> *Me granny sat in a wooden chair*
> *She had a stiff face, wrinkles and straight black hair,*
> *But if I ever needed comfort I found it there.*
> *Between her knees each day she'd have me stand,*
> *And look me head for nits, and I'd play the band*
> *Until she said, 'Here's a bullet*
> *Mind you don't choke yourself*
> *It'll stick in your gullet.*

Throughout the 1950s the condition of the homes in the four streets which made up the New Buildings had continued to deteriorate. On 12 October 1961 planners at South Shields Borough Council officially declared the fifteen homes in William Black Street a clearance area. It was three years before the last occupants had been rehoused and the bulldozers moved in to demolish the row. Phillipson Street was not abandoned by the council until June 1974. Again it was several years before the buildings were finally cleared. Today the site of No 10 lies within the Bede Industrial Estate.

Catherine vehemently defended her childhood home – the childhood she could 'still smell'.

'I get cross when I hear people say I was brought up in the slums,' she said. 'East Jarrow wasn't slums. It was a good working-class community with standards. High ones. Proper ones.' Sometimes, as Catherine well knew, those standards could be razor sharp.

A week after her comments on private health care, Catherine and Tom were under attack once again. This time they considered the attack so hurtful they seriously considered selling up their Corbridge home after just two years.

Their house, High Barns, overlooked a one-and-a-half acre rough field used for grazing cows. It had, however, been earmarked for housing. Worried at the prospect of the new buildings spoiling the view across the countryside, Catherine and Tom purchased the plot. Their intention was to turn the pasture into an ornamental garden as an 'asset for the village'.

Members of Corbridge Village Trust did not agree. They promptly sent the Cooksons a letter objecting to their plans to plant trees in the field because, they claimed, a medieval ditch ran across it. Other residents were less honest. One anonymous letter writer attacked Catherine by saying she should have spent her money on cancer research or a kidney machine instead of wasting it on safeguarding the view from her window.

Tom Cookson stepped into the row to protect his wife. 'Catherine is very sensitive to this sort of thing and if she thought there was any ill-feeling towards her in the village we would rather move out,' he said.

Two years later the couple had planned and paid for the planting of 20,000 daffodil bulbs, 6,000 crocuses, thousands of tulips and 700 saplings.

CATHERINE dedicated her latest novel: 'To the one and only to whom I owe so much'.

Her new book was the first since *Kate Hannigan* to make use of a central theme – a single thread – to hold the story together. In her very first novel Catherine had settled on a single day, Christmas Eve. Now, albeit less strictly, she used *The Cinder Path*.

The cinder path of the title is at Moor Burn Farm in Northumberland, where Edward Macfell, an Edwardian patriarch, metes out justice with a cane to wayward farm boys sprawled on the abrasive track. For Charlie, easygoing and with none of his father's inherent cruelty, each blow deepens the hatred he has for his father. Charlie forsakes his home for the trenches of Flanders. But among his 'comrades in arms' he finds new tormentors. When he fights back, the battle is not simply against flesh and blood, but against the ghost of his dead father, his own weak and oppressed spirit and the cruel significance of the cinder path.

In the autumn of 1978 executives from Granada Television approached Anthony Shiel about the possibility of adapting the Mallen trilogy. Catherine liked the idea. It was the first time one of her adult novels would be serialised.

Although the story is set near Alston in Northumberland, the series was filmed in the beauty spots of Derbyshire, close to Dovedale. Ilam Hall, a National Trust property in the valley of Ilam, was transformed into High Banks Hall. Location filming during the harsh 1978–9 winter caused enormous problems for the crew. A team of carpenters was cut off by snowdrifts in the first week of filming. The cast, including Caroline Blakiston, John Duttine, Ian Saynor and John Hallam, fared little better in the freezing conditions.

ITV had scheduled transmission of the first episode for the prime-time slot of nine o'clock on Sunday, 10 June 1979. Some weeks earlier Granada had sent Catherine videos of the first two episodes. She was impressed, but the sensation of watching the images of her mind's eye take on an existence of their own was an eerie one.

Catherine said after watching the episodes: 'I was full of anxieties and worries about how they would be translated to the screen, but I needn't have been.

'When I write, my characters are alive in my mind. The likenesses between some of my characters and the way they are portrayed in the series is uncanny.'

While the Granada crew were wrestling with the rigours of the weather, 73-year-old Catherine spent most of the winter at High Barns confined to bed. Her days remained long and the standards she set herself uncompromising. She was working on the *Tilly Trotter* trilogy.

The first book, simply entitled *Tilly Trotter*, was already with her publisher and due for publication in 1980. It was one of the longest and most densely populated novels Catherine had produced for years, with no less than fifty-four speaking characters.

The setting never strays far from Catherine's own birthplace, the south bank of the Tyne from Shields to Jarrow. The time – at the start of the Victorian era – allowed her to mix traditional village life with scenes of the Industrial Revolution, especially the appalling conditions in the mines. Tilly – 'fifteen gone, coming up to sixteen' – is living happily with her grandparents on the edge of the Sopwith estate in County Durham. She is still a teenager when the story ends. During this period Tilly is almost raped, is accused of witchcraft and sees her grandmother die in an arson attack on her cottage. When she falls on hard times Tilly has to work underground at the near-by pit and is trapped for three days by a roof fall – but holding her hand in the darkness is a man with the key to her future.

Although Catherine had written *Our John Willie* as a children's book, thousands of adult readers rapidly placed the story firmly among the United States top ten sellers. It was soon to become a favourite with British television audiences.

BBC director, Marilyn Fox, spent most of the early weeks of 1979 scouring the North-East looking for a yellow-brick row of Victorian cottages. Also on her shopping list were a workhouse, a drift mine and a little-altered rectory dating back to the middle of the nineteenth century. Filming for the five-part serialisation of *Our John Willie* eventually began in May. Taking the part of the deaf and dumb John Willie was thirteen-year-old Newcastle schoolboy, David Burke. His brother was played by teenager Anthony Manuel.

The location for much of the series was, in fact, the 200-year-old former rectory home of Sunderland bakery boss, Michael Milburn, at Whitfield. It was, coincidentally, the precise area in which Catherine had set *The Girl*. The rectory is even mentioned in Dr Arnison's volume of local history. While the Milburns' five-bedroom house suffered at the hands of a forty-strong film crew, part of it was converted to a modern-day classroom – to allow the two teenage stars to keep up with their schoolwork.

In 1979 – more than thirty years after she first joined the Hastings Writers' Group – Catherine agreed to sponsor a short-story competition. She was still its president. The winner of the annual event would receive the Catherine Cookson Cup and a cash prize.

For relaxation Catherine had turned once again to art. She was still using the easel she had bought from van der Meersch's widow during Tom's wartime posting to Hereford. One interviewer extracted from her a conviction that 'if I hadn't made it as a writer, I'd have made it as an artist.' She was completing about thirty paintings each year.

Although visitors were eagerly shown the sketches and paintings which decorated the walls of High Barns, Catherine had only once shown her work in public. Early in 1979 she was invited to join an all-woman exhibition.

Tom quickly dispelled his wife's initial reservations and helped decide which of her cathedral sketches, pastel work and oil seascapes to include. The five-week exhibition – Women Artists of the North-East – was staged at the Metal Art Precinct, South Shields. Catherine travelled from Corbridge for the preview.

Thirteen

Happiness is on a different plain: it is a state of mind, the main ingredient of which, I think, stems from kindness.

FOR HER READERS Catherine had been endowed with the ability to understand.

Despite the sex, violence and jealousy in her books she was judged entirely moral, endowed with an insight into feelings and human failings that, at times, seemed like second sight. Writing to Catherine – talking to Catherine – was like finding a long-lost member of your family or calling on a favourite aunt.

Some letters read as though confessing, as if their authors were seeking forgiveness from a greater power. Catherine had assumed the mantle of agony aunt; mother confessor; friend and confidant, all rolled into one. And she took on the responsibility of a thousand other tragedies without complaint.

'If I have been ill, the mail mounts up tremendously and I get very worried about it,' she admitted. 'My publishers have been at me for ages to get stereotyed letters done. They couldn't believe I received so many letters; some people have been writing for twenty years. I would rather not answer at all as send a stereotyped letter.'

Although she was employing a part-time secretary to transcribe her tapes and retype the manuscripts, Tom continued to act as his wife's correspondence secretary. By the early 1980s as many as sixty letters a week were arriving at High Barns, an average of 3,000 unsolicited letters each year.

With the letters from all over the world came the gifts – a box of flowers from a reader on holiday in Guernsey; beautifully knitted shawls or sweaters; a silver coffee set from America – 'But the dishcloths I got from one old lady were just as precious.'

Money to Catherine had always been a way of helping others. It also magnetised those – honest and dishonest – begging for cash. Catherine read every letter. 'Some stories would break your heart,' she said, 'but I had to keep my reason.'

Catherine, more than most, had reason to feel aggrieved at the incompetence and fallibility of doctors. She was also convinced the specialists treating her telangiectasia were going a long way to keeping her alive. In February 1980 she decided to repay a fraction of that debt by donating £27,500 for research into blood disorders at Newcastle Haemophilia Reference Centre, part of the Department of Medicine of Newcastle University and based at the city's Royal Victoria Infirmary. 'I have learned to live with my condition,' she said, 'but haemophilia can have a devastating effect on young people. This grant is an attempt to relieve some of that suffering.'

Eleven months later she stepped in to buy desperately needed life-saving equipment for Newcastle General Hospital's maternity unit. Her £12,800 gift paid for an incubator, ventilator, heart monitor and special drip feeds for premature babies. It was the biggest single donation received by the department.

Other grants included cash to support the work of the spinal implant programme at Newcastle's Freeman Hospital and £250 to a North Shields school helping physically and mentally handicapped children.

In the autumn of 1980 Catherine's first appearance on Independent Television's top-rated *This Is Your Life* had to be abandoned at the last minute. The target for the 2 November 1980 edition was to be Southampton Football Club manager and fellow North-Easterner, Laurie McMenemy.

Their unlikely friendship began when Catherine and McMenemy both appeared on a live television programme hosted by Melvyn Bragg. They were speaking from separate studios hundreds of miles apart. When Catherine was criticised for dwelling on the past in her books, McMenemy sprang to her defence. His wife Anne, admitted the soccer personality, was a great fan of her books.

'Kitty wrote afterwards to thank him and sent a book for his wife,' explained Tom. 'He later sent her his own book.'

The programme is produced in absolute secrecy, and a *This is Your Life* researcher had approached Catherine to ask if she would be willing to appear on the programme as a surprise guest and meet McMenemy face-to-face for the first time. At the last minute she suffered a severe bleeding attack and had to be rushed by Tom to Newcastle's Royal Victoria Infirmary for treatment.

TO everyone's surprise *The Man Who Cried* failed to take its expected place as the country's bestselling paperback.

Under pressure from the book trade to issue more titles in July 1980, Corgi had brought forward the novel's publication date from 25 to 18 July. News of the revised, earlier release date failed to reach half of the eighty bookshops around the country taking part in the *Sunday Times – Bookseller* bestsellers' list scheme. They recorded a scrupulous 'nil', while the forty who were aware of the change recorded heavy sales – still enough to put *The Man Who Cried* into fourth place in its first week.

Since 1979 the greater part of Catherine's working day – and most of the night when her mind refused to surrender – had been devoted to her second trilogy. The proofs of *Tilly Trotter* had been read and corrected. By March Catherine had completed the second book, *Tilly Trotter Wed*.

Events have moved on twelve years from the end of the first book, which left Tilly, still a lanky teenager, looking after crippled mine owner Mark Sopwith. Tilly refuses to marry Mark. When he dies, leaving her four months' pregnant, Mark's spiteful daughter throws Tilly out. But before long she is back at the manor, this time at the invitation of Mark's eldest son Matthew, newly returned from making his fortune in America. The pair eventually marry and return to the American pioneer territories, where Tilly finds herself fighting both a grizzly bear and irate Indians.

The conflict of personalities between the forceful and domineering Matthew and Tilly, his beautiful and fiercely independent housekeeper and wife, occupies the central part of the book. It is classic Cookson and, many critics agree, Catherine at her most skilled and confident best. Transporting a major part of the action not only out of Tyneside, but across the Altantic to Texas in the 1850s, did give her second thoughts, however.

Catherine studied Sue Flanagan's photographic record *Sam Houston's Texas* and read T. R. Fehrenbach's *Lone Star* and *Comanches*. In the author's note she confesses: 'It wasn't until I was advised to read these books that the audaciousness of my effort opened up before me and I hesitated whether to continue with my story.'

Tilly Trotter Wed appeared in January 1981. The final part of the trilogy, *Tilly Trotter Widowed*, was published twelve months later. Tilly is white-haired, although still mysteriously attractive, at the age of thirty-five. First a rich man's mistress, then a frontier wife, she is now a widow with two assorted illegitimate children to bring up – one half-blind, the other a Mexican girl. Her husband has died in the previous book from wounds received in an Indian skirmish. Tilly returns from Texas to take up her role as lady of Sopwith estate, a full circle for the servant girl who once scratched for coal in the pit she now owns.

DURING the late 1970s the Cooksons decided to purchase the property next to High Barns at Corbridge. Although only yards from the main house Catherine and Tom used Trinity Barns as a weekend retreat and as extra accommodation for guests and relatives.

On 12 January 1981 they returned to find Trinity Barns broken open and ransacked. A pair of antique candlesticks Catherine had purchased from a charity sale, a Chinese table and an antique plate were missing. At first the police assumed the raid to be the work of antique thieves. It soon became obvious local teenagers were involved. A fourteen-year-old boy and three fifteen-year-olds later admitted in court they had entered the house when they noticed a smashed window. They were bored because a village dance had been cancelled.

Catherine was angry and upset by the theft and the damage. Tom felt a deeper hurt. Since their move to Corbridge he had involved himself with the youth of the village, supporting clubs and sports and social events. 'It hurt Tom a great deal,' she said.

Catherine had long overlapped work in progress: dictating a raw and unrefined story on to tape; reading and correcting a typescript of a second; cutting and polishing the manuscript or proofs of others. On 20 June 1981 she celebrated her seventy-fifth birthday by completing the last of four new novels. It would be another five years – and Catherine would be eighty – before the final book found its way into print.

Five years after her return to the North-East Catherine found she was still recovering from the surfeit of enthusiasm her homecoming had generated. During her first year back she had seldom refused an invitation, sometimes attending as many as four a week. Her writing output and her health began to suffer. Not since she was asked to rewrite the *Rooney* script had she put in so many night shifts. Thankfully the novelty wore off. For a while, at least, Catherine's dubious relegation from news to newsworthy provided the bonus of a little more peace.

Her health and her obsessive need to work now confined her to the two-and-a-half acres of her Corbridge home. Six months of each year were spent in bed. The rest of the time, when the unpredictable Northumberland weather allowed, Catherine shared between her vast study and even more impressive garden.

Catherine was always anxious to remain in control of her public image. Her agent, friends and relatives sent cuttings of newspaper and magazine pieces in which her name appeared. Inaccurate news reports and features were swiftly followed by corrections or apologies. Childhood anecdotes and details of her adult life were dispensed in strictly measured doses. When, in 1981, her former agent John Smith admitted he was working on a Cookson biography Catherine was dismayed.

Smith was already an accomplished poet with seven collections of his work in print. The biography, he explained, would bypass the *Our Kate* years and concentrate more on Catherine's career as a writer. Catherine agreed to co-operate because she 'preferred it to be written while I am alive and by someone who knows me'. The biography was never published, however.

The burglary – and the publicity engendered by the resultant court case – had somehow spoiled Trinity Barns. The couple put the house up for sale and bought themselves a new weekend retreat, this time in the hamlet of Langley, less than ten miles west of Hexham.

For the first time in their lives the break-in also fanned a sense of vulnerability. In one way the Cooksons – whose openness and trust so endeared them to friends and strangers alike – had been betrayed by Catherine's 'ain folk'. They took steps to protect their property. Collapsible grilles were fitted to the insides of windows and iron gates protected entrances.

Their apparent – and misunderstood – need to escape also produced a pack instinct among journalists and photographers, to many of whom Catherine would gladly have granted an interview. Rumours of the 'celebrity' owner of Bristol Lodge leaked out. Catherine and Tom awoke one morning to find a reporter from a national newspaper peering through a window. The couple attempted to buy the weekend peace they needed by 'leaking' details of their latest retreat through media friends. One report placed them in a cottage near Ashington on the other side of Northumberland.

Life back at High Barns was equally hectic and frustrating. In October 1981 her latest children's story – *Lanky Jones* –appeared. For some reason it generated almost as much interest as *Tilly Trotter*. Tom and Catherine once more packed their car and headed west down the A69 beyond Hexham.

They both cherished the long breaks at Bristol Lodge. 'It's peaceful and it's quiet and it's in the wilds.' That first winter they deliberately cut themselves off for six weeks. 'And we enjoyed every minute of it,' admitted Tom.

Catherine spent the long winter retreat gathering material for a new story. Surrounded by open countryside and overshadowed by sparse upland she could not shake off her fascination with industry. In the early years of the nineteenth century the area had reeked with the fumes of lead smelting. Derelict furnaces and workshops still pock-marked the landscape. Catherine consulted local historians and read *Forster's Strata* on the industry.

Once back at Corbridge Catherine began dictating a new novel. Although little more than fifteen miles separated High Barns from Bristol Lodge, Catherine still found she needed the act of departure and arrival to focus her thoughts. She opened the story with the arrival of young Roddy Greenbank at the remote community of Langley in 1807. Its climax was already set in her mind. She was intrigued and pleased by her narrative. The first draft was completed in a matter of weeks. She felt it was 'a bit like *Katie Mulholland* – or even better'.

For a title she turned to Proverbs: 'Better a *dinner of herbs* where love is, than a stalled ox and hatred therewith.'

Heinemann, although delighted by the new book, insisted it take its place among the novels already awaiting publication.

There were at least four more 'big books' on hold. *A Dinner of Herbs* would not be released until 1985.

Since the publication of *Kate Hannigan* thirty-one years earlier, a total of fifty-six Catherine Cookson and Catherine Marchant stories had appeared – every single title still in print. Her books had been translated into fifteen languages. And Corgi had issued 27,500,000 Cookson paperbacks.

Still working at least seventy hours a week on her stories – and many more answering letters – an accumulation of fatigue and ill health finally caught up with Catherine.

On 22 September 1981 she was due to open a £500,000 housing project for the elderly at Simonside, East Jarrow – almost within sight of her Leam Lane birthplace. Tom was forced to call the organisers and apologise after her doctor ordered his wife to remain in bed for at least a week. The forty residents at Queen Elizabeth Court replied with a get-well telegram.

A month later, at the end of October, Catherine finally arrived at the South Shields home to enact a fantasy she had nurtured for almost seventy years. While walking through South Shields market as a child before the First World War, she had watched delighted and horrified as a woman shopper accidentally dropped a £1 note. Although her family desperately needed the extra money, Catherine picked up the note and handed it back. For years she had fantasized of returning to the market to distribute cash to the poor and needy. At last Catherine had her chance. Every one of the forty-two residents at the newly opened home was treated to a crisp £5 note and a signed photograph of the writer.

Mary Ann Shaughnessy – the girl from the dog-end of Jarrow who featured in eight of Catherine's stories between 1954 and 1967 – also made a reappearance in July 1981. Although Catherine was now with Heinemann, her first publishers, Macdonald, reissued the stories in a 756-page collection entitled *The Mary Ann Omnibus.*

Throughout the autumn and winter Catherine was in constant pain. The rest her doctors ordered somehow eluded her. A coughing fit – even a bout of laughter – could start the flow of blood from her nose and tongue. Wrapped in the dressing gown she calls her 'blood coat', Catherine would sit in the back of their five-year-old car as Tom drove her through the night to hospital in Newcastle.

On one occasion Catherine and Tom had invited her doctor and his wife to visit them socially at Langley. As she arrived the doctor's wife said to Catherine, 'Isn't it lovely to see you dressed!'

Catherine was now under the care of three specialists, one looking after her injured back, a second her blood disorder, and the third acting as 'general adviser' – 'All three are great friends.'

Christmas, a time Catherine admitted long ago she never really enjoyed, brought with it the usual round of family visits and the deluge of letters, cards and gifts. On 1 January she and Tom decided 1982 was to be a lazy year. The resolution had worn thin within days.

During the summer of 1982 Catherine allowed readers of a Newcastle newspaper a rare insight into her working day.

Well, there I am in the black dark at two o'clock in the morning grappling with characters. I always use the same process in my writing . . . the characters come first, not the plots, ever.

I try to pretend to be asleep but Tom always knows: 'Aren't you ever going to sleep?' he says.

The next morning I get started on my tapes at about half-past six: I always have them there by the bed.

Tom goes downstairs and makes a cup of tea while I talk my stories on to the tapes. At a quarter past eight my dear husband brings my breakfast to bed; this he has always done. It's usually grapefruit and toast; porridge in winter, perhaps, but mostly very plain.

It takes me only five or ten minutes at the most to eat my breakfast and, even then, I'm looking at my scripts. Then I get up, come down to the study at about ten o'clock and do a half-a-dozen or so telephone calls, mostly business, London probably; then I get started on the mail.

But the day goes on. Mostly I stay in the study until twelve or half-past and get as many letters off as I can.

We have a break at about twelve or twelve-thirty, maybe half-an-hour but no longer. I have what I call my 'American bit' – two Vitawheats, an apple cut up, a handful of raisins, a piece of cheese and a glass of milk. In the kitchen, usually, sometimes in the conservatory.

In the afternoon I start again, get to work correcting the roughs that my secretary has typed from the tapes. I might go over manuscripts three or four times, correcting. If, by this time, my mind is going round and round and dizzy, I might go to the conservatory and start on a picture. It's the starting on it that's difficult . . . once I've started it's all right because I can then do maybe half-an-hour or an hour's work on it.

Then we have dinner about half-past five. After dinner? Well, what they call comedies on television now, one is afraid to look at. You can hardly see one without somebody jumping into bed.

I like M.A.S.H., though. And I like anything with that girl . . . you know, the To the Manor Born *girl [Penelope Keith] in it. I love* It Ain't 'Arf Hot, Mum; *my tastes are very simple.*

If I am very tired I might go to bed at half-past nine, but not to sleep . . . to work again on my scripts. Even if I am ill and stay in bed I am always working; I've got to be very, very ill to stop work altogether. I would go bats if I just laid in bed and did nothing.

I might go on working until eleven; my mind is always very alert.

I know that I overwork. I know I exhaust myself and am sometimes flat out and speechless . . . But I ENJOY *working.*

Accolades for her work arrived year after year – almost month by month. In 1981 Catherine was awarded a trophy in recognition of her 27,500,000 paperbacks sales. And 1982 saw another award take its place in the Cookson study-cum-office, this time a silver book to commemorate one million sales of *The Mallen Streak*.

Late in 1981 Macdonald had approached Catherine to ask if she would consider writing a book for five- to seven-year-olds. It was a new challenge. The inspiration was an old one.

Catherine could still feel the bubbling excitement of reading – of owning – her first book, a birthday present from Mrs Romaines. She could also see herself eagerly studying a picture in the story book Jack McMullen had stolen from his school billet in 1914. It showed a cosy room, warmed by a blazing fire, and lived in by a little girl who had her own cup and saucer, her own teapot, and her own kitten which sat on the floor. From the memory Catherine created *Nancy Nutall and the Mongrel*, published in September 1982.

Nancy is a child with a houseproud mum and a noisy baby brother, who longs for the same picture of privacy as her creator once did. Catherine made one change. She swapped the family cat for a dog. 'I changed it to a dog because I love dogs so much,' she admitted. The current dog in the Cooksons' life is Sandy, a nine-year-old white poodle which whispers in Tom's ear and 'plays football better than most professionals'.

After a relatively peaceful summer, shared between Corbridge and the secrecy of Langley, the final three months of 1982 were to prove hectic for both Catherine and Tom.

In October Catherine received two prestigious awards – one she collected personally, the other was delivered.

Troughout the summer readers of *Woman's Own* magazine had been voting to elect their Fifty Women of Achievement. The poll was to celebrate the publication's fiftieth anniversary. Catherine was overwhelmingly voted Britain's number one creative writer. Six other award winners attended the presentation at London's Café Royal on 11 October, including Margaret Thatcher, cellist Jacqueline Du Pré and charity organiser Sue Ryder. Catherine was determined to attend, whatever warnings her doctors gave.

The 650-mile round trip left her exhausted. Although Catherine had thought of asking her agent John Smith to stand in for her at the second presentation in Leeds, the Variety Club of Great Britain would have none of it. Its members had voted her one of the organisation's Women of the Year and wanted to honour her in person. Michael Land, chairman of the Woman of the Year competition, and regional committee member Laurie Higgins, drove up to Corbridge to present Catherine with an inscribed jewellery box.

Never a great admirer of newspapers – and what Catherine called 'their version of the truth' – she and Tom nevertheless used them to keep in touch with charity appeals and pleas for financial help. In the late autumn of 1982 Catherine took time off from working on her seventy-fourth novel to write to specialists at the infant intensive care unit at Newcastle's General Hospital to see how she might help – they didn't expect her to donate a complete ward.

Two years earlier she had handed over a cheque for £12,800 to pay for life-saving equipment at the unit. This time the hospital sent her a new list of equipment it required. Instead Catherine offered to pay for badly needed space. Her cheque – for £40,000 – would allow doctors to take the pressure off the twenty-four-foot ward which accommodated babies with breathing problems and add a third room to the infant unit. It would also allow mothers to remain with dangerously ill babies.

Catherine's latest gift brought her total donations to hospitals and medicine since 1976 to almost £150,000. During 1982 alone she had given more than £48,000 to appeals, not all of them medical. Among others to benefit were handicapped sportsmen and women in near-by Hexham, a schoolgirls' rowing team and a fund to floodlight the seventeenth-century St Andrew's Church at Corbridge.

Early in 1983 the Cooksons watched the progress of yet another campaign – this time to buy an American-built Cavitron ultra-sonic scalpel. When the £60,000 appeal appeared to be faltering, Catherine stepped in with a £20,000 donation. By the end of the year the organisers of the appeal had collected £150,000. The Cavitron Ultrasonic Surgical Aspirator would be used for the removal of difficult tumours in the brain or spine. The additional funds would allow doctors to purchase ancillary laser equipment.

But three days before Christmas 1982 one couple were given the chance to thank Catherine for saving the life of their baby daughter – in front of millions of television viewers.

Catherine had arrived at the Tyne Tees Television studios in City Road, Newcastle, expecting to take part in a live two-minute interview with presenter, Tom Coyne. Instead she was greeted by the soft Irish accent of Eamonn Andrews who told her: 'Catherine Cookson . . . *This Is Your Life.*'

Close to tears, Catherine sat next to Tom during the thirty-minute programme and listened as Gateshead mother Jill Carr described how her daughter, Alison, had been born eleven weeks' premature and weighing just 2lb 15oz. The baby was rushed to the infant intensive care unit at Newcastle General Hospital. 'The incubator Alison was placed in and the monitoring machines she was attached to all had plaques on them saying they were donated by Catherine Cookson,' the former policewoman explained. 'We are just so grateful you helped save our baby's life.'

As usual Thames Television had gone to extraordinary lengths to protect the programme's secrecy. Even management at Tyne Tees were only told the London-based television company needed the studio for 'an evening of light entertainment'. For Tom – an attentive and kindly husband for forty-two years – it was an even bigger problem.

Catherine unwittingly helped by slipping and injuring her ankle ten days before the broadcast. 'It came as quite a relief,' Tom admitted later. 'At least it kept Kitty upstairs and out of the way for a while.'

His ever-increasing activity came to a head when he disappeared for an entire afternoon and refused to explain his absence. All he would tell Catherine was that he was preparing an extra special Christmas present. In fact he was at the Gosforth Park Hotel, north of Newcastle, for a rehearsal with the programme's other guests.

At the end of the programme, and with the cameras still rolling, Eamonn Andrews presented Catherine with the *This Is Your Life* album used during the recording. She was not allowed to keep it. Those honoured received a personal and permanent, leather-bound copy – 'it took months to come.' But once it arrived Tom would ensure the large red book and his wife's other awards, were on display whenever guests arrived.

NEVER shy to include scenes of sex and violence in her novels, Catherine took many of her critics and readers by surprise with final chapters of *The Whip*. Published in the first week of January 1983, its climactic scene involves a sadistic whip attack on a naked and bound woman. At nearly 400 pages it was one of her longest books. It remains one of her most popular.

The story's central figure is Emma who, half-Spanish, half-English and orphaned at seven, is sent to an unknown and uncaring grandmother in a village near Gateshead. Her late father, a Spanish fairground entertainer, has already taught her how to protect herself with a whip and dagger. Emma survives the cholera epidemic which swept through Tyneside in the early years of Queen Victoria's reign, but her grandmother's death from the disease leaves her little choice but to marry a farmer's son. He breaks his back in a fight with his wicked twin brother – over Emma – and she is left to bring up a daughter, who turns out to be a natural whore. Emma's further involvement with the local parson triggers another scandal before a vengeful relative exacts a terrible retribution.

Less than three weeks after the launch of her latest novel, Catherine suffered one of her severest bleeding attacks for many years. She was losing blood internally as well as from her nose and tongue. An added complication was her ever-increasing allergy to the drugs used to control the condition. She was taken by ambulance from High Barns at Corbridge to Royal Victoria Infirmary.

While being treated in hospital the Department of Education and Science announced a survey of 11,000 schoolchildren had put the 76-year-old writer among the top four authors read by teenage girls in England and Wales. Among her rivals in the Government backed study were Agatha Christie, James Herbert and James Herriot.

Her recovery was hastened still further with the news that Newcastle University wanted to award her an honorary degree.

The full impact of the Master of Arts degree did not hit Catherine until she stepped up to receive the honour on 13 May 1983. Her recent and prolonged illness had taken its toll. Catherine looked frail and unusually old. She moved slowly and unsteadily. But there was a new strength in her voice.

'Next to my wedding day and being given the freedom of Shields,' she confessed, 'that was the day that I'll remember. I think, subconsciously, that university degree must have been one of those things I'd wanted all my life.'

The Sunday after the presentation Tom opened the door of High Barns to a man holding a copy of *Our Kate*. It was the caller's second attempt to get Catherine to autograph the book. He had, explained the man, travelled up from London to attend the university ceremony. After returning home empty-handed, he decided to try again the following weekend. The procession of unannounced visitors to High Barns was becoming intolerable.

Tour operators were openly including 'Cookson hunting' stops in any journey between Scotland and the south. Autograph-seeking Americans took to planning their summer holidays with a pilgrimage in mind. And several North American holiday brochures offered a visit to 'Catherine Cookson's Corbridge' as part of a UK holiday.

Catherine and Tom once again sought refuge at Bristol Lodge, their home at the end of a road that provided no known route to anywhere.

For the first time guests were screened. Those who did not know the way were met at Hexham railway station and ferried in by Tom. As compensation they were treated to an impromptu Mallen tour – 'There on that hill is the drovers' inn where Constance met Michael. Down in that valley is the ravine where Donald died.'

One London journalist – whose lack of research was only surpassed by her total ignorance of Catherine's ill health – described her as 'an upright, attractive woman, looking a little like the headmistress of a select girls' school'.

Her description of Bristol Lodge was a little more accurate. From the outside the house, which backed on to a reservoir, appeared small. Inside it contained a series of vast rooms. Two great drawing-rooms, a long dining-room with a mahogany table for sixteen and upstairs – reached by a wrought-iron staircase –an immense study. It was the only room in the house which Catherine and Tom had attempted to make an absolute replica of its predecessor at High Barns. The whole house was neat, tidy and warm with rich deep patterned materials, flock papers and damask, flowered linen. Off the main bedroom was a Hollywood-style bathroom with a round, raised bath.

It wasn't until January 1984 – several months after High Barns at Corbridge had been sold – that Catherine finally admitted the major reason for moving out of the village. In a characteristically frank letter to Corbridge councillor Sandy Mearns, Catherine claimed she and Tom had been subjected to a daily campaign of harassment following their decision to landscape the field adjoining High Barns.

The issue had surfaced once again because of an application by a property developer to build three houses on the field the Cooksons had spent thousands of pounds landscaping. Councillor Mearns, hoping to draw Catherine into the debate, wrote to her thanking her for what she had done for Corbridge. Catherine lashed back: 'You say it was very much appreciated by the village. I can only say, by some. Only I and my husband know the extent of the upset that followed. After the initial explosion, the niggling continued daily until we were forced to move.'

Before she moved Catherine offered to donate the garden to the village. The parish council shunned the idea, claiming it could not afford the upkeep. 'I was left with no option but to sell the land with the house,' she told the councillor. And, in a rare display of pique, she suggested that the houses might even 'enhance' the view across the valley.

Adding insult to injury the developer, to whom the Cooksons had sold the land, offered to sell the two-acre field – ready landscaped – to the village for £80,000 . . . only weeks after Catherine had offered it for free.

On 15 August 1983 Catherine published her sixtieth novel, *Hamilton*. It was written, as Tom recalled, in the style of the early stories she had shown him and then destroyed in the late 1930s. 'I intended this book to be a funny book, a one-off,' Catherine said.

Her publishers, Heinemann, were hesitant. They believed her image as a chronicler of the nineteenth century was so entrenched that a tragi-comedy about a modern, lonely young woman who talks to an imaginary horse for comfort might be rejected by loyal Cookson fans. It was hinted that *Hamilton* should be shelved. Catherine dug in her heels, convinced she knew what her readers wanted. *Hamilton* is still her only book to go through three impressions in six weeks.

LONDON Weekend Television producer, Jack Bond, spent most of July 1983, with a picture of the young Kitty McMullen in his briefcase. He was looking for a face to match – 'Small, bright, intelligent eyes and a neat turned-up nose.'

When he walked into Dunn School, Jarrow, he saw the same face with its quiet peaceful look once again. This time it belonged to eight-year-old Gina Scott. 'As soon as I set eyes on her sitting in a corridor I knew she was the answer,' said Bond. There was another coincidence. Gina's birthday was 27 June – the same date as that recorded on Catherine's birth certificate.

In August the writer came face to face with her childhood look alike. 'She has the same rather lost look that I used to have,' conceded Catherine. Bond intended to use Gina for flashback sequences in a future edition of London Weekend's arts programme, *The South Bank Show*.

The 54-minute programme was eventually broadcast on Sunday, 20 November. It contained a montage of interviews, flashbacks and period scenes filmed at an open-air museum. Catherine was not happy with the documentary. 'She hated it,' recalls Heather Ging, a Tyne Tees Television producer and long-time friend. 'She really hated it. It seemed so condescending and added no authority to her work at all.'

Catherine was also to have the final say over the choice of another actress.

After spending two hundred hours auditioning more than three hundred actresses, Newcastle Playhouse director John Blackmore had settled on Malay-born Prue Clarke to star in the first stage production of a Cookson novel. The musical adaptation of Catherine's 1967 bestseller *Katie Mulholland* was the idea of North-East composer Eric Boswell. He had explained his idea when he went to see Catherine at High Barns a year earlier. She liked Boswell, but thought his scheme 'pie in the sky'.

Within weeks he telephoned to arrange a second appointment, this time to play through several tunes he had composed for the production. Catherine began to take notice.

In March 1983 Boswell presented the idea to Blackmore, head and driving force behind the Tyne Wear Theatre Company. Within eight weeks – the kind of speed Catherine admired – Blackmore and director of production, Ken Hill, had produced a draft script.

Catherine read the script with growing apprehension. 'She hated it,' admitted Hill. 'And Catherine doesn't need a brandy before telling you what she thinks.'

The problem was obvious. Hill – who at six-foot towered over Catherine – had not even read the original novel. 'What you have to remember is that I wasn't even asked to read Catherine's book,' he said in defence. 'Eric had already had the idea and approached her. It was only then that I became involved.

'And then, because we were working under such pressure, I had to show her a draft that normally I would have shown nobody. My first script is a very shorthand, stuck-together thing. I had set some scenes in the bawdy house and she hated that . . . and she was right. I'd probably have cut them, myself.'

The second draft, however, was more to Catherine's liking. 'I can't speak for Catherine and say she approved of it,' said Hill. 'But she passed it – put it that way.'

He also makes the point that there is a considerable difference between writing novels and writing for the theatre. 'Sometimes you might have a kind of sub-text going on which isn't immediately apparent on the page, and reading a script requires a certain amount of experience. It's not the same as reading a novel.'

Time was running out. There were just over six weeks from the day that Hill settled on his leading lady to the first two-and-a-half hour production on 29 September. Rehearsals were hard and energetic, but Catherine and Tom made sure the cast relaxed in style. Actor Alan Hockey remembers Catherine sitting quietly watching the rehearsals. 'After, she would invite us out to dinner at a restaurant – the entire cast – or back to her home at Corbridge,' said Hockey.

Management at the 449-seat theatre had not underestimated the pulling power of Catherine Cookson. Two days before the first night only 400 of the 12,572 tickets available had not been sold. By the end of the twenty-eighth performance every seat had been filled. It was the first sell-out in the company's chequered twelve-year history.

Catherine still had doubts. She and Tom attended the first night with a party of twelve friends. 'I just hope people will clap,' she said drily.

The audiences, who arrived in bus loads from all over the north of England, did applaud. The critics, both local and national, found the musical too parochial.

'The show has little hope of repeating its popular success outside Tyneside,' predicted David Isaacs, arts editor of the Newcastle *Journal*.

His colleague on the city's evening newspaper, the *Chronicle* was less forgiving. 'Were it not for the name of Cookson emblazoned on poster, programme and leaflet . . . the theatre would be sparsely attended each night.'

And, he went on, 'Having lured their audiences in the performers hoof and mug their way amiably through a musical which at times falls only a degree or two short of pure farce . . . Eric Boswell's music is eminently forgettable, trite and frequently so banal as to make one cringe with embarrassment . . . Ken Hill meanwhile has given us a cliché-ridden script.'

Worse was to come. Most national newspaper critics also, it has to be admitted attracted by the Cookson name, saw it as a 'wafer-thin attempt at a home-grown show', appealing only to 'northerners besotted with Ms Cookson'.

The only newspaper to carry a favourable review was the *Shields Gazette*. Catherine promptly telephoned to thank the editor personally.

Plans to tour the musical were abandoned. Catherine, however, continued to defend the production. 'This was a book of 200,000 words, remember. It was a colossal task trying to cram all that into a musical,' she said. 'Anyway I enjoyed it.'

FOR years Tom Cookson guarded his own private thoughts, just as he physically protected his wife.

His need for Catherine – who he often teasingly referred to as 'She' – had grown into a passion. He once claimed he never closed both eyes when he went to sleep in case Catherine had one of her bleeding fits and needed him. His voice broke and he found it difficult to answer when one journalist asked him what life would be like without Catherine: 'Life without Kitty would be no life at all.'

But in October 1983, he did confess his love – briefly – in a three-part Newcastle *Journal* feature. He also proved that the finding of Tom Cookson had undoubtedly saved Catherine's life. His was the unshackled spirit for whom she had been searching, magnetically opposite to the male bigotry which had played a part in her departure from Tyneside.

She's the most wonderful person on earth. I always hoped she was meant for me.

People always assume I'm in the background and always have been throughout our marriage, that Kitty was the strong one, pushing me. But deep down I never believed I was inferior. With her beside me I felt there was nothing I could not do. There was this person who to me exuded such magnetism that I must have craved it all my life.

She believes in herself and in me and she made me believe in her and me too, by golly she did. If she asked me to swim the Channel for her, you know I would.

I have learned that if a man is only prepared to let go of his ego and let a woman have the reins where she clearly has the strength, then there's nothing that can't be achieved. She really is an inspiration.

It pleases me. I feel as though I'm putting back some of what has been put in.

I'm proud to stand just behind her shoulder. People say, 'Who's that?' when they see me, then, 'Oh, he must be her husband.' Well, that doesn't bother me. Not a bit. I know who I am.

My only regret is that she is not in good health. It is terrible to see her bleed, truly terrible.

Her talent you know is quite wonderful. She was always telling stories, right from when we first met in Hastings. I used to teach on a Saturday morning and I would tell my boys that if they were good all week, then I'd read them one of my wife's stories on the Saturday morning. They never misbehaved.

I always liked it when she went to the pictures. I didn't have to go. Hearing her tell me about it was always far better than it would have been seeing it for myself. She makes everything come alive.

Today I still have to shake my head when I watch her working. You should see her. The words just come out of her mouth. You tell yourself that you are an agnostic and then you watch this gift materialise.

It has to come from somewhere, doesn't it? She makes words of wisdom come out of the mouths of ordinary people. I used to criticise back at the beginning. Now I don't think I can find anything to criticise.

And when she took me back to Tyne Dock and the area she'd been brought up in, I felt, well, exhilarated, excited by it, thrilled and proud not that she'd left it behind particularly, but so glad that she wouldn't have to go back there again.

Tom has always refused to discuss his early life. He couldn't remember much of it. It didn't matter anyway. 'My life only began when I met her,' he said defensively. 'Everything stems from that.'

In November 1983 Tom found himself with yet another of his wife's awards to bring to the attention of guests.

It was Catherine's second award from the Variety Club of Great Britain. Jointly organised with BBC Television's *Look North* programme the ceremony, at Newcastle's Gosforth Park Hotel, honoured the achievements of people born in the region. Another recipient was world-champion runner, Steve Cram.

A month later Catherine achieved a different kind of immortality. The Guardian Housing Association sought permission to name a block of twenty-two retirement flats after her. The flats, in Westoe Village, South Shields, would be called Catherine Cookson House.

Fourteen

I am capable of doing everything that I make my characters do: good, bad or indifferent. I am quite capable of doing the worst things possible.

CATHERINE CELEBRATED HER seventy-eighth birthday by cutting a huge cake decorated with the words: 'Spellbinder in person to her friends. Spellbinder to millions through her books.'

The cake – and the champagne lunch which preceded it – had been arranged and paid for by Book Club Associates, the publishing house responsible for releasing special editions of Catherine's novels. 'Giving the world's top-selling author a birthday party was just too good an opportunity to miss,' Lawrence Cotterell, BCA's literary adviser told the guests at Ramblers Country House Restaurant, not far from the Cookson's former home at Corbridge, and a long-time personal favourite.

Catherine and Tom had also just celebrated their forty-fourth wedding anniversary. 'I'm often asked how I manage to continue to write two books a year. I'll tell you,' Catherine confided to her guests. 'I have an excellent staff . . . a marvellous butler, footman, a first-class secretary, a very good chauffeur and part-time gardener and a day and night nurse – all embodied in one man – my husband Tom.'

Her sense of comic irony was never far below the surface. In an earlier interview marking the anniversary she had berated her marriage and career: 'I'm a very unfortunate woman. I've got an honest agent, a good accountant and a marvellous manager in Tom . . . I'm saying unfortunate because there's never any scandals or drama.'

That was not quite accurate. Catherine had started the year by giving her readers a new novel overflowing with scandal and suspicion. She had provoked the 'drama' in her own life by defending the way she saw her own work and how others interpreted it. Written at Corbridge during the long-running campaign of petty prejudice over the field, Catherine's latest novel, not surprisingly, centred on the sinister side of close-knit communities. Woven with sub-plots, it won almost instant critical acclaim for its historical accuracy and reflection of the cruel social conditions of the 1830s. It is still regarded as one of her finest works.

Nine people die on the first page of *The Black Velvet Gown*, taken by a fever that 'emptied the stomach both ways and brought water from the pores likes tears from the eyes'. The momentum never falters. Riah Millican, widowed by the cholera, lurches the six miles on a carrier's cart from a County Durham pit village to her native North Shields. Lodgings for Riah and her four children – with a bowl of broth before sleep – cost 10s 6d a week. The only work available is at the blacking factory, where little imps of children work for 3s a week.

Throughout her life Catherine has remained rigidly apolitical. Yet in her writing she never lost an opportunity to emphasise the politics of poverty. In 1835 – the first year in which the word 'socialism' was used – six- and seven-year-old children were paid just 6d for a sixty-hour week to pick stones from farm fields; kitchen devils earned 1s 6d; and men with families brought home little more than 3s for a week's labouring.

Early in 1984 Catherine heard an American magazine had nominated her as a candidate for its annual romantic writer award. Catherine hastily wrote back, refusing even to be considered. She was not, the editor was curtly informed, a 'romantic' writer. 'I'm a story-teller, a novelist . . . you can't get romantic about a pit lad or dock worker earning 3s 6d a shift.'

American and Australian critics – eager to perpetuate the myth of swashbuckling lords and innocent beauties – quickly dubbed her stories 'bodice rippers'. Catherine has always defended them as unromantic, unsentimental social histories of the north. A view supported by the growing number of sociology students advised to study her autobiography and early works. 'The people who call me a romantic writer have never read me. It's a prejudice. I've written as Catherine Marchant for a woman's magazine because they wanted lighter stories. They could be called romantic,' she said. 'But I wouldn't write them under the name Catherine Cookson. Catherine Cookson is not a romantic writer.'

Her other disagreement that spring was with her former publisher Macdonald over its decision to launch a new collection of her early books.

Issued as the Cookson Library series, Catherine felt the pastel shades and modern, well-fed faces on books such as *Roony* and *The Blind Miller* did not portray the harshness suffered by many of the characters. She also felt a British artist should have been used instead of one living and working in Spain: 'They look like modern novels and certainly my earlier stories are not like that.

'A lot of my books are set at the beginning of the century. They're about the pits and factories, poverty, hardship and sometimes middle-aged characters like Fanny McBride, but these covers give no idea of that.'

Four days after the birthday celebration Catherine was guest of honour at another gathering, this time to lay the first stone of a sports centre for the disabled. She had launched a £140,000 appeal, to pay for the facility in the grounds of Hexham General Hospital, with a £2,500 donation.

In August 1984 her sequel to *Hamilton* was published. Both *Hamilton* and now *Goodbye Hamilton* made use of Catherine's fear-fuelled imagination during her fifteen-year breakdown. In the second book she gives Hamilton a mate called Begonia. Maisie, the lonely and battered heroine, has now dispensed with her awful first husband, and is about to marry again – to the publisher of her first book.

Catherine would continue the story of Maisie in a final novel – *Harold* – already completed and due out in the autumn. Maisie, now a successful author, has adopted a six-year-old Cockney boy, following the death of her second husband. As she struggles to teach him good behaviour, she finds herself caught up in the mysterious doings of a strange young man with a Mohican haircut who offers to help her retrieve her jewellery, which has been stolen by a con-man. This leads her into the hands of criminals and a near-fatal fall.

For the first time in Britain writers were being paid each time one of their books was borrowed from a public library. When the

Public Lending Right scheme began in 1983 only 6,113 authors had registered. The maximum annual payment any writer could receive was £5,000. Catherine agreed to donate her cheque to the Royal Literary Fund to help struggling writers.

The long-fought-for scheme also provided an instant league table of the country's most widely read authors. Of the 100 most borrowed books during 1983 the Register of Public Lending Rights showed Catherine had written no less than 33. Her nearest rival, with just 9 books, was the historical novelist Victoria Holt. Catherine shrugged off the official compliment. 'I don't think about numbers,' she said. 'I just carry on writing.'

While his wife was writing, Tom pottered in the vast garden at Bristol Lodge. His favourite plants were rhododendrons and azaleas, a genus ranging from large big-leaved trees to small alpine shrubs. Both varieties were a regular feature of every garden the Cooksons had owned and Tom had studied them in detail. In the autumn of 1984 he added roses to his list – especially the one named after his wife.

The rose, a light creamy pink, with a deeper pink centre, had been bred by retired pitman, George Davison, in the garden of his Northumberland home. It took him seven years of trials and building up stocks to perfect the forty-petal classic, hybrid tea. The name was suggested by a Hexham nursery. Catherine agreed, only if a proportion of the profits went to local charities to help children and the disabled.

'I Won't Send Roses' – a ballad by Robert Preston – was one of the eight records Catherine selected for her sojourn as a resourceful castaway on the BBC's mythical desert island. For years Roy Plomley had interrogated personalities before their imagined departure. Because of her health Catherine revealed her choice of *Desert Island Discs* during a recording at Bristol Lodge. She chose to take with her Elgar's *Salut d'Amour*, as well as pieces by Schubert and Hoffmeister. In addition to the Robert Preston ballad she wanted 'Thora', sung by Robert Wilson and accompanied by the National Philharmonic Orchestra. As light relief she chose Joyce Grenfell and Norman Wisdom's duet called 'Narcissus'. Her one luxury, Catherine admitted, would be a piano. And, if she were restricted to a single book, it would have to be her own, *Our Kate*.

The idea of spending months on a desert island – even months getting there – also appealed to Tom.

Part of the garden at Bristol Lodge ran down to a small lake, a feature which had been a large part of its attraction for Tom, with his fascination for water. It was not surprising his mind should also return to adventures unlived. 'I would have loved to sail round the world single-handed,' he admits. As a mathematician the navigation would have presented no problems. The days of solitude filled with good books and kind music – 'except I would never leave Kitty.

'I've always had a great desire to sail and it still gives me a great thrill when I see a five-tonner yacht, just the right size.'

On 10 October 1984 Catherine was back at Harton workhouse – almost sixty years to the day after she first took her place among the laundry staff. Long since renamed South Shields General Hospital by South Tyneside Health Authority, Catherine had responded to an appeal for cash to buy baby-monitoring equipment.

Expecting a formal presentation the gathered dignitaries were thrown off balance when Tom produced a blank cheque. 'How much do you need?' Catherine asked the authority chairman, Bill Darling. 'Was it £6,000?'

Darling nervously reminded Catherine the sum mentioned had been £5,000. There was a moment's silence. 'OK,' said Catherine, 'we'll split the difference.' Tom wrote out a cheque for £5,500.

EVER since the Queen Mother had requested a special showing of *Jacqueline* at Windsor Castle in the 1950s, rumours had circulated that Catherine's novels were required reading among certain members of the royal family, a fact Buckingham Palace has always refused to confirm. The proof came in August 1985 when the National Book League let slip that *A Dinner of Herbs* was among a consignment of books it had recently delivered to Balmoral. Published the previous February, four years after it was written, advance bookshop orders made *A Dinner of Herbs* an instant bestseller.

Catherine had set the book among the lead-smelting and farming communities of Allendale and Tynedale, the area dominated by the Mallens. It opens in 1807, with a murder discovered and a second committed. The survivor, a little boy called Roddy Greenbank, is left without a memory of his father's death. It returns to him as a young man when he is attacked by hired thugs of a local landowner, as a punishment for daring to court his daughter. Roddy unmasks his father's killer and solves the mystery of the disappearance of the father of his best friend Hal. But the traumatic experience splits the friends. Roddy goes off to London to learn to be an artist, leaving his childhood companion Mary Ellen pregnant – and dependent on Hal.

While the public was still eagerly buying *A Dinner of Herbs*, Catherine's paperback publisher announced it was producing a special hardback edition of *The Black Velvet Gown*.

The Corgi book, which had a gold-cloth binding to mark the fiftieth Cookson title in paperback, also contained a letter from the novelist. Only 1,000 copies were issued. The majority were given to members of the book trade; others were distributed as prizes through newspapers.

South Tyneside Council, formed from the old and now defunct borough authorities which had shared administration south of the river, also announced a plan to celebrate Catherine's success – by inviting visitors to tour Catherine Cookson Country. Against a backdrop of severe unemployment and declining industry the council hoped its £50,000 campaign would attract Cookson fans into the area. Maps and guidebooks would direct tourists around the borough, while plaques would mark sites such as her 1906 Jarrow birthplace – a petrol station by the mid-1980s – the now demolished New Buildings and Sts Peter and Paul's Church in Tyne Dock.

Catherine had her doubts as Peter Gillanders, the council's publicity officer, recalls. 'Mrs Cookson was afraid it might be construed as an ego trip on her part. She was wary at first and it was only because we convinced her of the potential for bringing new jobs and money into the area that she finally agreed to back it. People assumed there was something in it for her, but she got absolutely nothing.'

Less than two weeks after unveiling its plan, the council announced it was also considering opening a Catherine Cookson Museum, possibly in the historic Old Town Hall in the centre of South Shields Market Place, in the shadow of which the poor but honest Kitty McMullen had returned the pound note to a woman shopper.

The 78-year-old writer drew the line, however, when she was asked to lend her name to a public house. Infected by the Cookson Country fever, licensee Vincent Dingwall wrote asking if he could change the name of his Allison Arms pub in East Jarrow to the Catherine Cookson. He had, he explained, several good reasons. His public house was the only building left in the village where the novelist was born; his children went to St Peter and Paul's School, South Shields, which Catherine had attended and where his aunt had been a classmate, and his father used to live in William Black Street, where the writer grew up.

Catherine's firm, but friendly reply, informed Dingwall she had been connected with enough pubs in her younger days and didn't wish to be so again.

SCHOOLBOY Mark Campbell was playing with friends on waste-ground in the Slatyford area of Newcastle when he heard whimpering coming from a water-filled manhole. Looking down, the boys saw a small, grubby poodle hanging on to an iron grid by its front paws, desperately trying to stop itself being swept away by the fierce current.

The teenager climbed down the fifteen-foot drain and dragged the dog to safety. What he didn't know then was that he had just rescued a future member of the Cookson household.

When Tom and Catherine read news stories of the dog's lucky escape they immediately contacted Newcastle Cat and Dog Shelter where the bitch – dubbed Sue by the staff – had been taken. After a two-hour session at a local poodle parlour Sue was delivered to Langley to meet the Cooksons' other poodle, Sandy.

DURING May 1985 the postman delivered a white envelope to the Cookson's Langley home. There was no stamp. In its place was a circular, dark-blue frank enclosing the words 'London M.L.O.' and below the date and time of posting. In the opposite corner of the envelope was a paler blue rubber stamp, this time enclosing a crown and beneath it the letters 'E.R.' On the reverse was a red embossed royal crest.

Catherine read the letter with growing excitement. Her name, it said, had been put forward as someone deserving consideration in the Queen's forthcoming birthday honours list. Would Catherine Cookson, the letter's writer wanted to know, accept an honour should it be offered?

It wasn't until the afternoon of 14 June that newsrooms around the world – confined to a midnight embargo – were informed Britain's bestselling and best-read novelist was to receive the Order of the British Empire. She was just five days short of her seventy-ninth birthday. The next day Tom was forced to field the scores of telephone calls. Catherine had laryngitis.

One event Catherine could talk about in advance – she had been bound by a promise of silence over the OBE – was her birthday launch of the Catherine Cookson Trail. On the morning she was too ill to attend and sent a good-will telegram wishing the campaign success.

Since the sell-out production of *Katie Mulholland*, management at Tyne Wear Theatre Company had not lost sight of the financial necessity of adapting a second Cookson novel. Early in 1985 the company asked Catherine to suggest a suitable follow up. Her choice was *The Gambling Man*.

Ken Hill, the Playhouse's resident director, thought the adaptation – as a play rather than a musical – would be an excellent start for the company's 1985 winter season. Before he could finish the script the play had already broken a British box-office record. Three days before the theatre's front office was due to start selling tickets for the September production the company had already received more than 3,000 reservations. The figure represented a fifth of all the seats available during the run and was the highest recorded in advance of an official opening. The cast had not yet been auditioned.

Hill eventually settled on Brendan Price to play the part of Rory Conner – all Price had to do now was to learn to speak Geordie. The Coventry-born actor had exactly a month to turn himself into the brash Jarrow lad those life was governed by chance. 'It was one of the most difficult of all the regional accents to get right,' he remembers. 'I went to see a dialect coach in London and listened to tapes of Geordies talking.' He also conducted his own research in several Tyneside pubs.

Throughout the summer of 1985 Catherine had been working

on a new story *The Black Candle*. Although it would not be published for another four years she dedicated the manuscript to Brian Enright, the Newcastle University librarian, for his hours of painstaking research on her behalf. During one telephone discussion, the librarian recalls, 'Mrs Cookson asked if there was anything she could do to help the library. It was then I thought of the thousands of Tyneside unemployed.'

Within days Catherine had arranged to donate £32,000 to the university library. It would be used over the next two years to create four new library assistant's posts and pay the wages of school leavers who would otherwise have been forced to join the dole queue.

Thursday, 7 October 1985 was investiture day at Buckingham Palace. Catherine spent the day in bed at Newcastle's Royal Victoria Infirmary. The previous weekend Tom had written to the Palace informing them his wife was too ill to make the three-and-a-half hour rail journey.

There were around sixty other people living in the north-east who suffered from the same hereditary blood disease which, once again, had forced Catherine into hospital. Her next donation attempted to ease the painful condition for future generations. It would also be the biggest single financial gift she was to make.

On Monday, 2 December Catherine was admitted to the Royal Victoria Infirmary for the second time in less than a month. Two days later – from her bedside – she handed over a cheque for £250,000 to Newcastle University. The money was to be used to launch the Catherine Cookson Foundation. With additional donations, and the creative use of tax schemes, it meant the university would eventually receive almost £900,000.

Part of the money was used immediately to fund research into blood disorders and to create a lectureship in haematology. The idea behind the research was to study the abnormalities of blood cells at a molecular level, find the cause and then, possibly by genetic manipulation, correct the disorder. 'I have a vested interest in this,' Catherine said less technically. 'I thought I was the only one in the world suffering from this, but now I know there are many riddled with this pest.'

Much of the cash was to be used at the Royal Victoria Infirmary, where Catherine had received treatment from specialists over many years. For the first time she would benefit directly from one of her own donations. A second £40,000 cheque was used to buy a laser to treat bleeding in the intestines. Catherine was one of the first patients.

On the same day she parted with a third cheque – this time for £50,000 – to pay for the purchase of equipment to help diagnose and treat deafness in young children.

Catherine has always remained defensive about her alleged wealth. *The Times* once claimed she was worth £20 million. Another newspaper said that with a fortune of some £17 million she had written her way to being Britain's fourteenth wealthiest woman. She dismisses most claims as 'ludicrous', explaining her financial donations are possible, not because she is earning more but because the Government is taking less. At one time Catherine was paying 83p in tax for every pound she received in royalties. During the 1980s – and under Margaret Thatcher's 'more in your pocket' policies – the deduction dropped to 60 per cent.

Since their return to the north – and prior to establishing the Catherine Cookson Foundation – Catherine estimates she and Tom have given away at least £250,000 of their own money. To receive and process more formal appeals for financial assistance the couple formed the Catherine Cookson Charitable Trust.

Never a lover of Sundays – 'I always work hard on Sundays. It's to stop myself thinking about what day it is' – Catherine and Tom used the quiet hours of the afternoon or evening to read and consider the hundreds of requests for help. During 1984 the trust sent cheques to 120 charities.

Tom shares his wife's philosophy about their alleged fortune. 'Since we haven't any children it would go to charity in the end. It may as well go now.'

Catherine, as always, is a little more practical. 'The only thing I want from my money is to die in comfort. *That* I'm looking forward to and I'm really going to get my money's worth.'

After the loss of her faith in the Roman Catholic Church, Sundays in the Cookson homes were relegated to yet another working day. The 6.30 am starts were the same as Tuesdays or Fridays. Traditional Sunday lunches were abandoned – partly for health reasons.

In 1982 Catherine gave up meat. Instead she was eating more

cheese, fish and eggs. Tom's specialities became soufflés and cauliflower cheese with fresh vegetables. There was one other benefit. 'Since I stopped eating meat I can now eat chocolate,' Catherine explained. 'Before it used to make me feel ill. Now I have two chocolates every night as a treat.'

Throughout the summer hundreds of visitors had descended on Jarrow and South Shields. Day trips to walk the Cookson Trail had become a regular offering by coach operators from Scotland and the Midlands. Now South Tyneside Council sought Catherine's help to bring in even more visitors.

During the coming winter the authority intended to build a full-scale replica of the William Black Street kitchen. The £50,000 project, eventually housed in the Ocean Road Museum at South Shields, would draw on Catherine's description of the room in *Our Kate*. She agreed to scrutinise items like linoleum and light fittings to ensure they were as close to the original as possible.

The plan was not without its critics. Many councillors felt the money would be better spent on housing repairs. One, George Smith, condemned the New Buildings by saying, 'The place wasn't a monument to the town – we pulled it down. I think we want to forget it.'

Members of the town's libraries, and millions of others around Britain, did not agree. For the third year running Catherine Cookson was the nation's most popular author. Releasing the 1985 top 100 books under the Public Lending Right scheme John Sumsion, the Stockton-based registrar, confirmed, 'One per cent of all the books borrowed from libraries in Britain are Catherine Cookson novels.'

Her latest stories, *The Black Velvet Gown*, *Goodbye Hamilton* and the Tilly Trotter series, featured most strongly in the list. Intriguingly, some of her older novels, such as *The Nice Bloke* (1969) and *Feathers in the Fire* (1971), were also included. But if Catherine continued her domination, writing 23 of the top 100, the public's taste in reading matter was changing. Wilbur Smith took second place with 9 books on the list, Victoria Holt had 7 and Dick Francis had six.

Once again Catherine donated her lending rights' cheque to the Royal Literary Society.

A BITTER wind whipped up the Tyne on 6 February 1986. Among the crowds surrounding the Business Enterprise Centre in Eldon Street, South Shields, were 76-year-old Sarah Rose and her sister Violet Butterworth. But it wasn't Prince Charles the elderly sisters had come to see. Both women were clutching copies of *A Dinner of Herbs*.

Catherine, who had been confined to a hospital bed and unable to travel down to London to be invested with her OBE, had arrived at the new complex early. The Prince had agreed to present the decoration as part of his day-long tour of Tyneside.

As the crowd cheered the royal guest, Sarah, who suffered from pernicious anaemia, collapsed and found herself being returned to her South Shields home in a police van. As special constable Sandra Nesbitt made the disappointed woman a cup of tea, she heard how the sisters had waited for hours for Catherine Cookson's autograph.

The 79-year-old writer emerged from the meeting with Prince Charles clutching the leather case containing her award, only to be confronted by a policewoman holding two copies of *A Dinner of Herbs*. Catherine signed both books – and added a get-well message for Sarah.

February also saw the publication of *The Moth*. Long before it won critical acclaim the novel had come to mean something special to its author. It is a short book by Catherine's standards, yet it contains a distillation of everything she had taught herself as a writer. It is a love story uncluttered by excessive emotion; a summoning up of times past without the sentiment of nostalgia. Seldom given to passing judgment on her own efforts, Catherine later admitted she regarded it as one of her finest works.

Robert Bradley, a carpenter, leaves the relative security of Palmer's Jarrow shipyard early this century to work at his uncle's old-established workshop at Lamesley; a time and a place which itself had a special association for Catherine.

Women would cause Robert's downfall, if he let them: first, the brazen Nancy Parkin, in the market for any man; then his luckless cousin, Carrie, who blames him – conveniently but wrongly – for making her pregnant; then the less than plain but good-hearted Maggie, who finds his is the only shoulder to cry on. Flitting ghost-like through the book – but hardly making a tangible impression – is *The Moth* of the title, Millie, who loves Robert with the same, simple trusting love she gives her puppy. Robert eventually marries Millie's sister, Agnes, mistress of 'The Big House'.

The book ends with the start of the First World War, but even the wartime horror is eclipsed by the actions of a mad, jealous arsonist set on destroying 'The Big House' and everyone in it.

Catherine's imagination had worked its magic on her own house just as easily as if it had been one of her stories. 'I knew just how I wanted it to look . . . with as many windows as possible so that whichever way you look there's something lovely to see.'

When the Cooksons purchased it, Bristol Lodge was a 300-year-old single-storey building. It was set in two-and-a-half acres of garden and bordered a man-made lake built as a reservoir in the eighteenth century to provide hydraulic power for machines in the local lead-mining industry.

Part of the house's attraction, like High Barns, was an indoor swimming pool where Catherine swam each day. When even swimming became too painful, the pool was filled in and the area was converted into a forty-foot drawing room. In pride of place, on an antique reading table, stood a copy of the Domesday Book, duplicated on parchment and bound in wood, an exact replica of the original in the British Museum. Tom acquired it when a limited number of copies were produced while the original was being restored. His idea was to use the historic book to practise the Latin he had once enjoyed and taught. Between the arrival of the replica, and the bound English translation several months later, Tom had managed to read most of the handwritten text.

During the 1980s the original house was extended to incorporate two near-by farm cottages to provide extra living accommodation, jokingly dubbed by Catherine the 'sick bay'.

Leading off the hall are the sitting room, dining room, spiral staircase and then, beyond the conservatory, the vast drawing room. Above it is the main bedroom with its sloping ceiling and views across the countryside.

Each morning Catherine's cousin and part-time secretary, Sarah Sables, would take the day's tapes to the first-floor study for typing. The study – at the top of the wrought-iron spiral staircase – also houses a collection of leather-bound first editions of all

Catherine's books. Beside them are her OBE, the scroll granting her the freedom of South Shields and the honorary degree from Newcastle University. As in every Cookson home, correspondence is everywhere. At Bristol Lodge an entire room is devoted to files of readers' letters.

Also on the first floor are the main bedroom and en-suite bathroom. All the fittings are gold-plated. Either side of the bath stand a pair of sculptures, women of Italian origin. One Tom acquired, the other was Catherine's find.

When Catherine is ill, the daily routine remains on the ground floor, sometimes for as long as three months. Tom brings the typewriter down from the upstairs study to a room adjoining the 'sick bay' bedroom.

As Catherine's eightieth birthday approached she was torn between starting a new novel or saving her energies for the celebrations. She had just finished correcting the proofs of *Bill Bailey*, due out in October.

Finally, on Sunday 25 May, she gave in to the story nagging at her mind; to the 'swirling wind' which kept her awake long after Tom had fallen asleep and sometimes woke her long before he stirred. The research, which Catherine had always considered a kind of extension to her own education, once again became intense. This time it centred on the tobacco industry. Always a non-smoker, Catherine was fascinated by how many different kinds of cigars there were and which countries produced them.

Since the Cooksons first purchased Bristol Lodge in 1981, Catherine's health had progressively deteriorated. Her sight in one eye was failing and the arthritis in her back kept her almost permanently confined to bed. Although her days were never idle, Catherine's appointments outside her home were kept to a minimum. In May, however, Tom drove her to Durham for a BBC television interview with Cliff Michelmore.

Sitting in the Galilee Chapel of Durham cathedral, she chose some of her favourite music to be played by members of the Northern Sinfonia. They included Mozart's *Eine Kleine Nachtmusik* and Massenet's 'Meditation' for *Thaïs*. During the *Home on Sunday* programme, broadcast in August, Catherine also requested the Sinfonia Chorus to sing 'Amazing Grace', 'Ave Maria,' 'Bless This House', and the 1960s pop hit 'Windmills of Your Mind'.

At home she often listened to Jim Reeves – 'His voice is so soothing to listen to.'

Throughout May 1986 John Wilkes, the curator at South Shields Museum, had been tracking down items of old kitchen equipment and furniture, but there was one thing he had failed to locate – a picture of Lord Roberts sitting on a horse next to a negro. The picture, which had so often attracted the drunken abuse of John McMullen, was the only major item he could not include in a re-creation of the William Black Street kitchen. The £50,000 display incorporated a full-size bricks-and-mortar street façade and a reproduction of Cissie Affleck's shop. Catherine had helped with the design and layout of the kitchen. 'Everything that happened in that kitchen,' she said, 'everything I thought, everything that I have written since, seems to have been bred in that kitchen.'

The decision on whether she would attend the official opening on 25 June would not be made until the day.

Her fans were soon to get another chance to see the streets and buildings and industry that had been part of her early life. The previous year writer Piers Dudgeon had been looking for a sequel to his recently published Thomas Hardy's England. He discovered old photographs of Catherine's Tyneside and its urban industrial landscape were complimentary opposites to Hardy's rural scenes.

Dudgeon's idea was to dovetail sections of fiction and biography with new elements from interviews with Catherine. As he explained it to Catherine: 'The book would not only be a literary statement, but also a history and evocation of the spirit of the industrial landscape of the north.' She instantly agreed.

After approaching both Heinemann and Transworld at the 1985 Frankfurt Book Fair a deal was eventually struck between Dudgeon's company, Pilot Productions, and Catherine's hardback publisher to produce Catherine Cookson Country: Her Pictorial Memoir.

Three long taped interviews at Bristol Lodge with Dudgeon provided additional material. Catherine and Tom also agreed to sift through hundreds of photographs. The proofs arrived while she was ill. One mistake slipped through. Dudgeon had located St Peter and Paul's Church in Jarrow instead of Tyne Dock.

The book itself is a skilful grafting together of passages from

Our Kate and extracts from Catherine's novels. Much of its worth, as its name suggests, lies in the photographs. Any new insight into the writer's background is found, not in the main body of the text, but in the notes at the beginning and end of the book and the captions to the pictures.

It opens, not with an introduction by Catherine, but with a foreword by Tom. Except for brief newspaper features it was the first time he had written in detail about Catherine's life. More importantly he attempts to place his wife's work in context, to point out the social milestones she passed along the way.

> *one must again remember her upbringing in the years prior to and during the First World War: no wireless – this came in the 1920s – no TV; only reading, if possible; but certainly there was the listening to tales told and retold by members of the family, detailing events which had occurred much earlier, perhaps going back even to her great-grandmother's time before the 1850s . . .*

And the start of the journey. The quirk of fate which thrust Catherine forward at a given time and at a given moment.

> *Had she been born twenty or more years later than she was, she would undoubtedly have profited from the formal education that would then have been available: 'winning a scholarship' to High School, and then proceeding to university; and even being the age she is, had she been born in better circumstances in the sense that books would have been readily to hand, as well as guidance from educated people around her, she would have taken full advantage of both.*

There is one other product of her years as a writer which Catherine allowed readers of Cookson Country to experience for the first time – her 'prose on short lines'.

Much of Catherine's poetry had been written during the merciless years of her breakdown or at more recent moments of emotional pressure. Others she produced as warming up exercises for her writing. Some – like 'Nostalgia' – echoed the book's theme.

> *Oh would the North were as it was*
> *When I was little Katie*

When ships were born from Palmer's womb
And slag lit scarlet and black night sky
And rivets flew like sparks from stars
And men were proud to work and sweat.
And yet?
This is just reminiscing talk
No – I would not have the North
As it was
When I was little Katie
For then no workman owned a car
Or took a holiday across the sea
Nor dare he stand and say to THEM
'Lad, I'm as good as thee.'
Oh, little Katie of long ago
Of long, long ago.

CATHERINE celebrated her eightieth birthday on 20 June 1986 with the publication of her illustrated autobiography – and by giving away £160,000.

The majority of the 140 guests who packed the orange and white ribboned marquee on the lawns of Ramblers Country House Restaurant at Corbridge were unaware of Catherine's birthday gift to Newcastle University.

The money would be added to the Catherine Cookson Foundation established a year earlier. In response the university announced it was setting up a new post within its medical school. It would be known as the Catherine Cookson Lectureship in Molecular Haematology.

Among the party guests, entertained by a wind octet from the Northern Sinfonia before sitting down to a lunch of Beef Wellington, were local and national television personalities Mike Neville, Bob Langley and Russell Harty. Asked whether civic dignitaries should be invited Catherine had replied, 'No, I want my friends around me.'

One of her most treasured presents came from Dr Brian Enright, the librarian at Newcastle University. It was a 136-year-old book, in almost mint condition, containing designs by Owen Jones, poetry by R. A. Bacon and drawings by E. L. Bateman.

Picking up the bill for the party were her three separate publishers, Heinemann, Corgi and Book Club Associates.

'Through her books Catherine Cookson has become a close friend of everyone,' Stan Remington, managing director of BCA told the gathering. 'She is the people's writer of this generation, the voice of the North and of real life, and her genius has served her own people in a very special way.'

Paul Scherer, of Corgi Books, added, 'I don't know anyone who is so positive about life, so direct, so unpompous, so generous and caring.'

Catherine, wearing an elegant mushroom-coloured dress with a matching bow in her hair, spoke for twenty minues. With a break in her voice, which reduced many of her guests to tears, she ended by thanking Tom. 'He has given me his life in order that I have the time to write,' she confessed.

Fifteen

They used to say I was a writer who became a business . . . and then an industry.

CATHERINE HAS HER own theory about the process which allows her to recall incidents and characters – even the smell and touch of places – with no apparent conscious effort.

She is convinced that in times of stress or illness her subconscious and conscious minds combine. Just as her conscious self feels fear, pain, or anger in the same way as anyone else, so the negative image, the stored emotion, is being etched on to her 'inner mind'.

Retrieving and viewing the experiences – one, two or even twenty years later – is a process she can only partly control. Always blessed with a remarkable memory, Catherine is able to return to her diary and make up lost days with total accuracy. Vivid memories require only a single prompt to set them playing on the white screen of her mind.

'I see everything in film form,' she says. 'I talk every piece of dialogue. I make love. I fight. I become very emotional with the characters and I laugh or cry with them.'

There is no conscious effort in the creation of her stories. No reaching out to grasp elusive images. No half-world populated by characters clamouring to be heard. The process is orderly and natural. Catherine produces the words – the sentences – as instinctively as though she were speaking to a perfect stranger. The reels of dialogue and action are played back without recognition, her subconscious rising to take control.

'When I'm dictating I have no memory,' she explains. 'It's not until I read the transcript, the words on the page, I recall where the inspiration for a story or character came from. It's as if the text prompts my memory and I remember it for the first time.'

There is no time limit on these subliminal images. They do not fade with the years, nor are they nudged aside by new experiences. Catherine claims they are as sharply focused as the moment they were recorded.

It is true Catherine was born in an age when childhood distractions were few, but thousands of children shared the same poverty; survived the same hardships. Few, however, endured the constant, gnawing mental stress which dominated her earliest years.

Her subconscious storehouse was already at work. There were happier memories. But the naked, hateful incidents of her illegitimacy; of Kate's drinking; of physical violence; of the degrading sights she witnessed – all were recollections of extreme stress.

Years later, as her life became easier, the moments of crisis diminished. But the process never ceased. It possessed her as much as she possessed it.

Catherine has never enjoyed riding in cars. She has repeatedly suffered from car sickness. She also suffers from extreme agoraphobia, the fear of exposed places.

After one speaking engagement in the Midlands Tom decided to drive back to Northumberland along the M6 motorway and over the Pennine ridge via Alston. The road each side of the remote Cumbrian town is flanked by open fells and deep scarps. As they drove higher and higher the fear inside Catherine became overpowering. She was forced to lie on the floor in front of the rear seats. All she could see was the sky and the tops of the snow poles which marked the edge of isolated road.

Tom pulled on to a flat parking area to let Catherine rest. 'He kept saying to me, "it's all right, you can come up now," ' she recalls. 'When I eventually peeped out over the top of the car door I could see a big ruined house beside the road. It had once been quite something, now it was in ruins and derelict.'

Almost three years later Catherine dictated a description of the house. It wasn't until she read the typescript of her day's work that she linked her fictional creation – correct in every detail – with that moment of fear high up on the fells.

'It was Tom who first recognised it,' she said. 'I had no idea what I had done or where the description had come from. It happens all the time, almost every day, as if I have imbibed the things around me.'

DESPITE four decades as a professional writer – two of them as the unrivalled mistress of her chosen genre – few interviewers have questioned Catherine on the practicalities of her craft.

In 1992, after an initial two-hour meeting, I requested a second interview, this time to discuss the practical aspects of her writing. Catherine was too ill to see me. Instead, it was suggested I submit a series of written questions. Almost by return I received her answers – handwritten by Tom – yet clearly in Catherine's own words.

The imaginary interview which follows is based on those answers.

CG: You crossed the threshold from amateur to professional when you started writing about your own background; how important was that?

CC: I even wrote plays about ladies and gentlemen and that sort of thing. Then I realised I knew nothing about these people. But I did know something about the ordinary people in the North-East. I dropped this veneer and started writing about things I knew about. Then I started getting things published.

CG: You have written so many books it is difficult to select the best – critically – as a work of art, as a great book. Have you written a great book?

CC: Every writer wants to write a great book. I get an idea and I think this is going to be it. I write it. And it isn't. Once I stop wanting to do this, I suppose I shall stop writing.

CG: But you never stop working.

CC: I do rest.

CG: Yes, but not for long.

CC: For about three days. Then I get another idea and I start off again.

CG: You also appear to be able to work anywhere. You said you wrote *The Fen Tiger* while on holiday on the Broads; can you write anywhere or are there some surroundings which inhibit your writing altogether?

CC: I can write anywhere.

CG: Can we turn to the inspiration for your stories? What kind of event would develop into a plot?

CC: I never think about plots. I think about incidents or personalities.

CG: Can you enlarge on that for a specific book; *The Menagerie* for example?

CC: I got the idea going past the war memorial in Hastings. It was showery, a wintry day, and right in front of me was this woman. She had a silk dress and flowing skirt, very thin stockings around her shanky legs and a big summer hat.

The memory stayed with me and she became the centre of a mining community in the north. From this came *The Menagerie*. The character gave me the story.

CG: Is it always a stranger? Always an unexpected incident?

CC: I never take a character from a person I know, but I take bits. Sometimes I see people for the first time in a hotel or restaurant and I recognise them as just like someone I have written about.

CG: So does a story have to gestate between the initial idea and having to begin work on it?

CC: I must know the end of a story before I begin. The characters might change here and there, but the main story remains the same.

CG: You appear to have been one of the most enthusiastic and forceful members of Hastings Writers' Circle; what lessons did you learn from your time as a member?

CC: To take criticism: to hear my work read out by others, when I had to admit it did not always sound as good as when I myself read it.

CG: What about your early failures, fifty rejections in one year wasn't it? Did they have any effect other than slow down your eventual success?

CC: No. But how right they were! I had talent but no training. You have to serve your time, and I did, and it was a very long time.

CG: It would be naïve to suggest that your name does not, in some respects, sell your books; but what – particularly in the early years – do you feel made your books so popular?

CC: Because they were written in simple and plain English following Lord Chesterfield's advice and, too, that of the Fowler brothers in *Fowler's King's English*.

CG: You have frequently credited Lord Chesterfield – and to

some extent Ralph Waldo Trine – with providing you with personal guidance. What writers have contributed most to the development of your work?

CC: None; except Chesterfield.

CG: Why have you never owned and written on a typewriter?

CC: You mean why do I not write on a typewriter?

CG: Yes.

CC:Not having used a typewriter before – I was forty in 1946 when I started to write seriously – I did try it, but found it too slow for my way of thinking.

CG: Did you find the change to dictation – allowing your thoughts to flow naturally rather than be slowed by the act of writing – improved your work in any way?

CC: Yes, because I am a story-teller. But it meant a lot of work and correcting afterwards. Nevertheless, I enjoy this part of my work too.

CG: In the early years you would write on scraps of paper during the day, while doing your housework.

CC: That's right. Whenever I could.

CG:Yet you have only recently found it necessary to make brief biographical notes while working on a book; have you never kept a writer's notebook?

CC: No, as I said earlier, the story is there, in my mind, albeit with slight variations.

CG:Can you describe the various stages a manuscript goes through before submission. Do you revise each day's output, or wait until the story is complete?

CC: Wait until the story is complete. But I do much preparation in my mind in bed; always have done.

At night I go as far as acting the characters and speaking their dialogue. Tone of voice is important to what is being said and so what is conveyed to the reader.

CG: Do you allow a story to ferment before revising?

CC: Yes.

CG: And do you revise mainly characters or do you adjust the plot?

CC: I don't think of plots, never have. I place a character in an environment and generally the environment guides their behaviour.

CG: How do you select the names of your characters?

CC: I think of the character and the name becomes applicable.

CG: Some of your books have as many as fifty characters. How do you keep track of the different plots and sub-plots and the dozens of characters?

CC: They never go away, even if I were to want them to. They will always be there when I want to draw them up.

CG: Your early works were largely based on your personal experiences; how emotionally involved are you with your later characters?

CC: Just the same as I ever was.

CG: Do you still experiment in your work?

CC: I have never experimented.

CG: You have been widely praised for the accuracy of your novels. But researching can become addictive; at what point do you decide enough is enough and you must write the story?

CC: I find, now, I need do little research for my writing, my particular way. Over the years I did much research before starting a story. Remember too, I can go back a long way to people and conditions in the early part of this century.

CG: How important is revision? How many times do you rewrite a manuscript before you are happy with it?

CC: I go through a script three, four or five times from taking it down in the rough.

People say: 'I love reading your books. They're so simple to read.' They don't know that simplicity is the hardest form of writing.

The true praise for a writer is the verdict, 'I couldn't put it down.' And the best way to achieve that is to put your heart into your work.

If you want to touch the heart of a reader, then write about the kind of people you know from the inside, whether your acquaintance with them was in the slums, in the middle class, or in a stately home, because only then will you get your heart into your work.

CG: Surely there must be something else? Some other vital ingredient?

CC: People have the idea that if they put sex into a book it will sell. It may do the trick for a first novel, but what about the second and third?

The people with all the good ideas can't always follow them through. They don't possess the stamina or the determination. I've had to revise my opinion and alter my views. Everybody can't write.

CG: You must have had hundreds of new writers seeking your advice over the years; if you could give them one single piece of advice what would it be?

CC: Write something every day, even if it means stealing an hour from the night.

I don't believe in these schools teaching people to write. If you are a writer you will write.

CG: And the process of writing – every day – is a learning process?

CC: Yes. I have always looked upon writing as a trade. I simply apprenticed myself to it.

Writing doesn't get easier, but you learn more. I have learned to be my own critic. If something is not up to my standard it doesn't go out.

CG: Would you discourage anyone from becoming a writer?

CC: If you have it in mind to try the trade of writing there are one or two precautions you must take.

You must first of all make up your mind to turn deaf ears to all those well-wishers who say the trade is swamped already and that there is not a hope in hell for newcomers. Or that there is no money in it so you had better settle for a steady wage and pension.

CG: You have frequently said that you would have to be very ill to stop working altogether – and sometimes you were forced to – but how true is the reverse? Has not your work provided you with the motive and strength for you to overcome your ill health?

CC: That would need much discussion, but you are probably right.

Now I am losing my sight, the only thing left to me is my tape recorder. My work must now be read out to me for me to correct orally.

CG: You have earned a good living from your writing, but what else has it given you?

CC: It's better than money hearing that your work is encouraging people. If they read me and then go on to other things – then I feel that things have been worthwhile.

266

Sixteen

I'm rotten from the eyebrows downwards, and spend most of my time in bed or in hospital, but as long as my mind is active I'll carry on.

O N 25 JUNE 1986 Catherine was presented with a belated birthday present from the people of South Tyneside. The crystal ship in a bottle had also been intended to commemorate the Cutty Sark Tall Ships Race, coming to the Tyne for the first time that summer. It reminded Catherine of the mast-tops she had watched above the staithes of Tyne Dock.

Bolstered by her birthday celebrations, Catherine had been well enough to make the journey to the South Shields Museum to open the reconsruction of the street she grew up in.

While at the opening, she learned of the fate of her former Tyne Dock school from the head teachers of the new St Peter and Paul's Junior School, James MacKay. Three months later, at the start of the new academic year, he opened his morning mail to discover a donation from the former pupil. The money was used to buy computer equipment.

So often the butt of injustice, Catherine has never missed an opportunity to defend those whom she considered victims – even against those she considered her friends.

In September management of Newcastle's General Hospital issued a circular warning staff that using hospital milk or sugar would be regarded as theft. Nursing staff at the hospital – to which Catherine had donated thousands of pounds – considered the implication a 'slur'. So did Catherine.

She wrote to the Confederation of Health Service Employees condemning the theft warning. 'Throughout my long life I have had experience of hospital beds and my husband, sitting by my bedside both night and day, being a heavy tea drinker, has had great comfort from the cuppas offered by the nurses,' said her letter.

'A hospital is not a factory, it's not an office, it's a place which deals with disease, with the curing of it on the one hand, and with the dying from it on the other.

'Consequently, it houses, beside patients, an army of caring and compassionate men and women who carry out very unenviable jobs. Many times from my hospital bed I have asked myself why they have chosen to do it, and now they are accused of stealing a cup of tea and the required milk and sugar.

'The whole idea smacks of pettiness,' she went on. 'I can understand the nurses' anger and their being demoralised by this slur on their integrity.'

That autumn Catherine agreed to two deals – one covering some of her past books, the other on novels yet to be published.

News of the first deal leaked out during a meeting of South Tyneside Council's economic development committee. Catherine had agreed in principle to give a new company the film rights to several of her books.

Catherine was still bitter over Rank's treatment of both her scripts and her stories. ITV's attempt to turn *The Mallens* into a television serial had received some critical reviews and did not entirely please its author. When businessman, Roger Neville, asked permission to film several Cookson stories Catherine was sceptical.

Neville was managing director of Newcastle-based film makers, Storyline. His company had already completed a series of promotional films for the council as part of its Cookson Country campaign. Storyline's consultant was Tony Baker, a presenter with the BBC's *Look North* programme, which was broadcast from the city. Between them they hoped to form a new company, enticingly called Chesterfield Films after Catherine's mentor.

Neville and Baker explained they wanted to film Catherine's stories on Tyneside, using local labour and from a base on the Simonside Industrial Estate, only yards from the site of William Black Street. Their initial request to adapt *Our Kate* was swiftly rejected. Instead, Catherine allowed them temporary rights to five of her novels. 'Mrs Cookson's stories are so powerful I'm sure a lot of people would love to see a lot more of them on film,' said a confident Baker. After a feasibility study into the scheme – and an approach to the Urban Development Council for part of the one million pounds start-up costs – the idea was dropped.

Anthony Shiel, meanwhile, had selected the Frankfurt book fair to auction his client's next ten books. The two contenders were Heinemann, which in 1972 had outbid Macdonald, and Bantam Press, an imprint of Transworld whose Corgi paperbacks had become Catherine's primary publisher. When the bidding stopped Transworld's Paul Scherer had signed an author he had known as a friend for many years and Catherine had earned herself something in excess of 4 million pounds. The exact figure has never been disclosed.

At Heinemann, which still had two Cookson books in the pipeline – *The Parson's Daughter* and *The Cultured Handmaiden* – Brian Perman was philosophical. 'There is nothing in our business that prevents overbidding. But there must come a point when affection and admiration give way to commercial common sense.'

To Catherine and Shiel the move made perfect sense. As it did to Transworld's chief executive, Paul Scherer. 'Since we started Bantam Press I made it very clear I would like to publish her in hardback as well,' he said. 'The advantage of joint marketing and vertical publishing must have the scope within it to improve both her hardback and her paperback sales.'

For Catherine, who had already completed some of the novels to be included in the ten-book package, it demonstrated the commercial value now being placed on her work.

As a rule of thumb publishers are prepared to advance an author two-thirds of the royalties they expect a book to generate from its first edition. In thirty-six years Catherine had seen her advances jump from £100 for *Kate Hannigan* to £15,000 for *The Dwelling Place*. Her latest deal would give Catherine an initial £400,000 for each new story. Print runs were also increasing with demand. In the early days with Corgi, sales of Catherine's novels were around the 100,000 mark. Now a new title received a first printing of not less than 600,000. A successful hardback title like *A Dinner of Herbs* was selling around 90,000 copies in its second year.

The Bantam Press contract would commence in October 1987 with the publication in hardback of the second book in the Bill

Bailey trilogy, *Bill Bailey's Lot*. The first – *Bill Bailey* had been published by Heinemann a year earlier. Bantam would release the final story – *Bill Bailey's Daughter* – in the autumn of 1988.

The latest returns from the Public Lending Right scheme confirmed Catherine's hold over the British reading public – the eighty-year-old writer had gained in popularity over other best-selling authors.

Twenty-nine out of every 100 books borrowed during 1986 had been written by Catherine Cookson, compared to 23 in 1985. Second place went to thriller writer Dick Francis, with 10 books; followed by Wilbur Smith, 9, and Jeffrey Archer, Jack Higgins and Alastair Maclean, who had 6 each.

As well as seeing the appearance of Catherine's latest novel – *The Parson's Daughter* – the spring of 1987 also brought three new honours – two of them in stone.

Early in February the council of Newcastle University met to discuss naming a seven-story campus building after the writer. The vote was unanimous. The block would house the university departments of anatomy and physiology, the medical and dental library and the medical school offices. Appropriately it would also accommodate the newly appointed Catherine Cookson Lecturer in Molecular Haematology, Dr Peter Middleton, as well as John Birchall, whose laboratory was equipped by a £50,000 grant from the novelist.

The second tribute was a little more down to earth. A year earlier South Shields artist, Bob Olley, had presented Catherine with a bronze statuette of her 'Gambling Man' during the opening of the Cookson exhibition. He now returned to the museum with life-size figures of Catherine as a young girl and her step-grandfather John McMullen sitting in his high-backed chair.

On Thursday, 23 April Tom drove Catherine from their Northumberland home to attend a dinner at Gosforth Park Hotel, north of the city. She had been honoured by the Variety Club before. This time the North-East members had named her female personality of the year. Looking frail and very tired, she was greeted by a standing ovation.

Even before its official publication, *The Parson's Daughter* had appeared in the bestseller list. Book shops were ordering so many advance copies of the 400-page novel that it was 'outselling' books already on the shelves.

The parson's daughter of the title is Nancy Ann Hazel from County Durham. The period, with its changing moral climate, is the last quarter of the nineteenth century.

Nancy Ann, who begins the story as a poor but virtuous virgin, ends by having three husbands. The three men in her life are a dissolute gentleman – she marries him to please her dying mother –who fathers her children but loses his fortune through gambling and bad company; the saintly landowner to whom she turns for solace; and the romantic hero, who begins the book as the illegitimate son of a servant girl, locked in the attic of a big house, but returns from Australia as a millionaire seeking revenge for the privations of his childhood.

Eric Griffiths, Royal Doulton's art director of ceramic sculpture, spent the early months of 1987 attempting to improve on one of Catherine's characters.

The company, which had first started making figures six years after Catherine was born, had decided to break with tradition and design and sell a collection of characters taken from the works of a living author. The first was Kate Hannigan.

Despite numerous book jackets and illustrations since *Kate Hannigan* had first appeared, only Catherine could focus the heroine in her mind's eye. Griffiths consulted the writer from initial sketch to production. The nine-inch, bone china figure, which sold for £79.95p, was an immediate success. Even before the launch the Stoke-on-Trent company had begun work on a second, this time of another Cookson favourite, Katie Mulholland.

ROB Bettinson couldn't sleep. He tossed and turned until his frustration solidified into anger. Reaching across the bed he picked up a book his wife, Shirley, had put aside several hours earlier.

'I started reading it thinking it would send me to sleep,' admitted Bettinson. 'I thought it would be a nice Mills and Boon-type thing leading up to a happy ending.

'But then half-way through there is this great shock ... I couldn't believe it. I thought, "She can't do this." '

The book was *The Fifteen Streets*. Bettinson knew he had found the book he was looking for.

Within days Bettinson, the son of a Cleveland sheet-metal worker, had contacted Catherine. She was very ill. Her spirits were low.

Since its publication in March 1952, its readers had always found something magical in *The Fifteen Streets*. The latent energy in the book had kept it in print and among her bestsellers for more than thirty-five years. Even so Catherine had 'qualms' about Bettinson's stage production. 'I was against him doing it,' she admitted. 'If I had to be asked which book I wanted to go on to the stage, that would be the last one I would have picked.'

With tentative approval Bettinson set about transferring the story of the battling O'Briens from the pages of the bestseller to the confines of a stage. The daily round of writing was not his only battle. He still had to convince potential backers that the story was more than a simple romance – the same image Catherine had been struggling to shed for almost four decades.

'The public perception of Catherine Cookson was such a false one,' Bettinson admitted later. 'Everyone thought she was like Barbara Cartland. But all her stories are deeply rooted in reality.

'*The Fifteen Streets* may be a microcosm of the North-East, but Catherine knows people like the back of her hand. The main character is not romantic, he is a six-foot-four docker – a man with all his faults.'

Stage adaptations of Catherine's works had generated mixed reactions. While rated as successes by the public – and box-office managers – they failed to attract critical acclaim or, more importantly, interest from other theatres. Many producers feared the stories were too parochial for a West End theatre.

In a perverse way they were right. The enthusiasm needed to visualise the transition from page to stage appeared only to be shared by those born or who had lived in the North-East. The latest production of *The Fifteen Streets* was no exception.

Its first run – extended by three weeks – took place at the Belgrade Theatre, Coventry, early in 1987. Both the leading actor and actress came from the North-East. Peter Marshall, who portrayed the imposing father in the O'Brien family, and Margo Stanley, who played his wife, had Tyneside connections – Stanley was born in South Shields less than four miles from Catherine's birthplace.

Throughout the summer Rob Bettinson, the play's producer and associate director at the Belgrade, had attempted to capitalise on the critical capital amassed by the Coventry production. On 12 December he announced plans to take the Cookson story to London's West End following a national tour. Not surprisingly Sunderland and Newcastle were included in the tour.

Three days later on 15 December Catherine found herself attracting attention at two events 300 miles apart.

In London a Sotheby's auction was offering forty-four literary items for sale in a bid to raise money to help support writers around the world imprisoned for their beliefs. Approached by Lady Antonia Fraser, chairman of the British organising committee of International PEN, Catherine agreed to donate the manuscript of one of her books. Other items snapped up by collectors had once belonged to Harold Pinter, Alan Ayckbourn, Tom Stoppard, Auberon Waugh, Graham Greene and Thomas Hardy.

In Newcastle Catherine announced she was giving something else away – thirty letters. Among the thousands of letters she received each year were a handful Catherine wished never needed to be written. Most thanked her for drawing attention to the daily suffering endured by telangiectasis victims. All were from people who, like her, had inherited the mysterious condition from a parent. She now contacted the writers again, this time asking if she could disclose their names to doctors as part of new research into the previously ignored disorder.

Catherine announced her involvement in the research minutes after unveiling a plaque to commemorate the naming of the building at Newcastle University. The new laboratory block, to be known as the Catherine Cookson Building, was to be home to the country's first research programme into telangiectasia, financed largely by her one-million pound gift to launch the Catherine Cookson Foundation.

The ceremony also gave Dr Peter Middleton a chance to meet his benefactress. His hope was to raise the level of understanding of HHT – hereditary haemorrhagic telangiectasia – to the same level as other diseases like cancer. The research technique involved 'reverse genetics', examining genes to find the 'lock' to hereditary disorders. 'We hope that eventually this might lead to screening

273

for carrier status,' explained Middleton. 'We may, in future, be able to give a woman who had haemophilia in her family a risk assessment of her chances of passing it on.'

Not satisfied with her million-pound donation, the university also announced the writer had recently parted with an extra £100,000. The extra money was to be spent on purchasing medical equipment and to fund improvements at the university's Hatton Gallery. Part of it was also earmarked for an ongoing project close to Catherine's heart, the conservation of rare books at the university library.

There was a moment of unease among members of the university governing body when Catherine ended her impromptu speech by telling them, 'I knew what I really wanted, and that was to be a lady and talk proper.' Waiting in the wings was her surprise gift, a glossary of Tyneside dialect. The two volumes, beautifully bound by trainees at the university library, were the original 1892 work of Oliver Heslop for the English Dialect Society. It had the formidable title *Northumberland Words: A Glossary of Words in Northumberland and on the Tyneside*.

WHILE Bettinson struggled through the final months of 1987 against a continual round of auditions and rehearsals for his latest production of *The Fifteen Streets*, Catherine found, for once in her life, she had lost the will to write.

'I am very down and have no energy,' she said early in 1988. She had remained in bed for months. From 2 January until well into February she bled practically every day. On two occasions she was too weak to move and her Newcastle specialist visited her at Bristol Lodge.

Her days, too, were now being rigidly screened: first by her London agents, whose office in Doughty Street, was receiving all her unsolicited mail; second by Tom.

One invitation she was forced to decline was the Sunderland première of *The Fifteen Streets* on Tuesday, 16 February. The first night, already a sell-out, was to have special significance for a cancer charity Catherine had agreed to help. Management at the Empire Theatre had agreed to donate all 300 dress circle seats to the Marie Curie Cancer Care organisation. Priced at £25 each, all the ticket receipts were to be donated to a £2.5 million appeal to find a replacement for an ageing Newcastle cancer home.

Like all previous attempts to adapt a Cookson novel for the stage Bettinson's production was applauded by her fans while suffering at the hands of the critics. One commented, 'Unfortunately the designer poverty of the young O'Briens owed more to Laura Ashley than Tyneside of 1910.'

Bettinson's promise to make the production the first Cookson story staged in London also proved hard to keep. Negotiations with various theatres proved fruitless. It was not until the end of March, less than six weeks before it was due to open in the capital, that *The Fifteen Streets* was finally booked into MP-turned-writer Jeffrey Archer's newly refurbished Playhouse Theatre near Charing Cross station. It eventually ran for five-and-a-half months.

But the producer, Philip Talbot, still had plans for the play. After a month's rehearsals it re-opened at York's Theatre Royal in March 1989, at the start of a nine-month tour. Early in April *The Fifteen Streets*, with a cast of thirty-two including eleven children, returned to the North-East, this time for a booking at Newcastle's Theatre Royal.

Although Catherine had been too ill to attend the Sunderland performance, she insisted she would not miss it this time. Tom reluctantly agreed to drive her the thirty miles from their Northumberland home to Newcastle. Catherine looked tired. As a precaution – and as a 'thank you' gesture – she was accompanied by two of her doctors and their wives. 'It has been a great effort to get here,' she admitted to a friend, 'but it is probably my last chance of seeing it.'

Despite fears the poverty and petty squabbles of a nineteenth-century working-class family would prove unpopular with affluent 1980s theatregoers around the country, *The Fifteen Streets* played to packed houses. 'The further south it went, the more letters I got,' Catherine recalls.

An invitation to attend the Women of Achievement presentations at the Dorchester Hotel in London was also to prove out of the question. Catherine, voted Writer of the Year, shared the honours with Raisa Gorbachev, wife of the Soviet leader, who had been voted International Woman of the Year, and Prime Minister Margaret Thatcher, who was Politician of the Year.

Her latest award, and the success of *The Fifteen Streets*, once again brought her to the attention of Radio Four's popular *Woman's Hour*. Its producers needed a local personality to celebrate the programme's first broadcast from the BBC's Newcastle studios on Friday, 19 February. Once again Catherine hid her ill-health with a joke. 'It shouldn't happen to a dog what's happening to me,' she said. 'I should be enjoying all this glamour. It should have happened thirty years ago.'

After thirty-eight years as a professional writer, committing millions of words to paper, the spring of 1988 was to see two of Catherine's shortest letters.

Earlier in the year Newcastle University librarian, Brian Enright, had been asked by Catherine whether he thought the library project she had funded, providing work for four school leavers, should be continued. His reply was emphatic. The project had been very successful, he informed Catherine by letter, both for the library and the teenagers concerned.

Two days later Catherine's three-line response arrived: 'Here you are. Cheque for £18,000. Get on with it.'

The subject of her own wealth returned yet again. Catherine had fought for years to keep her public and her private money separate. She did not object when her cash gifts to appeals and charities hit the headlines: on more than one occasion the publicity had attracted more donations. But when *Money* magazine placed her among 'Britain's Richest 200' she lashed out.

Without attributing the story, the Newcastle *Journal* claimed she was the country's 187th richest resident and worth at least £10 million. It was an old claim, more annoying for its persistence than its inaccuracy. Four days later, on 29 February, the newspaper published her response: 'If any one of your readers can tell me where I can lay my hands on the £10 million I am supposed to possess, I shall be only too pleased to give him a substantial reward.'

In March 1988 Heinemann published its last Cookson novel. *The Cultured Handmaiden* is the story of Miss Brownlow, the ugly duckling of the typing pool, whose conscience and manners are pushed too far. A goody-goody, trying always to be liked and anxious not to rock the boat by speaking to anyone out of turn Miss Brownlow finally snaps. Her rise from the lowly typing pool to the top floor is swift. Despite his gruff, aggressive chauvinism, she soon becomes the apple of her boss's eye. In the end she admits, 'I think perhaps I do love him.'

Catherine had always been sensitive to the hidden suffering of those whose physical or mental condition placed them on the fringe of more public medicine. In July she responded to a statement made by Professor Sam Shuster. The head of Newcastle University's department of dermatology at the Royal Victoria Infirmary had claimed his staff treated more eczema, psoriasis and other skin complaints than medical and surgical patients combined. Many, said Professor Shuster, were forced to live in a 'half-world of shame and shadows' because of their conditions.

Catherine side-stepped an existing £80,000 appeal for new dermatology laboratories and posted Professor Shuster a £50,000 cheque on condition it was used for the direct treatment of patients. She hoped others would step in and support the laboratory fund.

DURING the early summer of 1988 programme executives at Tyne Tees Television gave producer Heather Ging the go ahead for a documentary she had wanted to make for a long time. Within six months Catherine found herself confessing some of her innermost secrets – and writing one of the books she is most proud of.

Ging, born just 400 yards from Leam Lane End on the other side of the Tyne Dock arches, first met Catherine in the early 1970s. Each time they renewed their friendship for a filmed interview or documentary, the writer caught up with Ging's developing career. It was a field in which Catherine had gathered some expertise of her own.

'She is always at ease in front of the camera,' Ging explains. 'Catherine never needs prompting. The words just flow out.' It is an attribute which has caused problems in more than one editing room. 'Catherine doesn't talk in phrases,' adds Ging, 'which makes it very hard to edit an interview once she has started speaking. Her sentences flow into each other. There is never a natural break.'

As a film crew was setting up its equipment or taking a break between shots Catherine would bombard its members with questions. What lens were they using? How was the light? 'She is very film-literate,' says Ging. 'She will suss out the cameraman and sound man from the moment they arrive to see if they know what they are doing.'

The thirty-minute documentary, eventually screened on a Monday afternoon before Christmas 1988, was a 'no budget' production. 'I was told I could do it as long as I poached a crew from one department and other facilities from another.

'It was something I had wanted to do for a very long time. I wanted to explore Catherine's philosophy of her early life: how she had coped with it and what effect it had had on her thinking and behaviour in later years.'

Ging had still not settled on a title. Although the producer was to provide the inspiration, the title – which all but chose itself – needed to be triggered by a colleague. Ging and Tyne Tees researcher, Malcolm Gerrie, had driven out to Langley to discuss the documentary. Catherine suddenly produced some sheets of her poetry and began to read aloud. Both listened in silence. Their suggestion that the pieces be used in religious epilogues surprised and horrified Catherine. She agreed, however, to meet Maxwell Deas, head of religious broadcasting at the Tyneside studios. A few days later, as he walked through the door of Bristol Lodge, Catherine announced: 'Now let me make myself plain, I'm an agnostic.'

Ging had her title. Now all that remained was to film the interview.

'Catherine was very much confined to her bed at that time,' says Ging. 'But when we arrived at the Langley house she was up and dressed in a superb black dress, with pearls, and wearing make-up.

'She was too ill even to be filmed in the garden. She sat down in the house and we shot it there. When we had finished Catherine got up and changed into a dressing gown and we all had a cup of tea. The whole thing was an act of willpower.'

A few days later, when Ging had finished editing, the telephone rang. It was Catherine. She asked how the programme was going and what Ging thought of the finished product. 'It's nice,' Ging told her. 'What do you mean nice?' Catherine snapped back. 'What kind of word is nice?'

Meanwhile, Deas had persuaded Catherine to record a series of Saturday-night epilogues. It was the first time Catherine had spoken directly to a mass audience since her radio talks of the

1940s and 1950s. The resulting requests for copies of her scripts and poems were overwhelming.

Anthony Shiel suggested that she combine the scripts, the previously unpublished poems and other fragments of memories into a new book of autobiography, to be called *Let Me Make Myself Plain*. Its gestation, although not as long, was as protracted as *Our Kate*'s.

For weeks Catherine and Tom considered the exact format the book should take. 'Whether this poem should go there . . . or perhaps it would be better here . . . whether piece twenty-three should come after thirty or before twelve . . . it went on for days,' she remembers.

In the end her editor from Bantam Press arrived to find the manuscript laid out in neat piles on a table. The debate started once again. 'That's it,' he said, scooping up the typed pages. 'We're going.'

'When it came out, I couldn't look at it,' said Catherine. 'Tom sat down and read it through, but for six months I couldn't even open it. And then one day I read a little bit and I thought to myself, "This isn't too bad," and slowly I re-read the whole book. Now I'm quite pleased with it.'

She has already completed the sequel, *Plainer Still* which awaits publication along with ten other books.

THE previous December Catherine had made the mistake of announcing her New Year resolution for 1988: 'I feel better and this is going to be a marvellous year.' She spent the next three months in bed.

Her health improved as the year progressed. But the drugs she took to control the bleeding and suppress the pain in her back were creating other problems. She could no longer eat anything sweet, and the eggs and fish she enjoyed after giving up meat now produced an allergic reaction.

The Cooksons did manage a brief holiday during 1988. They spent five full days in the Lake District and another forty-eight hours away from home later in the year. It was their first holiday for twenty years. By September Tom, too, had succumbed to the ceaseless demands on his time and energy and went through a 'bad period' of illness. 'We both should rest,' said Catherine, 'but this is a treadmill we are on and you cannot rest.'

January 1989 brought the not-unexpected news that Catherine had once again topped the list of authors whose books are borrowed from public libraries. Twenty-nine of her novels featured in the 100 most borrowed books for 1987, compared with twenty-three the year before. It was a position she had held since the introduction of the Public Lending Right scheme in 1982. The latest returns showed her titles accounted for one per cent of the country's 624-million library loans during 1987.

Catherine celebrated in traditional style, by donating more than £75,000 to local appeals and campaigns during the next eight weeks. The largest cheque, for £40,000, was for a cause she understood only too well.

On 24 February Catherine and Tom prepared Bristol Lodge for a deputation of trustees from the Pilgrim Street Trust, an organisation which raises money for the North East Council on Addictions. Catherine's donation would complete a £500,000 refurbishment of premises in Mosley Street, Newcastle, which had been opened by the Princess of Wales three years earlier. The council, Britain's largest regional alcohol and drug-abuse charity, offers treatment and training to 10,000 clients.

To the guests attending the mid-week presentation, Catherine appeared 'tired, but very much in control'. She told them, 'I have a lot of knowledge of alcoholism and how it affects families and individuals.' She recalled the effect drink had had on her childhood. 'In my days there was far too much drinking, and far too much money spent on alcohol. There was only a certain amount to go round but filling the grey hen was always a priority. Until I was fourteen I was sent on far too many errands to get drink, and I saw too many pubs and outdoor beer shops.'

A second appeal triggered more kindly memories. Doctors at South Shields General Hospital – part of which occupied the former Harton Workhouse – had written asking for a donation to a £150,000 fund to upgrade the hospital's postgraduate medical centre. Catherine responded with a cheque for £25,000. Making the presentation in person, however, was out of the question.

One date Catherine was determined not to miss – no matter how ill she felt – was an appointment with a five-month-old royal baby.

Catherine and Tom were long standing friends of Princess

Helen of Romania and her Northumberland-born husband, Dr Robin Medforth-Mills. When Princess Helen gave birth in January to a daughter the couple asked Catherine and Tom to be the child's godparents. 'They are the most lovely people we know,' said Medforth-Mills, a Durham University lecturer.

The baby, regally named Elisabette Karina de Roumanie Medforth-Mills, is related to every royal family in Europe and is fifty-sixth in line to the British throne. Her other godparents included King Michael of Romania and the Duke of Aosta. 'We feel that Catherine will be a great person for Elisabette to grow up to,' added Dr Medforth-Mills. 'Catherine is one of the women in the world that Princess Helen and I admire most.'

The writer's attendance at the June christening was planned with military precision. Two cars, one as back-up in case of mishap, ferried the Cooksons from Bristol Lodge to the chapel at Durham Castle. During the service Catherine began to feel ill. The strain left her weak and in pain for several days. It was the last time she was tempted to leave her home for a social outing.

Despite living almost thirty miles from Tyneside Catherine's reputation as the area's number one celebrity was as strong as ever. In the first eight weeks of 1989 the area's two leading newspapers carried ten news stories on Catherine, and there were almost as many mentions on regional television. But an attempt by two fans to spread even more details about her life and work met with a swift refusal from Catherine and a harsher threat from Tom.

The previous summer David and Kathryn Higginbottom, and their son Jonathan, had been injured in a car crash. As the South Shields couple recovered, they both read *Our Kate* for the first time. They were 'inspired'. After reading more Cookson novels they tried, without success, to learn more about Catherine.

'It occurred to us there must be many people similarly inspired by her own personal story and by the books that capture emotions and feelings we can all identify with,' explained 38-year-old David Higginbottom. 'When we tried to locate an appreciation society, we were astounded to find there wasn't one.'

The couple wrote to the author informing her of their plans to start a Cookson Fan Club. Within days Catherine had replied thanking them for the suggestion, but explaining she had tried to answer all letters of appreciation personally. Both were sure

Catherine had 'got hold of the wrong end of the stick'. A second letter prompted a stronger refusal, this time from Tom. He explained his wife was 'against the formation of any type of appreciation or fan club bearing her name' and, if plans went ahead, she would 'with great sadness' make her feelings public.

An appeal to Catherine's London agent, Anthony Shiel Associates, received an equally cold comment. 'The author has always resisted anything like this, otherwise I'm sure there would have been such a society in existence long before now.' Catherine, went on a spokeswoman, was a 'very private person, in poor health, who likes to keep a very low profile. We all respect her wishes.'

In July 1989 Catherine received a new request to make use of her name. This time she consented without hesitation. Carnation expert, Jack Wandless, had taken three years to perfect a new bloom. He now wanted to register the yellow and pink flower with the Royal Horticultural Society as 'Catherine Cookson'. Catherine, who already had a rose named after her, said she 'would be very pleased' by the honour.

RAY Marshall, an enthusiastic Yorkshireman, had been appointed to lead World Wide International Television Productions' move from corporate film-making into small-screen drama.

While in Anthony Shiel's office Marshall noticed a display of Cookson novels. Shiel admitted there were no plans for any future adaptation of her books. He agreed to arrange a meeting between Marshall and the 82-year-old writer.

Marshall combined his trip north to Bristol Lodge with a meeting at Tyne Tees Television. Geraint Davies, director of programmes at Tyne Tees, conceded he would be interested in the possibility of backing a Cookson film. Within weeks Marshall was back with plans to turn *The Fifteen Streets* into a made-for-television, two-hour drama.

It would be followed, over the next three-and-a-half years, by more Cookson stories. Other novels World Wide had taken an option on were *A Dinner of Herbs* and *The Black Velvet Gown*. It also wanted to screen the *Bill Bailey* trilogy as seven one-hour episodes and turn the *Tilly Trotter* stories into a mini-series.

Marshall admits he could not understand why Catherine's stories had not been adapted and screened more widely. 'I must confess I was amazed to discover a writer of Catherine Cookson's calibre, who outsells every major British writer, has been largely ignored by television. Her work is ideally suited to television adaptation.'

Shooting began in April 1989. Marshall asked Rob Bettinson, who originally adapted the book for the stage, to write the screenplay. He was equally sure about his choice of actor Owen Teale –who had headed the West End cast – for the roll of docker John O'Brien.

The part of the treacherous Dominic O'Brien went to Sean Bean, who had never heard of Catherine Cookson. 'Until I read her book I didn't realise how much powerful drama she packs into her work,' he admitted later. Other members of the cast were equally accomplished. They included Ian Bannen, Clare Holman, Billie Whitelaw, Frank Windsor and Jane Horrocks. The film was directed by Sunderland-born David Wheatley.

One immediate problem facing Wheatley was finding a Tyneside terraced street, still cobbled, and with a shipyard within sight. An impossible task. In the end his team settled on Richardson Street in the Heaton area of Newcastle. The road was cobbled and working gas lamps were fitted. A huge shipyard backdrop was hung across the end of the street. The transformation was so startling that the residents later petitioned Newcastle City Council to have the area renovated in the 'Cookson style'.

When *The Fifteen Streets* was screened on 20 August it attracted more than 10 million viewers. Not everyone was pleased. Catherine endorsed several viewers' complaints about the inclusion of a four-letter word in the script, claiming such words were never used during the period in which the book was set. Catherine had objected before the film was televised, but was told the offending word could not be deleted.

The Tyne Tees production won almost instant recognition from the public and professionals alike. Book shops nationwide sold out of the novel within a week. In October 1989 the film won the Best Network Programme title at the Royal Television Society's annual regional awards presented in Newcastle.

On the same day Catherine admitted in a regional magazine what many people had realised a good many years earlier – only her writing was keeping her alive.

'Active: There is the crucial word with regard to old age, and I think being so is the solution. Perhaps not the whole, but in good part, because stagnation of the mind can create boredom, and this becomes the breeding ground of depression, when loss of the will to live can take over.'

Seventeen

I wake up most mornings and wonder what I'm still doing here!

FOR SIX DAYS in May 1990, Catherine's millions of fans – and many of her friends – were unaware she was in hospital fighting for her life.

Catherine had injured her leg and, for the first time in days, she was feeling a little more comfortable. Her bleeding attacks had abated. Only her failing eyesight troubled her. Tom now had to read the typescripts of her stories after they had been transcribed from the tapes. She was working on a new novel in the downstairs bedroom at Bristol Lodge on Saturday, 5 May when she collapsed. She was rushed the seven miles to Hexham General Hospital, where doctors in the accident and emergency department immediately diagnosed a heart attack.

News of Catherine's condition was kept secret until the following Friday. Tom had spent most of the preceding six days and seven nights at his wife's beside. Her cousin and part-time secretary Sarah Sables was deputed to make a brief statement. 'We were all very shocked,' she said. 'It was very sudden and there was no warning. It was a very big attack and has hit Tom very hard.'

On 12 May, exactly a week after her coronary, Catherine was back at Bristol Lodge. Tired and 'very poorly', she still found time, through Tom, to thank the medical staff who had saved her life. The couple also publicly criticised controversial plans to close the casualty department during evenings and weekends – the very time when Catherine received life-saving treatment. 'She finds it remarkable that a small cottage hospital like Hexham should be so adept at treating heart attacks,' admitted Tom. 'A place like that should never close because it is doing so much good for the community.'

On 1 June Catherine and Tom celebrated their golden wedding

anniversary. Visitors to Bristol Lodge were restricted to family and close friends. The same regime was enacted for Catherine's eighty-fourth birthday on 20 June. This time her readers responded with even more birthday cards, get-well cards and flowers.

Catherine found the idleness of her recovery irritating. She began to reach more and more for the microphone beside her bed. By July she was working on a new story. The strain proved too much. On the afternoon of Thursday, 9 August Catherine collapsed a second time.

This time news of her arrival by ambulance at Hexham General Hospital leaked out even before Catherine could be transferred to the coronary heart unit. Within hours the hospital switchboard was jammed with enquiries from worried fans. Officially a hospital spokesman was circumspect, admitting only that the writer was being treated for a 'heart-related illness'. It was left to Sarah Sables to confirm Catherine had, indeed, suffered a second heart attack. Once again Catherine was allowed to return to her Langley home after seven days in hospital.

News of Catherine's latest coronary reached executives at Tyne Tees and World Wide International Television as filming was about to start on a second Cookson novel. To follow the award-winning *Fifteen Streets* they had chosen *The Black Velvet Gown*.

The story focuses on the prejudices of the last century, with miner's widow Riah Millican moving into the local manor house as the owner's housekeeper. There she discovers love and the fact that it rarely runs smoothly. 'It is a complete contrast to *The Fifteen Streets*,' said producer Ray Marshall. 'It's strong on character and highly visual.' He was wrong when he described it as one of Catherine's most popular books.

Marshall had selected Bob Peck to play the part of embittered intellectual recluse, Mr Miller. The television film would be directed by North-East born Norman Stone and filmed largely in the region.

While his latest project was still in production, Marshall received news that *The Fifteen Streets* was among three films shortlisted from over 250 nominations for an Emmy award. The film had already been sold and screened in twenty-two countries worldwide. Video sales of 50,000 had pushed it to number five in the British video charts.

The simultaneous publication in October 1990 of *The Gillyvors* and the paperback edition of *The Black Candle* was part of a long-running campaign by Transworld to boost Catherine's sales still further.

During 1989 Bantam's marketing department had conceived a new 'message' for its future Cookson hardbacks. When it appeared in October *The Black Candle* carried a new cover style, with bold typography and a simple image of a candle replacing the illustrated designs used for her previous novels. It became her best-selling hardcover ever. *The Wingless Bird*, which followed in March 1990, again with the new-style cover, was her first novel in forty years to sell better in the south of England than in the north.

The new image was obviously a success. Scherer decided to capitalise on the move by initiating Transworld's biggest-ever sales Cookson campaign. From October he would spend £75,000 to promote three titles: her new Bantam Press hardcover, *The Gillyvors*; the Corgi paperback of *The Black Candle* and Catherine's personal anthology, *Let Me Make Myself Plain*, published in 1988. The message on the advertisements read: 'Catherine Cookson. More than meets the eye.'

The Black Candle would be the first paperback to appear with the new cover design. It would also be the first accorded 'hero' status by booksellers W. H. Smith.

As far as the reading public was concerned Catherine remained firmly in control of a title she had held for seven successive years. In the twelve months to June 1989 no less than 32 of the country's top 100 adult novels borrowed from libraries had been written by Catherine.

Not surprisingly the Public Lending Right figures recorded *The Fifteen Streets* as the most borrowed single title in Britain. The Bill Bailey and Tilly Trotter trilogies remained equally popular. Each time a Cookson title was date-stamped Catherine earned 1.39 pence. She was one of the few writers registered with the Stockton-based scheme to earn the maximum £6,000 payment, increased from its initial £5,000. She continued to donate the money to the Royal Literary Society.

Tom and Catherine still regarded Sundays as their 'giving day'. An early beneficiary in 1990 was a joint venture between the Northern Blood Transfusion Centre and the British Bone Marrow

Donor Appeal. It had launched an appeal to raise £40,000 to fund a tissue-typing laboratory in Newcastle to save the lives of leukaemia sufferers. The Cooksons responded with a £25,000 cheque.

For Christmas that year the couple continued a tradition they had initiated three years earlier. Each of the twenty pensioners living near their Langley home received a seasonal message – and a £50 note.

THE remoteness of Bristol Lodge and the near-by village of Langley had provided a physical barrier between Catherine's public and private life. Now, it seemed, it might also cause her eventual death.

Catherine had never fully recovered from the two heart attacks. For the remainder of 1990 Tom would continue to describe his wife's condition as 'very poorly'. Early in 1991 the bleeding from her tongue and nose worsened. On Sunday, 10 February Catherine suffered a sudden nose bleed, which showed no sign of abating. Tom wrapped Catherine in her 'blood coat' and drove her to Newcastle's Freeman Hospital. Three days later she was back at the Freeman for emergency treatment. This time her specialist refused to allow her home. It was Catherine's third unscheduled hospital stay within a year.

Catherine and Tom discussed the possibility of selling Bristol Lodge. It was self-evident, particularly to Catherine, that the thirty miles which separated her from her doctors was too much of a risk. After ten years at Langley – eight of them in full-time residence – the Cooksons knew they would have to swap the countryside for the city. They rented a Newcastle flat and began the search for a new home.

The Hexham chartered surveyor handling the sale ironically described the lakeside home as a unique 'gentleman's residence' – the same phrase which had first attracted Catherine to the Hurst. Yet the £425,000 price tag bore little relation to her original dream. There were several serious enquiries, one from America. In May the house and its acres of lakeside garden were sold to a family from 'outside the region'.

The Cooksons settled on a new home in the Jesmond area of Newcastle and almost within sight of the Freeman Hospital. The renovation of the bungalow and the rapid move were carried out in complete secrecy. It was two weeks after the move – on 4 March – that the local media carried news of the Bristol Lodge sale.

As painful as their decision to move was the realisation that many of their most treasured possessions would never fit into their new home. Smaller items the Cooksons gave to close friends and relatives. Hundreds of books were donated to Newcastle University library. The majority of furniture and paintings were auctioned.

Among the forty-five lots eventually sold by Newcastle auctioneers Anderson and Garland on 3 May was a huge mahogany bookcase in which Catherine had displayed the first editions of all of her books. It topped the day's bidding at £8,600. Other items included the Victorian davenport desk on which Catherine had written her early books and the first drafts of *Our Kate*. It was purchased by a literary collector for £1,300. A more modern desk used at Corbridge and Langley was bought for £820 by Tyne Wear Museum Service as an exhibit at the Catherine Cookson gallery at South Shields Museum. The sale eventually raised £42,000.

'I think the books were the most precious things of all,' said auctioneer Andrew McCoull. 'We had agreed to transport them to the university and Mrs Cookson was adamant the carriers be very, very careful with them. She was very upset when they went.'

The Cooksons agreed on the practicality of selling most of the items, including four three-piece suites, but Tom put his foot down over his wife's paintings. He refused to allow Catherine even to consider disposing of some of her scores of paintings and sketches.

One tribute that year did succeed in lightening Catherine's growing sense of despair. Four South Shields catering students had decided to name their entries in the national Taste of Britain competition after the writer's characters. Mulholland Mussels, Fanny McBride's Braised Lamb and Calfclose Mousse were a far cry from the 'fat brisket and runny cabbage' Catherine had endured as a child.

THREE days before her eighty-fifth birthday Catherine received the news that a trilogy of Cookson films had attracted almost thirteen million viewers – and nudged the long-running soap opera *Coronation Street* from its number one slot.

The Cookson mini-season had begun on 26 May with a screening of Ray Marshall's £1.3 million adaptation of *The Black Candle*. It was followed a week later by *The Black Velvet Gown* and concluded, on the third Sunday, by a second showing of *The Fifteen Streets*.

Catherine, recovering from a bout of pneumonia, remained laconic. 'It's rather wonderful news, but I don't think about figures,' she said. 'I simply hope that the readers will enjoy my books.'

Executives at Tyne Tees Television were less restrained. The company had topped the national ratings for a network programme for the first time in its existence. Their decision to screen the two new Cookson films on consecutive Sundays, followed by a repeat of *The Fifteen Streets*, paid dividends. *The Black Velvet Gown* and *The Black Candle* achieved the highest and second highest figures recorded on any channel for the previous twelve months.

The Black Candle attracted 10.8 million Sunday evening viewers. The next weekend *The Black Velvet Gown* had 12.8 million viewers glued to their television sets – 61 per cent of the national audience – and shared the number one spot with *Coronation Street. The Fifteen Streets,* screened on 9 June, topped the 10.2 million viewers it had attracted when it was first screened in 1989.

Again, not everyone was happy with the visualisation of the Cookson stories. Five viewers complained to the Broadcasting Standards Council about a murder scene in *The Black Candle*, in which a man has his head slammed against a tree and is then stabbed and choked. Although the actual blows were hidden from viewers, the victim's bloodied head was shown. The BSC upheld the complaints, ruling the scene was 'too long and graphic.'

Cookson books were in demand, just as they had been in the days following the first screening of *The Fifteen Streets*. Retailers nationwide, primed by Transworld, sold out of extra stocks of the adapted novels within days. Many libraries were forced to cut lending time on Cookson books from four to two weeks and Newcastle Central Library found itself with a six-month waiting list on Catherine's latest story, *The Rag Nymph*, four months before its publication date.

Public Lending Right figures, published later in the year, showed Catherine had written no less than 11 titles in the top 20 borrowed books and 24 of the top 100. Her nearest rival was Danielle Steel with 11 novels in all. For the first time Catherine's record had been ranked against the most popular classics. It showed her fans borrowed more Cookson novels than the top 20 classics combined.

Catherine had already been compared to Dickens and certain of her works with Greek tragedies. When she was compared with Chaucer she buried her face in her hands. This latest accolade came from Dr Anne Wright, Rector of Sunderland Polytechnic, during a brief ceremony at White Lodge, the Cooksons' new Jesmond home. Wright was presenting the 85-year-old writer with an honorary doctorate from the Council for National Academic Awards. Catherine, who had long fought to rid her books of the bodice-ripper image, was close to tears as Wright told the thirty guests: 'Her books are brim full of North-East life and steeped in social history. Catherine Cookson's novels have something to say to all of us.'

Entry to 'the box', as Catherine dubbed the bungalow, is by strict invitation. Interviews are prearranged, brief and always conducted by telephone. Those lucky enough to be granted a personal meeting are warned by Tom to expect no more than one hour. To discourage overtaxing his wife, he refers to such meetings as 'talks'.

The bungalow is built on two levels. To the right of the small hall, up two or three stairs, is a room crammed with antique furniture. As you walk through, the air smells of warm furniture; the predominant colour is blue. The bedroom is small. On the left of the door is a double bed, the cream headboard and side tables edged with gold trimmings.

Catherine is invariably lying on the left hand side of the bed, propped almost upright on the pillows. Her hair is white and thin. On the pink, quilted bedspread beside her is a radio. And beside the bed, within arm's reach, is a trolley with a dictating machine and a push-button telephone with outsized numbers.

The room is lit by a wall-to-wall picture window to the left of the bed. Opposite the window is the door to the bathroom. The wallpaper is again blue; bold, wide stripes and flowers. There is a framed collection of Catherine's own sketches. And, hanging between them on the wall to the right of the bedroom door, is the framed citation for her OBE. It is signed in the top right hand corner by 'Elizabeth R'.

Catherine still enjoys talking. She no longer wears her glasses, her eyesight registers only light and shade – 'I can only see your outline, no detail.'

As she talks she twists the white handkerchief in her hands. Her memory is still as strong as ever. It's not stories which trip her up, it's names or places or dates. She closes her eyes and throws back her head, gently tapping her cheeks with her clenched fists. When she remembers, Catherine looks at Tom or waves the handkerchief in his direction.

Tom, who frequently moves back and forth between his chair and sitting on the floor beside the bed, interrupts only occasionally. When he does it is not to correct, but to underline or reinforce the story his wife has just finished. 'You must remember,' he says, 'things were very different then . . .'

They clash only once. There is a silence. Tom apologises. Catherine smiles.

Since her first agent, John Smith, announced he was writing her biography Catherine has frowned at any attempt to tell her own story. Her will has long since included a clause forbidding her executors to approve any form of authorised biography. Anthony Shiel, her current agent, has received similar instructions.

Numerous requests, some by established and distinguished authors, to write her biography have been politely but firmly refused. During 1991 Catherine took drastic steps to forestall any attempt to publish her personal papers after her death. 'The doctors told me I was dying,' Catherine said. Seventeen diaries, covering some of the most productive and fascinating years of her life, were burned by Tom. 'We kept only a few, mostly for medical reasons.'

Catherine's other medical gifts were of more immediate use – and more personal

The Cooksons had long wanted to say 'thank you' to consultant Hugo Marshall, the Freeman Hospital ear, nose and throat specialist treating the symptoms of her telangiectasia. In August 1991 they responded by presenting his department with an advanced medical laser, the only one of its kind in Britain. The £65,000 machine can be used to destroy cancerous tissue or life-threatening growths. Catherine was one of the first patients to benefit from the machine. 'I only wish it had been invented forty years ago,' she said.

But her heart condition continued to cause her doctors concern. Within days of the publication in October of her latest novel, *The Rag Nymph*, she was admitted overnight to the Freeman Hospital with a 'heartbeat irregularity'. It was later confirmed as a mild heart attack, her third in less than eighteen months.

A year after America's Emmy Award judges had shortlisted Tyne Tees's film of *The Fifteen Streets* they were considering a second Cookson story. This time they were unanimous. *The Black Velvet Gown* carried off a prestigious Emmy.

The film also scored a 'perfect ten' in three classes at the annual International Film and Television Festival in New York – the first time in the festival's forty-four year history. The production, which starred Bob Peck and Janet McTeer, was awarded the Gold Medal for Drama, the Gold Award for Entertainment and Norman Stone was honoured with a Gold Medal as best director. When Catherine heard the news she burst into tears.

As so often happened during her writing career a woman had had a hand in Catherine's successes. Stone's wife, television personality Sally Magnusson, read *The Black Velvet Gown* while confined to bed through illness. She was so enthusiastic about its possibilities she convinced Stone to consider it.

A year later, in 1992, the Tyne Tees-World Wide film added yet another honour to its list. This time a first prize at Umbriafiction TV festival.

TRANSWORLD were so confident of Catherine's fans they decided to use one of her books as a guinea pig.

The Rag Nymph, originally published in October 1991, and due out in paperback twelve months later, was her first novel for many years not to appear in a book club edition. Paul Scherer wanted to see if the absence of a club edition would have any effect on paperback sales. He was taking no chances, however. Both *The House of Women*, Catherine's follow-on hardback, and *The Maltese Angel*, to be published on the same day as Corgi's *The Rag Nymph*, had already been sold to Book Club Associates.

Meanwhile, Anthony Shiel had succeeded in extricating the rights to thirty-four of Catherine's titles from the administrator of the now defunct Macdonald. 'Little, Brown were very sympathetic and understanding and, once they acquired the business of Macdonald, supported our efforts to revert the rights,' explained Shiel. He immediately sold on the rights to Transworld.

Catherine had, over four decades, so firmly established herself as story-teller supreme that her name had increasingly become synonymous with a style of writing. She had created her own genre, her own mix of social history, comment and addictive saga. Book clubs and publishers blatantly used her name to publicise other novels; 'in true Catherine Cookson style', 'in the best Catherine Cookson tradition'.

Hundreds of would-be writers – and a good many published authors – are still attempting to produce novels for the same readership, without possessing the depth of experience and enthusiasm Catherine has for her work. Yet Paul Scherer knew that if the Cookson tradition was to be kept alive his company would have to attract the best of a new generation of writers.

In February 1992 Transworld announced the Catherine Cookson Fiction Prize. The £10,000 award and guaranteed publication would go to an unpublished novel, of at least 70,000 words, which 'possesses the strong characterisation, authentic background and storytelling ability which are the hallmarks of Catherine Cookson's works'.

Meanwhile, a fourth television film was already in production. Ray Marshall, whose company had been renamed Festival Films-World Wide to reflect the American awards, had decided on *The Man Who Cried* as his next Cookson project. Scheduled for screening in January 1993, it would be the first Cookson adaptation to include location shots filmed away from Tyneside.

The £1.5 million epic would be the most modern of Marshall's adaptations. Spanning the years between 1932 and 1943, actor Ciaran Hinds played the central character of Abel Mason who leaves his shrewish wife in Hastings to search for work in the North-East, taking his young son with him. His luck changes when he befriends a wealthy garage owner. But Abel is soon involved in romance, deception and bigamy. Other members of the cast included Daniel Massey and Gemma Craven.

The sale of her stories to television, and the resultant increase in books sales, revived speculation over Catherine's wealth. In the 1980s one unconfirmed report had credited her with a personal fortune of some £20 million. Another had given her the unlikely title of being the fourteenth wealthiest woman in Britain. A new, and allegedly more accurate survey, had placed her sixty-fifth in the wealth league with a bank balance of £24 million.

This time Catherine refused even to discuss the subject. She responded as she had always done – by giving away more money.

In the late summer of 1992 management at Newcastle's Freeman Hospital launched a campaign to build a world-class liver transplant centre. Regular transplants were due to start at the hospital in the autumn. Extra finance was needed for the renovation of wards and the equipping of a high-dependency unit, caring for patients in the critical hours after surgery. Catherine, herself a regular patient at the Freeman, had initially donated £70,000 to the appeal. At the end of September she pledged an extra £50,000.

The donation was the second major cash gift that year. In March Catherine had agreed to give £100,000 to Sunderland Polytechnic to boost research into arthritis and autism. Half the money would go to the Tropical Disease Research Unit, investigating traditional Indian remedies for arthritis.

Tom still read and replied to most of Catherine's mail. Many of the letters, particularly those seeking help for individuals, deeply affected him. He was already drained by the extra care his wife now needed. In the final week of July he collapsed with exhaustion and was forced to spend several days in hospital before being allowed home.

Catherine immediately announced she and Tom were no longer prepared to consider the apparently ever-growing tide of 'begging letters' from across the north and around Britain. The Catherine Cookson Foundation – set up in 1985 – would restrict financial assistance to medical and academic projects. The fund stood at £1 million.

The realisation that Tom, at the age of eighty, was also vulnerable shocked and frightened Catherine. 'The people who send these letters don't know what they are doing to us,' she said. 'We like to help but things have gone too far. We have got to put our health first.'

The fact that she had survived to celebrate her eighty-sixth birthday – and was well on her way to her eighty-seventh – amazed Catherine.

Dictating a new foreword for the fourth edition of *Our Kate*, published in 1990, Catherine makes the innocent confession: 'Am I surprised? Yes, in a way. However, I shouldn't be, for if I look back over the years there seem to have been many times when I have said to myself "This is it!," only to answer, "Come on, you can't leave Tom, and anyway, even if the rest of you is rotten your ticker's all right, and there's certainly nothing wrong with your mind . . ." '

But a new sadness has developed through the good years. It is a fear they both share; silently, without words or elaboration.

When Catherine was too ill or tired to leave the house she would ask her husband to remain with her. To stay where she could see or hear him. Tom never refused. If anything were to happen to her husband, Catherine would want – would need – to be by his side.

'I can't imagine what life would be without him,' she says in a quiet moment. 'He . . . I . . . we would be nothing without each other.

'I could never have achieved so much in my profession without him. I would never have had the strength and will to keep going without Tom. He can't even bring himself to talk about what will happen if he's left behind. It's just too painful to think about dying. I wish there was a way we could go together. We talk about everything else, but the subject of death hurts too much.'

Does she ever worry about dying? 'I used to worry about it all the time. In fact I could write a book about it. But I have come to the conclusion that death is one of two things – either the start of a great adventure – if there is something after death – or, if there isn't, one long peaceful sleep.'

ON 1 January 1993 Catherine's childhood dream came true. In recognition of her services to literature and her tireless support for charities she was made a Dame of the British Empire.

Tom hugged his wife and they both cried.

Catherine Cookson was at last – a lady.

Chronology

1906:
20 June   Birth of Catherine 'Davies' at 5 Leam Lane, Tyne
                 Dock.
27 June   False date of Catherine's birth recorded at South
                 Shields Register Office.

1910:
2 September   Catherine attends Simonside Protestant School.

1912:
June   John, Rose and Jack McMullen and Catherine move
                 to upstairs house in William Black Street, East
                 Jarrow.
July   Family move to No 10 William Black Street.
Summer   Rose suffers from dropsy and Kate leaves service to
                 run the house.
                 David McDermott first visits No 10.

1913:
Spring   Catherine is moved to The Meases School, East
                 Jarrow.
June   She changes schools again, this time to St Bede's
                 Infants School, Monkton Road, Jarrow.
Autumn   Catherine is confronted with her illegitimacy for the
                 first time while playing with friends.

1914:
Spring   John McMullen receives £100 injury compensation
                 and retires.
                 Catherine is sexually assaulted by her mother's
                 boyfriend.

4 August	Outbreak of war. Within weeks Jack McMullen has joined the army.

1915: Summer	Catherine writes her first story, *The Wild Irish Girl*. She is refused entry to Belle Eckford's birthday party allegedly because of her illegitimacy.

1916: Spring	Catherine is moved to Saints Peter and Paul's Catholic School, Tyne Dock.

1917: 13 December	Rose McMullen dies at No 10 William Black Street.

1918: 5 September	Jack McMullen dies from 'wounds received in action' while serving in France.

1919: December	Catherine injures her leg in a playground fall; she never returns to school.

1920: Summer	Catherine enters service with the Sowerby family at 27 Simonside Terrace.
Autumn	After a thirty-minute art lesson she starts her own business pen painting cushion covers.

1922	Catherine completes her first long story, *On the Second Floor*. It is rejected by the *Shields Daily Gazette*.

1923: 30 June	Kate marries David McDermott.

1924: June	Catherine suffers from lead poisoning and is forced to give up her pen painting business.
Summer	She finds work as a companion-maid; the work is exhausting; Catherine shows the first signs of her inherited blood disorder.

22 October	Catherine begins work at Harton Workhouse as a laundry checker.
1926: Summer	Catherine submits a play to a national correspondence school; it is returned with the advice: 'Strongly advise author not to take up writing as a career.'
1927: September	When the workhouse assistant laundress leaves Catherine is promoted to take her place; four months later her application to become the laundress is refused.
1929: April	Catherine is appointed laundress at a workhouse at Tendring, near Clacton. Before she leaves the north she returns to Lamesley to learn more about her 'gentleman' father.
29 May	Catherine arrives at Tendring workhouse.
19 December	She is interviewed for the post of head laundress at Hastings Poor Law Institution, formerly the workhouse.
1930: 1 February	Catherine leaves the Tendring workhouse after 'eight lonely months'; she reports for duty at Hastings two days later; her first lodgings are in Clifton Road.
18 April	John McMullen dies at No 10 William Black Street. Catherine decides not to attend her step-grandfather's funeral.
1931: December	Catherine moves to a flat in West Hill House, Hastings.
1932 Spring	Kate visits her daughter in Hastings; she persuades Catherine to let her move south permanently.

1933
         Catherine buys the Hurst, a run-down 'gentleman's residence' in Hoads Wood Road, Hastings.

1936:
September
         Tom Cookson joins the staff of Hastings Grammar School; Catherine and Tom meet for the first time.

1937:
Summer
         Kate returns to Tyneside; Tom Cookson becomes a lodger at the Hurst.

1938:
5 February
         David McDermott dies after falling into the River Tyne.

1939:
August
         Catherine gives up job at institution laundry.
3 September
         Outbreak of war; the Hurst requisitioned for blind refugees.

1940:
1 June
         Tom and Catherine marry.
Summer
         Hastings Grammar School evacuated to St Albans; Tom and Catherine take a flat in Victoria Street.
7 December
         Catherine's first child, a boy, is born dead.

1941:
August
         Tom enlists in the Royal Air Force.
Autumn
         Couple move to Sleaford, Lincolnshire; Catherine suffers miscarriage.

1942:
Autumn
         Tom is posted to RAF Madley; the Cooksons are billeted at 31 Ryelands Street, Hereford.

1943:
         Catherine suffers her second miscarriage.

1944:

Spring   Catherine works at the Rotherwas ammunition factory; after five weeks she develops cordite poisoning and leaves.

Autumn   Confined to bed with phlebitis Catherine shows first signs of a mental breakdown.

1945:

May   Catherine admitted as a voluntary patient to St Mary's psychiatric hospital at Burghill, near Hereford; she discharges herself after six weeks.

July   Catherine returns to the Hurst.

Autumn   Her fourth pregnancy ends in another miscarriage.

1946:

February   Tom demobbed from RAF; Catherine struggles to cope with her ever deepening breakdown.

1948:   Catherine joins Hastings Writers' Circle; she reads the early drafts of **Kate Hannigan** and the episodes from her future Mary Ann stories.

1949:

15 August   **Woman's Hour** broadcasts Catherine's talk, **I Learned To Draw At Thirty.**

1950:

June   **Kate Hannigan** published; her second book is rejected.

1953:

Summer   Kate, suffering from terminal cancer, moves into the Hurst.

1954

May   Film rights to **A Grand Man** sold; it is retitled **Jacqueline** and released in 1956.

November   Catherine, Tom and Kate move to a new house, Loreto.

1956:

Spring   **Rooney** sold as a film; it is released in 1958; Corgi issue the novel as a paperback.

23 September	Kate dies at Loreto; within weeks Catherine begins work on **Our Kate**.

1961:

May	Writer's cramp forces Catherine to dictate her stories on to a tape recorder; she never 'writes' another book.

1963:

Spring	First Catherine Marchant story – **The Fen Tiger** –is serialised in **Woman's Own**; later published as first Marchant novel.

1967:

25 May	**Katie Mulholland,** Catherine's longest book so far, published; it is her first United States paperback.

1968:

Spring	Royal Society of Literature name **The Round Tower** as the year's best regional novel.

1969:

April	**Our Kate** published.
July	Tom retires from teaching.

1970:

February	Emergency operation saves Catherine's life after a prolonged haemorrhage.
Summer	Thirty manuscripts purchased by Boston University library.

1971:

March	**Joe and the Gladiator** screened as a BBC serial; it is the first Cookson story to appear on television.

1973:

January	Catherine moves to Heinemann after twenty-two years with Macdonald.
February	**The Mallen Streak** is voted Daily Express Book of the Month.

1974:

March   South Shields grants Catherine the Freedom of the
                 Borough.

1975:

October   Cooksons purchase 39 Eslington Terrace, Jesmond;
                 they commute between Hastings and Newcastle.

1976:

May   Loreto is sold; Catherine returns north to a converted
                 church near Morpeth, Northumberland.

Autumn   The Cooksons purchase High Barns in Corbridge,
                 Northumberland; they also buy adjacent Trinity
                 Barns.

1979:

June   Granada screen adaptation of the Mallen trilogy.

1980:

January   BBC screen five-part serial of **Our John Willie**.

1981:

January   Burglary at Trinity Barns; the property is sold and the
                 Cooksons buy Bristol Lodge at Langley,
                 Northumberland.

Summer   Paperback sales reach 27,500,000.

1982:

Summer   One-million copies of **The Mallen Streak** sold.

October   Readers of **Woman's Own** vote Catherine their
                 favourite creative writer; The Variety Club elect her
                 Woman of the Year.

22 December   Catherine is the subject of **This Is Your Life**.

1983:

Spring   Trinity Barns sold; the Cooksons move permanently
                 to Bristol Lodge.

13 May   Newcastle University honour Catherine with a Master
                 of Arts degree.

29 September   Musical of **Katie Mullholland** opens at Newcastle
                 Playhouse; the entire run is a sell out.

11 November	Catherine voted female Regional Personality of the Year.
20 November	**The South Bank Show** features Catherine.

1984:

Spring	Catherine refuses to be considered for American romantic writer award.
September	Catherine Cookson rose registered.

1985:

April	Limited Corgi edition of **The Black Velvet Gown** issued to mark the 50th Cookson paperback.
15 June	Catherine awarded OBE.
August	Cookson Country launched; fans walk the Cookson Trail.
5 September	**The Gambling Man** opens at Newcastle Playhouse.

1986:

6 February	Prince Charles presents Catherine's OBE on Tyneside
20 June	Catherine's 80th birthday; three publishers honour her with a celebration lunch.
25 June	Catherine Cookson display opens at South Shields Museum.
October	Bantam Press signs Catherine from Heinemann.

1987:

23 April	Variety Club name Catherine Regional Female Personality of the Year.
May	Royal Doulton issue Cookson character figures.
15 December	The Catherine Cookson Building at Newcastle University named.

1988:

February	Catherine voted Writer of the Year in the Women of Achievement awards.
20 May	**The Fifteen Streets** opens at The Playhouse, London; it runs for five-and-a-half months.
December	Tyne Tees Television broadcasts Catherine's series of weekly epilogues; the texts are published as her anthology, **Let Me Make Myself Plain.**

1989:
July   Catherine Cookson carnation registered with the
                Royal Horticultural Society.
20 August   Television adaptation of **The Fifteen Streets** screened;
                it attracts ten million viewers and is named Best
                Network Programme.

1990:
5 May   Catherine suffers heart attack.
9 August   She suffers second heart attack.

1991:
10 February   Catherine receives emergency hospital treatment after
                haemorrhage; the Cooksons decide to sell Bristol
                Lodge.
Spring   They move to a bungalow in Newcastle.
May/June   Three TV adaptations – **The Black Candle, The Black
                Velvet Gown** and **The Fifteen Streets** –screened in
                Cookson mini-series; they attract thirteen-million
                viewers; **The Black Velvet Gown** wins an Emmy.

1992:
February   Catherine Cookson Fiction Prize announced.
July   Tom collapses with fatigue and treated in hospital.

1993:
1 January   Catherine is made a Dame of the British Empire.

Appendix A

Catherine Cookson – publishing history:

1950:   Kate Hannigan

1952:   The Fifteen Streets

1953:   Colour Blind

1954:   Maggie Rowan
        A Grand Man

1956:   The Lord and Mary Ann

1957:   Rooney

1958:   The Menagerie
        The Devil and Mary Ann

1959:   Fanny McBride
        Slinky Jane

1960:   Fenwick Houses

1961:   Love and Mary Ann

1962:   Life and Mary Ann
        The Garment

1963:   The Blind Miller
        Heritage of Folly (as Catherine Marchant)
        The Fen Tiger (as Catherine Marchant)
        House of Men (as Catherine Marchant)

1964:   Hannah Massey
          Marriage and Mary Ann
1965:   Mary Ann's Angels
          Matty Doolin (for children)
          The Long Corridor

1966:   The Unbaited Trap

1967:   Katie Mulholland
          Mary Ann and Bill

1968:   The Round Tower
          Joe and the Gladiator (for children)

1969:   The Nice Bloke
          Our Kate (autobiography)

1970:   The Glass Virgin
          The Nipper (for children)
          The Invitation

1971:   The Dwelling Place
          Feathers in the Fire

1972:   Blue Baccy (for children)
          Pure as the Lily

1973:   The Mallen Streak

1974:   Our John Willie (for children)
          The Mallen Girl
          The Mallen Litter

1975:   The Invisible Cord
          The Gambling Man
          Miss Martha Mary Crawford (as Catherine Marchant)

1976:   The Tide of Life (initially published as Catherine Marchant)
          The Slow Awakening (as Catherine Marchant)
          The Iron Façade (as Catherine Marchant – originally pub-
          lished in the United States in 1965 as Evil at Roger's Cross)
          Mrs Flannagan's Trumpet (for children)

1991:   My Beloved Son
           The Rag Nymph

1992:   The House of Women
           The Maltese Angel

1993:   The Year of the Virgins
           The Golden Straw

1994:   Justice is a Woman

Appendix B

Bestselling Catherine Cookson novels in the UK.

	Estimated Sales
The Mallen Streak	1,027,000
The Black Velvet Gown	962,000
The Mallen Girl	937,000
Katie Mulholland	929,000
The Girl	914,000
The Mallen Litter	912,000
The Fifteen Streets	910,000
A Dinner of Herbs	909,000
The Moth	874,000
The Dwelling Place	858,000

* Source The Top Ten of Everything 1993 [Headline Publishing]

Appendix C

From January, 1983, the Public Lending Right scheme has issued an annual table of the one-hundred most borrowed books from British libraries. Catherine Cookson has dominated the list from the start.

The record number of Cookson loans in any one year exceeded five-million. The next best total was around two-million.

January to June, 1983.

Thirty-three of the top one-hundred books:

Tilly Trotter Widowed
Tilly Trotter
Tilly Trotter Wed
The Cinder Path
The Tide of Life
The Man who Cried
The Girl
The Gambling Man
Fenwick Houses
The Whip
The Mallen Litter
The Long Corridor
The Invisible Cord
Pure as the Lily
Hannah Massey
The Mallen Girl
Feathers in the Fire
The Nice Bloke
The Mallen Streak
Colour Blind

The Invitation
Fanny McBride
Kate Hannigan
The Fifteen Streets
Rooney
The Round Tower
The Dwelling Place

As Catherine Marchant:

Heritage of Folly
The Iron Façade
Miss Martha Mary Crawford
The Slow Awakening
The Fen Tiger
House of Men

July, 1983, to June, 1984.

Thirty of the top one-hundred books:

The Cinder Path
Colour Blind
Fanny McBride
Feathers in the Fire
Fenwick Houses
The Fifteen Streets
The Gambling Man
The Girl
Hamilton
Hannah Massey
The Invisible Cord
The Long Corridor
The Mallen Girl
The Mallen Litter
The Mallen Streak
The Man Who Cried
The Nice Bloke
Pure as the Lily
Rooney
The Tide of Life

Tilly Trotter
Tilly Trotter Wed
Tilly Trotter Widowed
The Whip

As Catherine Marchant:

The Fen Tiger
Heritage of Folly
House of Men
The Iron Façade
Miss Martha Mary Crawford
The Slow Awakening

July, 1984, to June, 1985.

Twenty-five of the top one-hundred books:

The Black Velvet Gown
The Cinder Path
Colour Blind
Fanny McBride
Feathers in the Fire
Fenwick Houses
The Fifteen Streets
The Gambling Man
The Girl
Goodbye Hamilton
Hamilton
The Invisible Cord
The Long Corridor
The Mallen Girl
The Mallen Litter
The Man Who Cried
The Nice Bloke
Pure as the Lily
The Tide of Life
Tilly Trotter
Tilly Trotter Wed
Tilly Trotter Widowed
The Whip

As Catherine Marchant:

> *Miss Martha Mary Crawford*
> *The Slow Awakening*

July, 1985, to June, 1986.

Twenty-nine of the top one-hundred books:

> *The Black Velvet Gown*
> *The Blind Miller*
> *The Cinder Path*
> *Colour Blind*
> *A Dinner of Herbs*
> *Fanny McBride*
> *Feathers in the Fire*
> *Fenwick Houses*
> *The Gambling Man*
> *The Girl*
> *Goodbye Hamilton*
> *Hamilton*
> *Harold*
> *The Invisible Cord*
> *The Long Corridor*
> *Maggie Rowan*
> *The Mallen Girl*
> *The Mallen Streak*
> *The Man Who Cried*
> *The Menagerie*
> *Pure as the Lily*
> *The Round Tower*
> *The Tide of Life*
> *Tilly Trotter*
> *Tilly Trotter Wed*
> *Tilly Trotter Widowed*
> *The Unbaited Trap*
> *The Whip*

As Catherine Marchant:

> *The Iron Façade*

July, 1986, to June, 1987.

Twenty-eight of the top one-hundred books:

> *The Black Velvet Gown*
> *The Cinder Path*
> *Colour Blind*
> *A Dinner of Herbs*
> *Fanny McBride*
> *Feathers in the Fire*
> *Fenwick Houses*
> *The Gambling Man*
> *Goodbye Hamilton*
> *Hamilton*
> *Harold*
> *The Invisible Cord*
> *Kate Hannigan*
> *The Long Corridor*
> *Maggie Rowan*
> *The Mallen Girl*
> *The Man Who Cried*
> *The Moth*
> *Rooney*
> *The Round Tower*
> *The Tide of Life*
> *Tilly Trotter*
> *Tilly Trotter Wed*
> *Tilly Trotter Widowed*
> *The Unbaited Trap*
> *The Whip*

As Catherine Marchant:

> *House of Men*
> *Miss Martha Mary Crawford*

July, 1987, to June, 1988.

Thirty-five of the top one-hundred books:

Bill Bailey
Bill Bailey's Lot
The Black Velvet Gown
The Blind Miller
The Cinder Path
Colour Blind
A Dinner of Herbs
Fanny McBride
Feathers in the Fire
Fenwick Houses
The Fifteen Streets
The Gambling Man
The Garment
The Girl
Goodbye Hamilton
Hamilton
Harold
The Invisible Cord
The Invitation
The Long Corridor
The Man Who Cried
The Menagerie
The Moth
The Nice Bloke
The Parson's Daughter
Pure as the Lily
Rooney
The Round Tower
Slinky Jane
The Tide of Life
Tilly Trotter
Tilly Trotter Wed
Tilly Trotter Widowed
The Unbaited Trap
The Whip

July, 1988, to June, 1989.

Thirty-two of the top one-hundred books:

Bill Bailey
Bill Bailey's Daughter
Bill Bailey's Lot
The Black Velvet Gown
The Blind Miller
The Cinder Path
Colour Blind
The Cultured Handmaiden
A Dinner of Herbs
Fanny McBride
Feathers in the Fire
The Fifteen Streets
The Gambling Man
The Girl
The Glass Virgin
Goodbye Hamilton
Hamilton
Harold
The Invisible Cord
The Invitation
The Long Corridor
The Man Who Cried
The Menagerie
The Moth
The Parson's Daughter
Pure as the Lily
The Tide of Life
Tilly Trotter
Tilly Trotter Wed
Tilly Trotter Widowed
The Unbaited Trap
The Whip

July, 1989, to June, 1990.

Twenty-two of the top one-hundred books:

> *Bill Bailey*
> *Bill Bailey's Daughter*
> *Bill Bailey's Lot*
> *The Black Candle*
> *The Black Velvet Gown*
> *The Cinder Path*
> *The Cultured Handmaiden*
> *A Dinner of Herbs*
> *The Gambling Man*
> *The Girl*
> *Goodbye Hamilton*
> *Hamilton*
> *Harold*
> *Harrogate Secret*
> *The Invisible Cord*
> *The Long Corridor*
> *The Moth*
> *The Parson's Daughter*
> *Tilly Trotter*
> *Tilly Trotter Wed*
> *Tilly Trotter Widowed*
> *The Whip*

July, 1990, to June, 1991

Twenty-four of the top one-hundred books:

> *Bill Bailey*
> *Bill Bailey's Daughter*
> *Bill Bailey's Lot*
> *The Black Candle*
> *The Black Velvet Gown*
> *The Cinder Path*
> *The Cultured Handmaiden*
> *A Dinner of Herbs*
> *The Gambling Man*

The Gillyvors
Goodbye Hamilton
Hamilton
Harold
Harrogate Secret
Harrogate Secret (Corgi paperback)
The Long Corridor
The Man Who Cried
The Moth
The Parson's Daughter
Tilly Trotter
Tilly Trotter Wed
Tilly Trotter Widowed
The Whip
The Wingless Bird

July, 1991, to June, 1992.

Sixteen of the top one-hundred books:

Bill Bailey
Bill Bailey's Daughter
Bill Bailey's Lot
The Black Candle
The Black Velvet Gown
The Cultured Handmaiden
A Dinner of Herbs
The Gillyvors
Goodbye Hamilton
Hamilton
Harold
Harrogate Secret
The Moth
My Beloved Son
The Parson's Daughter
The Wingless Bird

Index

colour Blind
Lilly Trotter "Trilligy"